HELENE SCHWEITZER

Albert Schweitzer Library

Other titles in the Albert Schweitzer Library

African Notebook
  Albert Schweitzer; Mrs. C. E. B. Russell, trans.

The African Sermons
  Albert Schweitzer; Steven E. G. Melamed Sr., trans. and ed.

Albert Schweitzer: A Biography, Second Edition
  James Brabazon

The Albert Schweitzer–Helene Bresslau Letters, 1902–1912
  Rhena Schweitzer Miller and Gustav Woytt, eds.; Antje
  Bultman Lemke, trans.

*Brothers in Spirit: The Correspondence of Albert Schweitzer
and William Larimer Mellon, Jr.*
  Jeannette Q. Byers, trans.

Memoirs of Childhood and Youth
  Albert Schweitzer; Kurt Bergel and Alice R. Bergel, trans.

*Reverence for Life: The Ethics of Albert Schweitzer
for the Twenty-First Century*
  Marvin Meyer and Kurt Bergel, eds.

Helene Schweitzer

A LIFE OF HER OWN

Patti M. Marxsen

Foreword by Sylvia Stevens-Edouard

SYRACUSE UNIVERSITY PRESS

THIS PROJECT WAS GENEROUSLY SUPPORTED BY THE STIFTUNG LAMBARENE SPITAL.

First Edition 2015
15 16 17 18 19 20   6 5 4 3 2 1

∞ The paper used in this publication meets the minimum requirements of the American National Standard for Information Sciences—Permanence of Paper for Printed Library Materials, ANSI Z39.48-1992.

For a listing of books published and distributed by Syracuse University Press, visit www.SyracuseUniversityPress.syr.edu.

ISBN: 978-0-8156-1051-9 (cloth)   978-0-8156-5326-4 (e-book)

Library of Congress Cataloging-in-Publication Data
Marxsen, Patti M., 1951–
    Helene Schweitzer : a life of her own / Patti M. Marxsen ; foreword by Sylvia Stevens-Edouard. — First edition.
        pages cm. — (Albert Schweitzer library)
    Includes bibliographical references and index.
    ISBN 978-0-8156-1051-9 (cloth : alk. paper) — ISBN 978-0-8156-5326-4 (e-book) 1. Bresslau, Helene, 1879–1957. 2. Schweitzer, Albert, 1875-1965. 3. Missionaries' spouses—Gabon—Biography. 4. Missionaries, Medical—Gabon—Biography. 5. Philanthropists—Gabon—Biography. 6. Nurses—Gabon—Biography. I. Title.
    CT1018.S45M38 2015
    361.7'4092—dc23
    [B]   2015002078

Manufactured in the United States of America

For Helen Marie Casey,
whose adventures in biography have inspired my own

Patti M. Marxsen is a journalist, essayist, translator, and independent scholar with a long-standing interest in the Francophone world. Her association with the Albert Schweitzer Hospital in Deschapelles, Haiti, from 1997 to 2007 led to writings on Haitian literature published in the *Journal of Haitian Studies, Caribbean Writer*, the *French Review*, and the *Women's Review of Books*, among other journals. As publications manager for the Boston Research Center for the 21st Century from 2000 to 2007 (now the Ikeda Center for Peace, Learning, and Dialogue), Marxsen developed books on global education and ethics that have remained widely used in college classrooms in the United States. Her own books include a collection of travel essays, *Island Journeys: Exploring the Legacy of France* (2008), and a collection of short fiction, *Tales from the Heart of Haiti* (2010). Her translation of *Albert Schweitzer's Lambarene: A Legacy of Humanity for Our World Today* by Jo Munz and Walter Munz (2010) was sponsored by the Albert Schweitzer Fellowship and eight international Schweitzer organizations. Marxsen lives and works in Switzerland and Maine.

Contents

◆ ◆ ◆

List of Illustrations   *ix*

Foreword, SYLVIA STEVENS-EDOUARD   *xi*

Preface   *xv*

Acknowledgments   *xxv*

1. In Search of Helene Schweitzer Bresslau   *1*

2. "You Seem to Be Someone"
   Coming of Age on the Grande Ile   *22*

3. In and Out of Africa   *42*

4. Divided Destinies
   A Sacrifice Observed   *73*

5. Against the Current   *96*

6. Madame Schweitzer in the Age of Obscurity   *117*

   Afterword
   The Lasting Legacy of Helene Schweitzer Bresslau,
   VERENA MÜHLSTEIN   *140*

   Chronology
   Helene Schweitzer Bresslau, 1879–1957   *149*

   Notes   *163*

   Bibliography   *185*

   Index   *195*

Illustrations

◆ ◆ ◆

Following page 62.

1. Helene Bresslau, c. 1906
2. Helene Bresslau on becoming a certified nurse, 1910
3. Albert and Helene Schweitzer correcting printer's proofs together, 1912
4. An outing in a pirogue on the Ogowe River, 1913
5. Helene as a civil prisoner of war in Garaison, France, 1917
6. Albert as a civil prisoner of war in Garaison, France, 1917
7. Albert, Rhena, and Helene in Strasbourg, 1924
8. Albert and Helene at the front door of their home in Königsfeld, Germany, 1932
9. The cottage in Königsfeld today
10. Helene Schweitzer, c. 1932
11. Nobel Peace Prize ceremony in Oslo, 1954
12. Helene's room in the renovated Historic Zone of the 1927 Schweitzer Hospital
13. Cemetery at the Schweitzer Hospital
14. Helene's 1905 file of notes for her index of *The Quest for the Historical Jesus*
15. Helene's 1915 edits to *Wir Epigonen*
16. Typescript with hand-written notes for Helene's US lecture tour, 1937–38

Foreword

◆ ◆ ◆

There is an old adage that says, "Behind every great man there is a good woman." In modern times, this statement has been updated to more accurately reflect reality: "Next to every great man there is an equally great woman."

Patti Marxsen's book focuses on the life and influence of Helene Schweitzer Bresslau and effectively illustrates the reality of her life as a young woman coming of age at the beginning of the twentieth century. We also learn of her life as the wife of Nobel Peace laureate Dr. Albert Schweitzer, who became an international icon for many people when he gave up a secure life in Europe to serve as a doctor in the region of Africa that is today the Republic of Gabon. Dr. Schweitzer is celebrated for his decades of humanitarian work and his philosophy of Reverence for Life. To most people, Helene is an afterthought confined to the role of Schweitzer's wife and help mate.

The traditional historical narrative describes how she became a nurse, took care of their daughter, Rhena, and raised money to help the Schweitzer Hospital in Lambarene, French Equatorial Africa. In other words, she assisted the great doctor in achieving *his* mission. And yet, as this biography makes clear, Helene Schweitzer Bresslau was a commanding figure in her own right and played a major role in Schweitzer's development as a writer and humanitarian as well as in his decision to become a doctor and go to Africa.

Through the exchange of letters and descriptions of historical settings, these chapters take us inside the world of this complex woman. More importantly, they allow us to see how her drive to be an agent of change influenced Schweitzer, helping him move beyond the intellectual pursuits of music, theology, and philosophy to become a man of action. We also experience the beauty as well as the cruelty of life in sub-Saharan Africa and Europe during a large expanse of time during the twentieth century. We feel Helene's conflict whenever she had to leave Africa and return to Europe, living apart from Dr. Schweitzer and their beloved hospital. We are also exalted by her determination to do whatever she could to keep the hospital running. Helene's life offers lessons in courage, sacrifice, loyalty, and service to family as well as compassion for the human race. One is left to wonder: If Helene Schweitzer Bresslau were born today, would she be celebrated as the wife of one of the world's great humanitarians or for her own humanitarian work?

We will never know the answer to this question, but this book makes it clear that Helene Schweitzer Bresslau was a force for good in this world. A living example of her goodness remains with us today in the form of the Albert Schweitzer Fellowship (ASF) here in the United States. This organization grew out of the seeds Helene planted during her lectures in the United States in 1937–38 in support of the Schweitzer Hospital. Initially a "Committee of Friends" led by missionary Emory Ross and Middlebury professor Everett Skillings, the ASF focused on providing support from US citizens to keep the hospital going during World War II. Continuing that mission, the ASF produced many programs and celebrations to promote and support the hospital. For example, Boston's Albert Schweitzer Festival raised ten thousand dollars in 1950 and another twenty thousand by the end of the decade.

In the 1970s, ASF president Larry Gussmann enlisted the assistance of Massachusetts senator Edward Brooke and his aide, a young lawyer named Mark L. Wolf, to negotiate a grant from USAID that helped build the modern Schweitzer Hospital in Lambarene. This institution was inaugurated in January 1981. Wolf subsequently joined the ASF Board and in 1979 initiated the Lambarene Fellows Program to send senior medical students to serve at the Schweitzer Hospital.

The Lambarene Fellows Program continues today, but Wolf and Lachlan Forrow, MD (president emeritus of the ASF and 1982 Lambarene fellow), soon realized that health disparities needed to be addressed in the United States as well. They took action by launching the US Schweitzer Fellows Program with the goal of developing emerging health professionals as "leaders in service" who, on completion of a year-long project, join an alumni network of Schweitzer Fellows for Life. Today, the ASF selects two hundred new fellows annually at eleven program sites across the United States and continues the Lambarene Fellows Program. With a network of more than two thousand Schweitzer Fellows for Life committed to addressing health disparities, the ASF's impact is magnified throughout the country and the world. These women and men committed to lives of service are living legacies of Helene and Albert Schweitzer.

For all this and more, Helene Schweitzer Bresslau deserves our recognition and gratitude. Her life, like her husband's, offers an important example of Reverence for Life.

Sylvia Stevens-Edouard, Executive Director
Albert Schweitzer Fellowship
Boston

Preface

◆ ◆ ◆

The first published writings about Helene Schweitzer Bresslau (1879–1957) began to appear in her last decade of life. In the summer of 1949, Albert Schweitzer's only trip to America created a media frenzy with newspaper and magazine coverage that sometimes took note of his wife's quiet presence and, in a few instances, quoted her directly.[1] Suzanne Oswald's memoir *Mon oncle Albert Schweitzer* (1974) includes a vivid portrait of an elderly Helene arriving in Lambarene to celebrate her husband's eightieth birthday. Two years later, when Norman Cousins was at the Schweitzer Hospital on furlough from his role as editor of the *Saturday Review,* he found himself enjoying conversations with Helene on the veranda and wrote about her with admiration in his best-selling book *Dr. Schweitzer of Lambarene* (1960). Meanwhile, German journalists such as the *Badische Zeitung* reporter who noted Helene's "intellectual vitality" during one of her last public lectures[2] and Otto Schempp, writing for *Christ und Welt,* were convinced of her significance but also aware of her enigmatic personality. "One sensed she preferred to be modest, inconspicuous, and to some extent incognito," Schempp wrote in 1956, a view reflected in the subtitle of his article "Helene Schweitzer: Am liebsten incognito."[3]

In the wake of her death on June 1, 1957, tributes to Helene settled around tropes of frailty and feminine sacrifice. Both were acceptable explanations for the apparent absences of "the wife of a great man" who had "not only married the man Albert Schweitzer, but also married his work."[4] Among the outpourings, the most level-headed was that by nephew Gustav Woytt.[5] In his careful account of Helene's professional life in Strasbourg before World War I, Woytt makes it clear that as far as he was concerned, she had accomplished her own work in the world and deserved to be remembered for it. Few mentioned the fact that she had spent more than a decade of her life in Lambarene—spread across nine sojourns—most often working as a nurse and sharing responsibility for the hospital and its connection to the larger world.

It was 1968 before a book-length biography about Helene was published. This book came from eastern Germany, where Schweitzer has always had a strong following. Unfortunately, although Marianne Fleischhack's 130-page effort lays out the facts of Helene's life, those facts are framed within the tiresome perspective of Christian sacrifice. A literal translation of the title says it all: *Helene Schweitzer: A Look at the Life of a Selfless Woman Who Gave of Herself and Sacrificed Herself for Brotherly Love.*[6] This biography is, indeed, little more than a "look" through the prism of Christian charity, with no primary sources consulted, one-fifth of the sources listed written by Albert Schweitzer, and no notes or annotations of any kind. In the end, Fleischhack's book does little more than reinforce a narrow understanding of Helene's life.

Another thirty years would pass before Verena Mühlstein's book *Helene Schweitzer Bresslau: Ein Leben für Lambarene* (Helene Schweitzer Bresslau: A life for Lambarene) became Helene's biography of record in 1998. Like Fleischhack's book, Mühlstein's work has never been translated into English or any other language. But unlike Fleischhack, Mühlstein presents a feast of information and analysis based on a variety of sources. Not only did Mühlstein consult the first edition of Helene and Albert Schweitzer's pre-Lambarene correspondence published in Germany in 1992,[7] but she had access to Helene's *Tagebuch* (diary) written during her first sojourn in Africa. Thanks to Mühlstein's personal friendship with the Schweitzers' daughter, Rhena, she also had access to Helene's correspondence with her sister-in-law and confidante, Luise Bresslau-Hoff. Mühlstein, furthermore, brought a feminist consciousness, a deep understanding of German Jewish culture, and the knowledge of a medical doctor to her project.

Consequently, her book succeeds as a thoughtful work of critical biography. If this is the case, one might ask, what else is there to say?

The present volume attempts to answer this question in a number of ways, beginning with the obvious point that until now there has never been a book about Helene Schweitzer Bresslau published in English. But that statement begs another question: Why do English readers need a biography of this particular woman? After all, there are more than enough books by and about Albert Schweitzer available in English. If she shared his world for more than half a century, why not rely on those texts to learn about the woman who married Albert Schweitzer in 1912 and cofounded the Schweitzer Hospital with him a year later?

This approach to Helene Schweitzer's life might work if Albert Schweitzer had said more about Helene in his writings. Unfortunately, she is mentioned only as his "wife," never by name, in his first book about life in Africa, *On the Edge of the Primeval Forest* (1921). And apart from a few facts, acknowledgments, and a veiled reference to her as the "most trusted friend" who knew before anyone else of his plan to become a medical missionary, Helene barely figures into his best-selling autobiography *Out of My Life and Thought* (1931).[8] Helene's voice comes down to us through journals, a limited number of letters, and a few published articles, but there is no single archive where her papers are preserved. Rather, Helene Schweitzer Bresslau's life story is scattered throughout the literature of Schweitzer studies so that a portrait emerges only through research in multiple archives and languages and with the assembly of fragments found in France, Gabon, Germany, Switzerland, and the United States. Necessary to the task is the art of reading between the lines, to say nothing of questioning omissions—which, in brief, describes my method. But, even so, interpretation is required, and aspects of Helene's personality remain undocumented, contested, or simply misunderstood.

At least the facts of Helene's early life are clear. We know she was born in Berlin in 1879 to Harry and Caroline Bresslau-Isay and spent her first decade in a warm and caring family, surrounded by an intellectual Jewish cultural milieu. Her father, Harry Bresslau, was a historian with the middle rank of *Privatdozent* at the University of Berlin.[9] A family move in 1890 was motivated by a position at Strasbourg's Kaiser Wilhelm Universität and the hope of career advancement, a hope that felt doomed to failure in anti-Semitic Berlin. After all, a decade earlier Bresslau had played an active, opposing role in a public debate with the outspoken anti-Semitic historian-journalist Heinrich von Treitschke. It was this experience, perhaps, that led to the baptism of the three Bresslau children by a Lutheran pastor in 1886, four years before the move to Strasbourg. In any case, Harry Bresslau's career flourished with his decision to move to the German Empire's most recently conquered region, Alsace-Lorraine.[10] In 1904, he became chancellor of the university in Strasbourg, a rare accomplishment for a Jew of his time.

Meanwhile, after her reluctant adaptation to the "New City" of Strasbourg—a phrase that typically referred to architectural expansion beyond the river Ill—Helene stood out at the private girl's school she attended before earning a teaching certificate at age sixteen.[11] By age twenty, she was studying piano at the Strasbourg Conservatory and singing in the choir at St. Guillaume, where she was known for her beautiful voice. She also learned foreign languages easily, a skill she often used on frequent travels throughout Europe with parents, friends, and family. Through a twist of fate, this young *citoyenne du monde* encountered a village pastor's son who was already making a name for himself in Strasbourg. She inspired Albert Schweitzer with her ideals and determination to be a modern woman at a time when there was hardly a role model in sight. As Jean-Paul Sorg notes in his introduction to the Schweitzers' pre-Lambarene correspondence, "The independence that she still confusingly aspired to had to be invented."[12] And so she invented it, though not without difficulty.

Apart from her intellect, character, and spirit, Helene deserves to be known in English because she was quite fluent in English from an early age. Although she did not want to be a schoolteacher as a way of life, she spent a semester in England teaching music, French, and English in the fall of 1902. Over time, her English skills facilitated Albert Schweitzer's social interactions, as her 1929 letter to the young Julius

Bixler written on her husband's behalf demonstrates.[13] Such letters also presented an opportunity to make herself known. When Bixler wrote a guest editorial entitled "The Miracle of Lambarene" twenty-five years later in honor of Schweitzer's eightieth birthday, he took care to acknowledge Helene's work. Her command of English also smoothed the way for her husband's travels to Great Britain in the 1930s, where he delivered important lectures and performed organ concerts. And although Albert Schweitzer was surrounded with interpreters on his trip to America in 1949, it is difficult to imagine him enduring it all without Helene at his side.

In the late 1930s, Helene Schweitzer moved to New York City with Rhena to offer her daughter a chance to develop her own English-language skills and to take a secretarial course far from the chaos of Europe. But perhaps she also wanted to spend some time in a wider world where she was perfectly comfortable linguistically. Helene's instincts were international, and with them she traveled as far as St. Louis to deliver lectures in English on the Schweitzer Hospital's behalf in 1937–38, an effort that helped to expand American awareness of Lambarene and planted the seeds for the Boston-based Albert Schweitzer Fellowship. With all of this in mind, my study "mines" English-language sources that have never been fully explored.

That said, the present book should not be approached as an updated, American English version of Mühlstein's biography. My primary goal has been to explore critical periods in Helene's twentieth-century life in some depth rather than to write a traditional "cradle-to-grave" biography. For this reason, Mühlstein remains the better source for Helene's early years. Another important aspect of my study is that it comes from the vantage point of an American feminist who understands Helene Schweitzer to have been an independent woman in perpetual motion, not a self-sacrificing or tragic figure, despite her lifelong battle with tuberculosis. I also approach Albert Schweitzer as a "mere" human being, not a saint or a hero or even a genius, despite my admiration of his enormous accomplishments. This stance allows me to interrogate his patriarchal view of the world often conveyed through self-serving language, habits, and omissions that clouded Helene's public image. If this study succeeds, it will offer a fresh and nuanced view of Helene's complex identity as an emancipated woman who struggled to be understood as an individual throughout her life.

Furthermore, although the outlines of Helene Schweitzer Bresslau's life have not changed since Mühlstein's book was published, time has passed, and new sources have come to light. First and foremost, the Antje Bultmann Lemke Collection Relating to Albert Schweitzer in the Special Collections Research Center of Syracuse University Libraries was not available for study until 2010. My discovery of the Helene Schweitzer Papers in this collection is an example of what can happen when a creative librarian takes time to respond to a doggedly curious researcher. Nicole Dittrich's "thinking outside the box" happily led to a box of documents that includes more than fifty years of Helene's day books and journals (1893–1951), writings related to her social work in Strasbourg (1907), and a typescript of her US slide lecture (1937–38) with hand-written notes. These treasures have allowed me to correct minor errors in previous works and to trace the day-to-day details of Helene's flight from Nazi Europe to Lambarene in 1941. Oddly enough, the combined resources of the Lemke Collection and the Albert Schweitzer Papers at Syracuse now make this modern campus in upstate New York the best place in the world to study the life of Helene Schweitzer Bresslau.

Of almost equal significance are Jean-Paul Sorg's three annotated volumes of pre-Lambarene correspondence of more than six hundred letters in their entirety, all translated into French.[14] This source constitutes considerably more material than previous editions, informative notes, and insightful introductions to the first and third volumes. Sorg's work, completed in 2011, resonates throughout the early chapters of my book. In another direction, my "shoe leather" research on the Schweitzers' internment in France during World War I draws on many sources, some published as recently as the late 1990s, and develops a more vivid portrait of Helene and Albert Schweitzer's World War I internment than has been previously available.

Finally, several new books have been published in the twenty-first century that add to our understanding of the Schweitzer universe, including works in English—such as the second edition of James Brabazon's masterful biography *Albert Schweitzer* (2000), Steven E. G. Melamed's translated edition of *The African Sermons* (2003), and Jo Munz and Walter Munz's firsthand account of the Schweitzer Hospital since 1965, *Albert Schweitzer's Lambarene* (2010), which I was privileged to translate and edit for American readers.

A new generation of Schweitzer scholars has also appeared in Europe in the twenty-first century, including Matthieu Arnold, Augustin Emane, Nils Oermann, and Thomas Suermann, to name a few. Meanwhile, Canadian historian Eric Jennings has broadened our understanding of French Equatorial Africa as a critical region in Charles de Gaulle's Free France during the early 1940s. As the history of Albert Schweitzer's life and work continues to be studied, surely it is not too late to give Helene her rightful place in the legacy of one of the most resilient humanitarian projects ever conceived.

လ

Each of the six chapters that follow focuses on Helene's character as she struggled through and adapted to important periods of her adult life in the twentieth century.

Chapter 1, "In Search of Helene Schweitzer Bresslau," begins with her absence from the standard narrative of Schweitzer studies and my quest to fill that absence. Because Lambarene was so central to Helene's life, I include perspectives on that faraway place from my own experience. These images and reflections are presented in italics and are intended to overlay my sense of "time travel" as I begin to assemble fragments of Helene's story, including the importance of other competent women to her husband's life and work.

In chapter 2, "'You Seem to Be Someone': Coming of Age on the Grande Ile," I rely on the pre-Lambarene letters to re-create the early years of Helene's friendship with Albert Schweitzer and her success in developing a professional life in the progressive city of Strasbourg during the reign of Kaiser Wilhelm II (r. 1888–1918). This period involves an emotional process of emancipation as well as a delicate balance of idealism and hard work. The overarching idea behind the chapter is that Helene Bresslau's independence was hard-won *by* her not created *for* her by Albert Schweitzer, as some scholars have suggested.

Chapter 3, "In and Out of Africa," does not recount the details that are easily found in other works (e.g., Schweitzer's autobiography and biographies by James Brabazon and George Seaver).[15] Rather, I focus on the Schweitzers' lives following the outbreak of World War I, including an in-depth exploration of their months as civil prisoners of war deported from Africa and interned in two camps in southern France. From this deprivation of freedom, a thread of compassionate indignation emerges that leads to a better understanding of how the war changed their lives and strengthened Schweitzer's resolve to return to Africa with or without Helene.

The theme of chapter 4 picks up this thread as Albert and Helene begin to live separate lives in the 1920s. "Divided Destinies: A Sacrifice Observed" interprets this critical period of change through social mores and biblical metaphor as it interrogates patriarchal notions of feminine sacrifice. Helene's health—the standard explanation for their separate lives—is put in perspective as I identify a gender-based connection between Helene's "frailty" and Schweitzer's heroic image. By the end of this chapter, Helene has found a way to adapt to circumstances and remain engaged in the work of Lambarene.

Chapter 5, "Against the Current," opens with an image of the ever-adventurous Helene returning to Lambarene and her husband after a difficult year in Nazi-occupied France. With this voyage in the summer of 1941 in mind, I navigate the pre–World War II years to address what has been almost taboo in Schweitzer studies: Albert Schweitzer's perceived failure to speak out against Nazism. I further accompany Helene to America in 1937–38, where she asserts herself as a public speaker, deploying her linguistic talents to bring support to the Schweitzer Hospital.

After the description of accomplishments in the previous chapters, chapter 6, "Madame Schweitzer in the Age of Obscurity," begins with Helene's postwar triage of her private papers, undertaken to ensure an accurate understanding of her role in Schweitzer's life. I then attempt to interpret her state of mind in the last decade of her life, including her adaptation to aging and the necessity of adopting a public persona that existed in contrast to that of her husband, even as she longed to be understood as a full partner. It is in this last chapter that I address the importance of new generations of modern women to Schweitzer's project, among whom Helene was the "prototype." To the extent that it is possible, I explore Helene's feelings about some of these women as age and health diminished her role in the work she had initiated with vigor so many years earlier.

Patti M. Marxsen
Ancien Presbytère
Gunsbach, France
March 2014

Acknowledgments

♦ ♦ ♦

All translations from the French are my own, unless otherwise noted in the bibliography. German sources have been translated with invaluable assistance from my husband, Dr. Hans-Peter Müller.

I am indebted to Verena Mühlstein for her insightful afterword and collegial spirit and for bringing Helene Schweitzer's unpublished Lambarene *Tagebuch*, 1913–1915, to my attention. I am also grateful to Albert and Helene Schweitzer's grand-daughters (Monique Egli, Christiane Engel, and especially Catherine Eckert) for encouragement and support.

Without the assistance of archivists, scholars, and librarians in Europe and the United States, it would not be possible to study the life of Helene Schweitzer Bresslau because her story is widely scattered in archived collections and embedded in books by and about her husband. For assistance in assembling the puzzle in Europe, I thank Jenny Litzelmann and Romain Collot of the Archives Centrales Schweitzer in Gunsbach, France, for their numerous contributions. Andrea Blochmann and Miriam Böhnert of the Deutsche Albert Schweitzer Zentrum in Frankfurt, Germany, shared useful examples of Helene's public life and private correspondence. Remi Venture of the Bibliothèque Municipale Joseph-Roumanille in Saint-Rémy-de-Provence, France, provided generous access to records of the Schweitzers' internment in 1918. In Switzerland, Rainer Walter and his colleagues in the Manuscript Department of Zürich's Zentralbibliothek greatly facilitated my research. I also acknowledge Markus Brandes's willingness to share his private collection of Helene Schweitzer letters in Switzerland.

In the United States, the Special Collections Research Center at the Bird Library of Syracuse University, where the Reading Room is diligently managed by Nicole Dittrich, houses the Albert Schweitzer Papers as well as the Antje Bultmann Lemke Collection Related to Albert Schweitzer. These rich resources make Syracuse University a major center of Schweitzer studies in the United States.

I am also grateful to my fellow travelers in the European Schweitzer world, from whom I have learned so much, especially Damien Mougin, Jo and Walter Munz, Sonja Poteau, Jean-Paul Sorg, Roland Wolf, and Christoph Wyss. Among works too numerous to mention, Jean-Paul Sorg's French edition of the Schweitzers' pre-Lambarene correspondence was an essential point of departure for my book. I thank him and his publisher, Jérôme Do Bentzinger, for illuminating Albert and Helene Schweitzer's early years with such care and attention to detail.

The present book, like all others, owes its existence to a number of people other than the author. Among them, my daughter, Kate Marxsen Bates, has offered a host of practical services as well as empathy, enthusiasm, and a willingness to read earlier drafts; Helen Casey has been a supportive voice from the beginning, without whose example I might not have found the courage to persevere; Sylvia Stevens-Edouard deserves special appreciation for her thoughtful foreword, written from her unique perspective as the first woman director of the Albert Schweitzer Fellowship; and Deanna H. McCay of Syracuse University Press has been a steady navigator since our first impromptu meeting in 2012. Indeed, all the dedicated professionals at the press have shared the goal of excellence that every author hopes for in the production of her work. It is also with particular pleasure that I acknowledge the generous financial support of the Stiftung Lambarene Spital in Switzerland *mit ganz herzlicher Dankbarkeit.*

Those who live with writers deserve a special kind of gratitude. With this in mind, Hans-Peter's positive energy, linguistic talent, hours of reading, and abiding interest in Helene and Albert Schweitzer's lives are reflected on every page. Without him, this book would not exist in its present form.

The publisher and I gratefully acknowledge the numerous permissions granted to quote from copyrighted material, especially from the archives mentioned here and from the Schweitzer–Eckert family. Every effort has been made to identify and contact copyright holders of material quoted, referenced, or reproduced in this work. We apologize for any omissions or errors.

HELENE SCHWEITZER

1

• • •

In Search of Helene Schweitzer Bresslau

A gust of heat invades the van heading south. Beyond the coastal concrete city of Libreville, bumper-to-bumper traffic gives way to red earth and a smear of green that seems to be moving at sixty miles per hour. Out in the country, children jump up and down as we drive past their huts, pink palms waving like blossoms. Their mothers doze in hollow doorways. Men sit elsewhere, lifting their heads from small plots of shade as we pass. They look at us, and we look back, bouncing on the two-lane road that was built here after World War II.

The road still feels new and out of place in this "primeval forest," as if the heaving green might swallow it whole any minute and hide these small houses from the curious eyes of strangers. Strangers like us—urbanized white people moving fast through an ancient world. Before the road was built, people traveled the Ogowe River in dugout canoes to reach Lambarene, that place that is an island and a town and an archipelago of sandbanks. "Lambarene," that musical name that became a myth in the middle of the twentieth century. Long before there was a myth to celebrate, people had come from far away to explore and exploit French Equatorial Africa. Others had come to convert the locals, as if the spirits inhabiting the jungle forest could be subdued by a thick black book. When a man and a woman arrived in the spring of 1913 to establish a hospital here, no one could imagine what would come of it.

The man was a doctor, a theologian, and a musician. His wife was a nurse, a social worker, and a natural linguist. They arrived in a paquebot *called* Europa, *leaving the ocean behind at Cap Lopez, now Port Gentil, to board the riverboat* Alembé. *They liked the way the Ogowe took*

1

them in and embraced their dreams. They liked the house on the hill pro-
vided by the Paris Mission Society, with its long view of the river winding
out of sight. They liked the sudden sunsets and the sound of rain in the
leaves. When the native people heard about Dr. Albert Schweitzer and the
woman they called "Madame Docteur," they followed the message of drums
out of curiosity and a desire to be cured, which is to say free of pain. In those
days, the river was their road, and the landscape varied from jungle forest
to ancient wetlands, with sedge and papyrus swaying in the current. Eyes
traveled the boundary of land and river, searching for crocodiles camou-
flaged as stone and deadly hippopotamus so easily mistaken for shadow.

☙

At the Schweitzer Hospital today, "the Great Doctor" is everywhere.[1]
His larger-than-life image greets visitors in the corridor of the administration building, an elderly face etched with compassion. A more pen-
sive expression gazes from a stone bust of Schweitzer in the main clinic,
where the waiting room is named for his wife, Helene Schweitzer Bresslau. It seems appropriate that we first encounter her name in this place
where people sit patiently on wooden benches. Elsewhere, down at the
water's edge of the hospital built in 1927 in what is now the Historic
Zone, Schweitzer's writing is literally carved in stone on pillars where
he recorded coworkers' names in the 1930s. His room and worktable
are part of a museum, the daily objects he touched preserved like relics.
He lingers here, as if he might return to take up a pen and write yet
another letter. Helene's room is here too, her cane and white cotton
dress evoking presence and absence in equal measure.

Helene Schweitzer's life in this place has been obscured by time
and by our cultural preference for male heroes. Apart from that cryp-
tic reference on old trunks and medical records stamped with "ASB,"
the imprint of Helene is almost invisible.[2] Her name does not appear
on the stone pillars, although she was here in 1930, again in 1939,
and again for five years during World War II (1941–46). There is no
portrait of her face etched with wisdom and no public statue, though
on postcards in the museum shop I find a few iconic images of Helene
with Albert in 1913. As I retrace her steps through the old hospital

village, Helene Schweitzer seems to stand just out of sight, working patiently on her husband's correspondence or talking quietly with a nurse weary from night duty. I pause in the shade of the cemetery where Helene's ashes are buried beneath the only visible monument I can find, a stone cross inscribed by Albert Schweitzer in his inimitable handwriting: "Here rest the ashes of Helene Schweitzer Bresslau, born 1.25.1879. Married to Albert Schweitzer 6.18.1912. Arrived in Lambarene 4.18.1913, to establish a hospital for the native people. Deceased in Zurich 6.1.1957."[3]

This cross was erected on what would have been Helene's seventy-ninth birthday in January 1958, and the matter-of-fact tone is one of Albert Schweitzer's familiar voices. His letters to Helene, though deeply affectionate in the early years and occasionally wistful in the 1930s, are often full of instructions, lists, logistics, and factual information. His notebooks record events, weather, names, addresses, and phone numbers. But here—especially here—something feels incomplete in this concise, factual statement. Some metaphor or call to God is missing. Some expression of love or gratitude for the woman Schweitzer famously described as "[m]y wife—my most loyal friend."[4]

Like that reductive, self-referential phrase, Helene Schweitzer Bresslau's gravestone says too little of her life—or, rather, of her *lives*—beyond marriage and medical skill. Lives—in the plural—because there was a European life and an African life; a personal life and a professional life; the cultivated life of a German Jewish girl baptized by a Lutheran pastor at age seven; the life of a mother without her child's father nearby; the life of a woman who felt history closing in around her in the 1930s and 1940s.

There is also what literary biographer Hermione Lee refers to as the all-important "posthumous reputation," that afterlife so carefully shaped to suit the living.[5] Even after her death in 1957, the difficulties Helene confronted during her time on earth—and her determination not to be defined by them—continued to develop into a generic "frailty" that serves to strengthen Albert Schweitzer's larger-than-life persona. Not until the centennial year of the Schweitzer Hospital in

2013 was Helene consistently evoked as an equal partner with the strength and energy to travel to Africa and establish a hospital. Did she go with him? Or did he go with her?

ରେ

Suddenly, in 1890, the world changed for the eleven-year-old girl who had grown up in Berlin. She was unhappy about her family's move to Strasbourg, even if it meant an opportunity for her father, a brilliant historian, to participate in the rise of the university renamed Kaiser Wilhelm Universität after the Franco-Prussian War (1871).[6] The Bresslaus lived in small apartments at first and eventually inhabited the elegant, leafy neighborhood along the Ruprechtsauerallee.[7] From there, Helene could easily walk to choir practice at St. Guillaume in 1898 when she was nineteen or to university classes in art history inspired by her six months in Italy in 1899. The location near the university was especially convenient for Professor Harry Bresslau, who was appointed chancellor of the university in 1904.

As a young girl, Harry's bright daughter could not know what it would mean to come of age in that city of progressive politics, architectural innovation, and social reform. She could not know that she would study art, music, history, and education. Even as she excelled in French at the Lindner School for Girls, no one could know that Helene Bresslau would spend four years (1905–9) as the first female inspector of the City Orphan Administration in Strasbourg. Her accomplishments in social work, such as the home for unwed mothers she would establish with a friend in the Strasbourg suburb of Neudorf in 1907, were still a distant reality.[8] And who would have guessed that a girl with early signs of tuberculosis from the age of ten, though known to be intelligent, would one day commit herself to rigorous training as a certified nurse (1909–10) or embrace the complex destiny of an emancipated woman?

By the time Helene achieved her nursing credentials, there was a plan in place to create a hospital in Africa with the man whose friendship had anchored her life since 1902, and she wanted to be prepared. Her active role in Albert Schweitzer's prolific writings—in theology, philosophy, and music—went along with these commitments, as did single motherhood through many of the years that followed because her husband chose to live and work on a different continent much of the time. By the time she reached age forty in January 1919, Helene Schweitzer Bresslau had experienced herself as a Jew and a Gentile, an exiled member of the colonizing class,[9] a professional woman in a managerial position, a globally minded humanitarian, an intellectual, a victim of tuberculosis, a prisoner of war, and the supportive wife of a famous man. In the twenty years that followed, she would also experience herself as a mother and a refugee in flight from Nazi Europe en route to a place she called home, a hospital village on the banks of the Ogowe River in French Equatorial Africa.

ତୄ

The overlay of Helene's *lives* may account for the sense of a "life in absentia" here on the ground in Lambarene. Though always here in spirit, she spent long stretches of time in Europe after 1913, traveling widely to Scandinavia, Great Britain, Czechoslovakia, and America. Her slide lecture and networking in the eastern United States in 1937–38 spread awareness of the Schweitzer Hospital. A few years later, another network involving the International Red Cross helped her survive in German-occupied France throughout 1940 and 1941 and, eventually, succeeded in arranging her passage out of Europe. After making her way back to Lambarene—traveling via Spain, Lisbon, Angola, and the Belgian Congo—Helene plunged into a five-year stint of nursing work soon after her unexpected arrival in the summer of 1941.

In 1949, Helene Schweitzer returned to America, making the journey to Aspen, Colorado, with her husband, where he delivered the keynote address at the bicentennial celebration of Johann Wolfgang von Goethe's birth. We also know that she insisted on joining Albert on the front row in Oslo for his Nobel Peace Prize ceremony in 1954. These acts can be "read" as living texts in place of published memoirs because Helene Schweitzer clearly preferred practical action to superficial celebrity. Furthermore, for her, action in favor of the Schweitzer Hospital was never confined to work "on the ground." She was, in this sense, one of the world's most efficient "virtual" professionals.

And yet there was a time in the beginning when she kept a diary of life in Africa for two years, from 1913 to 1915, as if already aware that the full meaning of this place would speak to a world beyond her own. From this 320-page document, we learn that it was on that first voyage that both Albert and Helene "truly fell in love with Africa" as the continent came into view from the deck of the ship *Europa*.[10] A few months later, despite oppressive heat and a daunting workload, Helene Schweitzer Bresslau allowed herself a poetic observation in a letter to her parents: "If I could, I would have our loved ones here and in the evening and could show them the wonderful performance of the full moon from our veranda as the glowing red rises and a streak of light scatters over the water." She felt close to her family, and so the letter continues, "[N]o homesickness—with the feeling that when thoughts and feelings are in harmony, there is neither a sense of separation nor of distance."[11] That thought echoes in the still heat of Lambarene today. She is here and not here, absent and present, a soul in harmony with this village and this river, regardless of her address. For a woman caught in the currents of history, Lambarene was the one place in the universe where Helene always felt at home.

Shortly before her death, she explained this feeling to *Saturday Review* editor Norman Cousins during his visit to Lambarene in March 1957. Too weak to leave the veranda, she took an interest in photographs of his daughters but also wanted to discuss world affairs. Cousins's portrait of Helene tells us a great deal about her state of mind. When he asked her where she felt most at home, there was no question for Helene that Lambarene was "home," regardless of long periods of time lived elsewhere.[12]

෨

Light snatches the surface of the Ogowe River like a thief, steals its jewels, and drowns the treasure. The river's surface can be burnished bronze or the color of mud. It can be iridescent, like blue silk, but today the sky is cloudy, and the light lies flat on the water. In the distance, I see the silhouette of a man standing erect in a dugout canoe, his pirogue, gliding and pushing with a long pole for balance.

From the riverbank where Albert Schweitzer built his own dock in the 1920s, a feature that made him as powerful as a tribal chief in African eyes, it is easy to see how geography determines life. I know of sandbars hidden in sweeping currents where some have been caught off guard and drowned while trying to swim ashore. I know of the concrete bridge that some who had never seen such a bridge could not believe would hold their weight when it was built in the 1970s, and so they crawled across it, slow and fearful, prepared to fall into the safer world of the river. Traveling the roads nearby, head down in the back seat of a makeshift "taxi" with torn vinyl upholstery and light crackling through a broken windshield, I ask the driver if he worries that the next pothole will fill the cab with shattered glass. "We are poor here," he replies, expressionless. The beauty Helene wrote of vanishes in the reality of poverty and disease that still exists here in Africa's second-richest nation. Both have always existed. Helene knew this; she also knew about the "Fellowship of the Mark of Pain" that she and her husband tried to honor.

௸

Here at one of the oldest hospitals in Africa, life has always been a struggle for Africans and Europeans alike. It was a struggle downriver when tam-tams announced the arrival of the Schweitzers in 1913 and later when Dr. Schweitzer returned without his wife in 1924 for three-and-a-half years. He was gone longer than expected because a dysentery epidemic made it clear beyond doubt that the first hospital jammed on the riverbank at Andende was too small to contain the suffering.[13] When a concession made the dream they shared seem possible—at last—another, longer struggle began on the hillside named Adolinanongo to rebuild an expanded hospital. By summer of 1927, two hundred patients were treated daily in the "new" hospital, which is now the old hospital, the one restored in 2006 as a "historic zone" to honor the past and attract tourists.

Schweitzer's books about his struggles have been widely read, but he rarely wrote about Helene. Neither did he mention the diary she kept here in the early years, those pages full of flowing German penmanship called *Kurrentschrift*, made in five copies at once to share with friends and family.[14] Nor did he mention the letters they wrote to each other before Lambarene. Words make fragile monuments. Ink fades and paper disintegrates. But how can the story of this place be told without Helene's voice? Helene's absence in Schweitzer's writings is like a stubborn root on a deceptively smooth path. Should his reticence be attributed to the discretion of bourgeois manners or to the blind insensitivity of an overblown ego? Is her invisibility a matter of omission, or is she a missing piece visible only to eyes "trained" by feminist consciousness?

It is tempting to dismiss these questions, knowing that even with the help of documents we can "read" only with the eyes and minds we possess. Perhaps "the Great Doctor" was simply a man of his time, incapable of perceiving—much less acknowledging—the enormous contributions made by often unmarried, frequently childless women to his life's work. In Schweitzer's case, however, that sort of magnanimity leads to a dilemma if we wish to preserve his "posthumous reputation" as a genius of humanist ethics whose existence rested on an instinctive respect for all life. Besides, it is no secret how conscious he was of his reliance on strong, resourceful women throughout his life or how consciously he nurtured those relationships.

To accept Helene's invisibility in Schweitzer's first account of their joint project requires an act of selective amnesia, for even a casual reading of his best-selling book *On the Edge of the Primeval Forest* demonstrates that the hospital's cofounder—as Schweitzer's chosen successor Walter Munz eventually described Helene[15]—does not appear as a named person at all. Rather, Schweitzer speaks of Helene only in relation to himself as "my wife" or "my almost utterly exhausted wife"[16] as he lavishes praise and admiration on his indigenous nurse, Joseph Azowani. Helene is a nameless shadow, if not a missing person, in what often reads like a directory of other named persons, including a small society of missionaries and their wives. If names do not matter, why does Schweitzer bother to name Mr. Haug, who was "the best wood expert on the Ogowe,"[17] or praise the hospitality of Mr. Cadier, at whose home "we ate monkey flesh for the first time"?[18]

In fact, we learn nothing from her husband of Helene's medical work in the early years of Lambarene until 1931, when he publishes his autobiography, *Out of My Life and Thought*. There he writes: "My wife, who had been trained as a nurse, gave me invaluable assistance at the hospital. She looked after the serious cases, oversaw the laundry and bandages, worked in the dispensary, sterilized surgical instruments, etc."[19] In the book published a decade earlier, readers can expect to learn very little of the hospital's cofounder from Schweitzer's peculiar anecdotal notes explaining that "[she] learnt how to solder, in order to be able to close up the flour and maize tins"[20] or how in a confrontation with traveling ants she demonstrated the presence of mind to "take the bugle from the wall and blow it three times."[21]

⁘

For a glimpse of Helene as a working nurse in Lambarene, we must turn to others who knew her, such as the young Dr. Victor Nessmann, who joined Schweitzer in Africa 1924 and took encouragement from Helene's words: "It's true what Madame Schweitzer says," he writes in an early letter to his parents. "'It is marvelous and magnificent work!'"[22] Or Frédéric Trensz, who came for a year in 1926 and later wrote of Helene in his own memoir: "In a recurring cycle of roles as doctor, surgeon, and architect, the doctor was supported only by his wife and a native nurse. Madame Schweitzer, far more than a housekeeper, concerned herself with preparations for operations at which she was present. The nurse served as the interpreter and administered intravenous injections."[23] Even Marie Woytt-Secretan, whose 1947 memoir does little to portray Helene as a full-fledged partner, takes care to describe Helene's work in the early years: "For operations, he [nurse Joseph] put red rubber gloves on his black hands and assisted the doctor while Madame Schweitzer took charge of anesthesia. . . . Madame Schweitzer managed the household, took over the care and feeding of the seriously ill, supervised the laundry, the bandages, surgical instruments, and the pharmacy."[24]

Through a narrow lens, Helene Schweitzer Bresslau appears to have been a bystander who weakened steadily as Schweitzer's "greatness" increased. Even people such as Miriam Rogers, who was instrumental in forming the Friends of Albert Schweitzer in Boston, kept "no recollection" of her first meeting with Helene in 1949. It is to Rogers's credit that she later reproached herself for this omission. "This is a typical and sad commentary on what it must mean to be the wife of such a famous man. I can only forgive myself because it was a large gathering and it was my first meeting with Dr. Schweitzer which was so very exciting and startling."[25]

A slightly larger lens, such as the one Miriam Rogers eventually possessed, reveals the hidden persona of "Madame Schweitzer," a woman worthy of mention as the loyal wife who—according to legend—became a nurse in order to follow her husband's dream. But here, as elsewhere, legends are deceptive. In truth, Helene's 1904 medical training predated and quite probably inspired Schweitzer's decision to become a doctor, as British biographer James Brabazon dares to suggest.[26]

In the July 11, 1949, issue of *Time* magazine, the story of Albert Schweitzer's first and last visit to the United States includes a 1924 family photo with a caption that chants the comforting refrain of the loyal wife-as-follower: "In June 1912, Schweitzer married Helene Bresslau. The daughter of a well-known Strasbourg historian, she had equipped herself for the life they were to lead together by becoming a trained nurse. They spent their first months of married life compiling lists and carefully purchasing and packing medical supplies. On Good Friday of 1913 they set out for Africa."[27]

Photographer Erica Anderson takes a similar, if less lucid, approach to Helene in *The Schweitzer Album*, her distillation of thousands of photographs taken between 1950 and 1965 in Europe and Africa. The brief text allotted to Helene romanticizes her wifely role and jumbles the facts as it focuses on Dr. Schweitzer, who went to Africa "with his bride Helene Bresslau, who alone among his friends encouraged him and who had trained as a nurse to be able to help him[;] he bought medicines and hospital equipment, and offered himself to the Paris Mission Society."[28] Anderson notes later that Helene "was in ill health for many years" and yet acknowledges that "in the 1930s she came to America to lecture for the hospital."[29] A similar ambivalence masquerades as tribute in the issue of the German Schweitzer Association's *Rundbrief* published two months after Helene's death. There, Dr. Peter Rinderknecht opens his article "Helene Schweitzer: The Wife of a Great Man" by repeating a statement that Pastor Karl Zimmermann had uttered on June 5, 1957, at the Zurich Crematorium: "'She not only married the man Albert Schweitzer, but also married his work.'"[30]

Through the larger lens we have today, it is not difficult to see Helene Schweitzer Bresslau as a woman with work of her own whose choices included—but were not limited to—her role as "the wife of a great man." Within months of Helene's death, a German postwar magazine devoted to women's emancipation made this point crystal clear by pointing out that "not only was she the wife of a great man, but a personality of her own worth mentioning in the same breath with Albert Schweitzer."[31] British journalist James Cameron echoed that blunt remark by describing Albert Schweitzer as "a doctor four times, a renowned organist and organ builder, a well-known humanist, and the husband of Helene Bresslau."[32] And Norman Cousins was surely ahead of his time when at the end of his book entitled *Dr. Schweitzer of Lambarene* he wrote: "I had several visits with Mrs. Schweitzer while I was at Lambarene. I came to admire her pride, her resourcefulness, her tenacity, her continuing interest in the outside world. . . . Her life had not been an easy one, but it had known purpose and hope and grace."[33] A similar admiration comes through in the fond memories recalled by Miriam Rogers, who eventually became friends with Helene, and in the astute observation made by Clara Urquhart, a journalist and trusted interpreter: "She [Helene] is a highly cultured woman and a most gifted linguist. She is frail to look at, but has an indomitable will."[34]

Finally, there is an important comment from one who knew Helene Schweitzer best. Daughter Rhena's unequivocal statement in the foreword to the first edition of her parents' pre-Lambarene letters would seem to set the record straight once and for all: "Since his time in Lambarene, my father has become world famous. My mother, who was his life partner and irreplaceable co-worker in the early work of setting up their jungle hospital, lived thereafter in his shadow. Only a few people know what an important part she played in his development and what an important role she had in the early years. She was a woman of achievement in her own right."[35]

৩১

Green is not a pure color. It is a trick of the eye made of blue and yellow. It sinks into violet at twilight, flickers in moonlight, turns black in fountains of ferns that choke the jungle forest. This "primeval forest" is known for its sudden power of erasure when it invades the silence of abandoned buildings and spills onto the road like lava. Green foliage takes a seat on the crumbling stone benches of bus stops unless someone cuts it back with a machete. It drifts and explodes where a trail was visible just yesterday. This profusion of green erases time.

I stand still for a moment on the road to Lambarene town, astonished at green clouds of mango trees overhead. Ivy crawls over gravestones in the above-ground cemetery, threatening to swallow the ancestors in their tombs within a mile of my hotel. There, everything has been clipped and scythed and mowed to create a false sense of order. Here, in the graveyard, there is no order among the broken gravestones disintegrating like calcified bones. In a country so proud of its ancestors, no one has been here in a while to honor the dead, a fact made clear by the tall, untrammeled grass and the indestructible plastic flower petals scattered by storms.

In the afternoon, I ride in another cab, facing yet another cracked windshield, returning to the old hospital grounds. There, in the house where Albert and Helene lived, their rooms are open to the public, a fact that I imagine would make Helene uncomfortable. Outside, the long wooden porch offers a bench, a respite from the heat, and a view of the old hospital village. There, another green shield rises above buildings carefully designed by Schweitzer as architect. He built natural ventilation systems into the rafters and insisted on an east–west orientation to avoid the direct glare of full sun. Helene lived in this house from time to time, but it occurs to me that she is much like the ancestors in the forest, a spirit

sleeping peacefully in a green world, half-forgotten but somehow alive,
holding fast to her own plot of memory.

ৎ৯

In the first decade of the twentieth century, Albert Schweitzer and
Helene Bresslau wrote to each other several times a week, a correspondence that now fills three volumes edited and (largely) translated
into French by Schweitzer scholar Jean-Paul Sorg.[36] The introduction
to the final volume makes it clear that throughout that decade Albert
Schweitzer's personality craved the company of women who were as
intelligent as they were independent. This was no unconscious habit.
Rather, he explained his strategy to Helene Bresslau in 1903 when he
wrote, "As long as a few women of noble spirit support me with their
fair sympathy, I can go my way alone."[37]

Schweitzer was never without "women of noble spirit," as Edouard
Nies-Berger observed fifty years later in a memoir of otherwise ques-
tionable accuracy: "He knew very well that he could never achieve
his Reverence for Life dream without the women who dedicated
their lives to his cause."[38] Helene Bresslau was the "noblest" of those
to fulfill this conscious need, though many others appeared as the
hospital evolved. There, much of the daily work was anchored by a
core of competent women that included Emmy Martin (1884–1971),
Emma Haussknecht (1895–1956), Mathilde Kottmann (1897–1974),
and Ali Silver (1914–1987). Each of these people devoted decades
of their lives to the Schweitzer Hospital. Furthermore, of those who
worked with Schweitzer in Africa during his lifetime, 65 percent were
women.[39] First among them, the skilled and liberal-minded Helene
Bresslau provided the "prototype" of precisely the sort of competent, adventurous, modern woman that Albert Schweitzer relied on
throughout his life.

Contrary to the commonplace view that Schweitzer shaped the
values and principles of his "most loyal friend," the facts of Helene's
life prior to 1909–10 confirm that she came into his life with a profound awareness of social needs and with ambitions of her own to
make a difference in the world. Part of her attraction to the man she
called "Bery" certainly included her realization that with him she

would have a role to play that she knew perfectly well how to fulfill. As Verena Mühlstein writes, "Helene Schweitzer Bresslau was always conscious of her own importance. She knew what a strong influence she had on Albert Schweitzer and what an important part she played in his work."[40] Likewise, James Brabazon explains that "Helene's social conscience was almost as highly developed as Schweitzer's and in addition she had enthusiasm, efficiency, and a fine disregard for social convention."[41]

It was this last essential trait that allowed her to adjust to Albert's insistence on partnership without marriage even if she initially experienced the idea as a shock. "I have gained new insights," she wrote shortly after his clarification of their "pact" on the Rhine in the spring of 1902.[42] As a modern young woman in a circle of young, affluent Germans coming of age in a germanized Strasbourg, Helene was open to new ideas and activities. She went out alone at night to sing in a choir and with her friend Elly Knapp organized a bicycle club. Her invitation to Albert Schweitzer to join the club drew him into her elite society, though he always understood himself as the son of a village pastor.[43] She was even willing to risk her parents' disapproval by accepting a salary for her work in Strasbourg when she began her job as city orphan inspector on April 1, 1905.

In his letters, Schweitzer addresses Helene as "My great one"— "Ma grande," in French, variously abbreviated as "mg," "Mg," and "MG"—often signing off with a capital G, to mark his own claim to grandeur. She eagerly echoed the compliment, thereby creating a special sense of intimacy between them. With letters flying back and forth, she also found precious time to devote to Albert's assorted agonies related to the demands of teaching and preaching, his hectic concert schedule, and his thorny negotiations with the Paris Mission Society between 1908 and 1912—to say nothing of the unpredictable personalities of other women.

Adèle Herrenschmidt, Albert's "Tata," was a strong-willed woman several years older who became vitally important to his emotional equilibrium.[44] Madame Fanny Reinach was less significant, but what are we to make of Schweitzer's declaration of affection for Helene that ends with instructions to send a particular book to "Madame R.," a book that happened to be Helene's first gift to Albert?[45] In keeping with such habits of apparent insensitivity, Schweitzer dedicated volume 1 of *Kulturphilosophie* (1923) to Annie Fischer, the wealthy widow and early donor who typed the manuscript, even though Helene had been the inspiration for this project—begun as *Wir Epigonen* (We, inheritors of the past; eventually published in English as *Philosophy of Civilization*)—and had shared in its development for decades.[46]

From letters in which Helene mentions Albert's ubiquitous female friends, it seems clear that she accepted them as part of the fabric of his life, especially the older ladies mentioned earlier. Perhaps this was because, as Sorg points out, Schweitzer expected his various female friends to know and enjoy seeing each other based on the rule of "two-way transparency."[47] Helene obliged: "I am so happy that you succeeded and are satisfied, and also that you have spent beautiful days with Madame R. Yes, I'll be delighted to meet her in October."[48]

But what of younger women such as Elsa Gütschow, Elly Knapp, or Hélène Barrès, all of whom were mutual friends of marriageable age? We can only wonder how Helene Bresslau felt when confronted with the opening lines of a letter like this: "Tonight Elsa Gütschow was at my place. I must spend a little time with her. . . . I hope to find the time to get her out of her boarding house at least once a week."[49] Perhaps we can deduce some process of resignation or adjustment from Helene based on comments often "positioned" as compliments: "Once again: I thank you for everything—everything, the good and the bad. The former made me happy and the latter helped me to move forward."[50]

In time, however, it was Helene Bresslau who became Schweitzer's most cherished friend as well as his most reliable editor, research assistant, and proofreader of book manuscripts. This work began with his invitation to her to help him with the index to the German version of *J. S. Bach* in 1904.[51] In the same period, he promised to write a philosophical book "for you alone" that would be called *Wir Epigonen*.[52] This project would occupy years of work in all imaginable situations, as Helene's careful copy of the final chapter, made during their 1918 internment at Notre Dame de Garaison, demonstrates.[53] But it was during their pre-Lambarene years, as their confidence in each other increased, that she became actively engaged in his work.

Among other things, she wrote extensive research notes and paginated indexes for *The Quest for the Historical Jesus*, in part because her German was highly evolved in comparison to his.[54] After all, Albert had grown up in a small village where his rural family was more at ease with the Alsatian dialect than with High German. Helene was a professor's daughter, born in the great city of Berlin and a member of Strasbourg's cultivated community called the "*Altdeutschen*" (Old Germans, in the sense of "authentic" Germans), whose skills were essential to the city's expansion. In time, she would even advise her "friend" on his manners vis-à-vis the marketing of his books, even scolding him for allowing Gerda Curtius to forge his signature in gift copies to colleagues.[55]

These cultural differences help to explain Mühlstein's description of Helene as "a great individualist,"[56] for she belonged to a world where travels, displacements, exile, and separation were part of a liberal familial and social milieu. As a young woman, Helene spent six months in Italy (1899), three months in England (November 1902 to January 1903), ten months in Germany with relatives (November 1903 to September 1904), and four months of convalescence in the refreshing air of the Black Forest when tuberculosis and the rigors of her nursing studies left her exhausted (1910–11). Later in 1911, she "took the waters" in Bad Schwartau, near the Baltic Sea, and visited Copenhagen, which she found "very beautiful and not tiring at all."[57]

A couple of months before her wedding in 1912, Helene made a last trip alone with her parents to Switzerland's sunny Italian canton, the Ticino, and wrote to Schweitzer describing the view from the Grand Hotel in the village of Brissago, "from which you only see the blue and green waves of the lake, crowned with little crests of white foam, and above that, the brown and green mountains whose peaks are still covered with snow."[58] She was, it seems, content.

ॐ

Helene's letters not only illustrate her social class but also say a great deal about her modern spirit, which Jean-Paul Sorg analyzes so insightfully within the framework of the Schweitzer–Bresslau relationship. "She understands she is free, thanks to her capacity of comprehension, her intelligence, her distance. She travels a lot in order to breathe at a distance, to take in fresh air, to unload her cares. A good method, as well, to revive her sense of freedom and find herself again."[59] In other words, and in contrast to Brabazon's identification of "the theme of renunciation, on which the whole relationship was based,"[60] Helene claimed her space without angst or apology, in part because it was normal for her to be learning, traveling, and interacting with others in comfortable surroundings. But it is very likely that the calendar she kept was also a way to avoid the loss of self that threatened to occur when she was too much in Albert's consuming presence. As Sorg illuminates Helene's critical role in providing Albert Schweitzer with a living example of the soul he wanted to possess, we also see how she became a symbol of the idealized modern woman, the Feminine Heroic, or, in Brabazon's language, Schweitzer's "guide and guardian angel."[61]

Helene's mobility was certainly among her most "angelic" talents. In her capacity to be simultaneously absent and present, she lived her independent life apart from Bery while holding her place in his thoughts. Indeed, from all the evidence, Helene was at ease with her pattern of oscillation between separation and devotion—a pattern that helped to set the tempo of the Schweitzers' ten-year courtship and forty-four years of marriage, during which months and sometimes years apart became a way of life. Despite the traditional view of Albert Schweitzer as the more active partner with a schedule full of sermons, concerts, students, academic work, and medical studies, in the early years it was often Helene who was on the move, asserting her need for solitude, a change of scenery, and stimulation apart from Albert Schweitzer's needs.

For the young Albert Schweitzer was most certainly demanding. His ambitions were great, and his days full to the brim with daily responsibilities. And then there were the writing projects swimming in his head, each with its inner force driving his moods. "I have not been able to concentrate in recent days: too much daily work and too little self-confidence. I dragged through without joy, avoiding any reflection on my life."[62] In March 1903, with Helene far away in Stettin, Germany, and his promotion to director of the Protestant Seminary imminent, he indulged in an outpouring of emotion, explaining how "[t]houghts chase each other inside my head and take my breath away." In this letter, he declares that his soul has been "too troubled and too full of struggles to remain 'noble,'" as he laments what "hours of insomnia will have cost me in terms of work." In this agitated state, he clings to Helene. "Only you understand everything," he writes before posing a question that must have given her pause: "Why have you chosen such a friend? I give you almost nothing and demand so much." And then, at the end, his mood shifts as he seems to tip his hat. "It was good to chat. Good night."[63]

If Helene was disturbed by such communication, there are no letters of hers to prove it.[64] Rather, it seems that as early as 1903 both felt connected to the other despite geographical distance. Was this a perpetual case of absence making the heart grow fonder, or did these two rather prefer physical distance to physical intimacy? For Schweitzer, the spiritual dimension of his love for Helene certainly seems to have been more deeply felt when they were apart. Then, he could imagine her as he wished and hold her up as a symbol, nearly transported, as he was when the ten o'clock bell of the Strasbourg Cathedral washed over the city and he wrote: "I sense your soul so pure around me and am comforted by it."[65]

But Helene, too, entered such states of reverie, as on a summer vacation to Trois-Epis (Alsace) with her parents when she slipped into the room once shared with Albert to remember "all the beautiful hours" they had spent there together.[66] If we allow that Helene and Albert were equally independent, the life they chose begins to look more like a mutual search for equilibrium than a pact of renunciation. In the end, their unconventional existence would not have been possible without Helene's particular mix of modernity, wanderlust, introversion, and self-reliance.

Long before their marriage on June 18, 1912, Albert and Helene had clearly established the terms that would shape their connection for the rest of their lives. As Schweitzer hoisted Helene Bresslau onto a pedestal, reaching for heaven, he enjoyed the way her noble character was reflected in his own striving soul. She, in turn, understood that she fulfilled a need without conventional constraints, which helped her to see herself as a modern woman instilled with strength and power. She must have been aware of these complexities even at the moment of their pact of March 22, 1902, though she may not have realized that she was promising herself to a grief-stricken man. Albert's beloved Aunt Mathilde had died in Paris on February 18, 1902. As soon as Helene appeared in Schweitzer's psyche, "[a] shift, a transfer, in the psychoanalytic sense too, from the deceased to the young woman was gently under way," writes Sorg.[67]

♋

Sooner or later everything vanishes into the river, merging with vast cycles of regeneration. More than a century ago, the river was a busy trade route where European "factories" such as Woerman's and Hatson & Cookson exchanged salt, rum, eau-de-vie, guns, and bolts of cotton for rubber, ivory, and ebony. It was also a world of missionary zeal, with mission stations strung like pearls along the Ogowe River where God's pious soldiers died willingly of "the fever."[68] A steady flow of people came and went long before Albert and Helene Schweitzer arrived: white people and black people, rich and poor, missionaries and explorers, ethnographers and entrepreneurs. Before them, the land swarmed with migrating tribes who worked their way along the river, gliding silently in their pirogues, eyes scanning the surface of the water for sandbanks and deadly hippos, black boulders hiding underwater.

Long before Albert Schweitzer was born in 1875, the Ogowe was here, winding through the long breath of green that presses forward as I watch the river. It carries people, memory, and sound. If you close your eyes to listen to the birds overhead, you also hear the buzz of motorboats and boys slapping the surface as they leap in to cool off at the end of day. I wonder what they know of the man they call "Schwei-zerrr." I wonder if they know anything at all about Helene. I assume they have never heard a recording of the doctor's pinched, accented voice unless they have seen Erica Anderson's 1957 film in school because it won an Academy Award in a place called America. And Helene's voice. Where is that recorded? I try to imagine the sound of it based on her photograph. It would be a clear voice, I think, a patient voice speaking the precise German she learned as a child. I search her letters for that forgotten sound—precise and melodious, self-assured.

⊙⌇

"Tell me, Bery, do you really believe that I would wish to restrain your freedom, and do you fear it? Don't you know that you will always be entirely free, yes m.g., entirely, from the moment you express it and wish it."[69]

Helene Bresslau asks her pointed question after a letter from Albert sheepishly mentions a "rendezvous" with Hélène Barrès. Perhaps his awkwardness arises because Hélène Barrès was as youthful as Helene Bresslau, whereas most of Schweitzer's "guardian angels" in this period were older women, such as "Tata," with whom he vacationed in Switzerland for weeks at a time, and Constance Harth, sister of his deceased aunt Mathilde. A few months before he became engaged to Helene, Albert felt compelled to write from the train, "I have a lot to confess: Madame Reinach is here again."[70] Some months before that, Annie Fischer arrived for dinner in the middle of his letter writing. "The door bell is ringing. It's Madame Fischer . . . I kiss your hand, your G."[71]

Helene's voice returns, as if in response to that perfunctory kiss. "Tell me, Bery, do you really believe that I would wish to restrain your freedom, and do you fear it?" There is something indisputably modern in the voice that frames this question. Helene clearly felt secure in Albert's affection—safe in her place as his very special "*amie,*" his "*grande,*" his "pure soul," either too "noble" or too busy to indulge in petty jealousies. Besides, the tone of her letter asserts her own claim to freedom that Albert must have felt as a veiled threat, even if he often urged her to find a husband other than himself prior to 1909.

The real challenges for Helene would come later, after World War I (1914–18) and their shared experience as civil prisoners of war interned in France. Life changed after the birth of Rhena in January 1919. And then there was the cottage in Königsfeld, Germany, where

Helene would raise their daughter after 1923, often alone as a "single mom," while Albert returned to Lambarene to rebuild the hospital. In July 1924, he was joined there by Mathilde Kottmann, then by Dr. Victor Nessmann in the fall. Dr. Markus Lauterburg and Emma Haussknecht followed in 1925 to form the first, on-site medical "team." As the hospital on the riverbank grew, Helene became a person whose health and parental responsibilities in Europe set her apart from the project that had been hers as much as his. Meanwhile, young doctors and very modern women begin to find their way to Lambarene, attracted by the humanitarian spirit and astonishing allure of the man Norman Cousins described as "a spiritual immortal."[72]

Albert's return to Lambarene in 1924 would mean a separation of three-and-a-half years from Helene and Rhena.[73] For Albert Schweitzer, humanitarian action mattered more than ever in the wake of World War I, and family life was a task he clearly felt free to delegate to Helene, even if he was well aware of her distress at being alone. Did he suddenly associate her with the bourgeois conventions he wished to leave behind? Had his "pure angel" cycled through a series of transformations to become his "most loyal friend," as he described her in the dedication to volume 2 of *Kulturphilosophie*?

Perhaps this is how history invades our most intimate lives. Perhaps Helene had always known—from the moment of her baptism in 1886 or maybe on the day she arrived in Strasbourg as a young girl—how fragile this quest for belonging was going to be. Perhaps her conscious choice to become an individual, which is to say a woman with work of her own, was the safest stance available to her, especially after meeting Albert Schweitzer. With or without him at her side, she knew she would survive in a world that allowed her to act. If Helene's life was a model of "purpose and hope and grace," as Norman Cousins describes it, it was also a monument stronger than stone, though much less visible.

2

◆ ◆ ◆

"You Seem to Be Someone"

Coming of Age on the Grande Ile

The more I understand life, our life, the more I understand about the necessity of work, about the fatigue of work and about work beyond fatigue, and the less I fear the consequences: that one day this work will reach the point of devouring those who have given into it[.] . . . And their life, even once passed, will have an impact— an impact! It's no small thing to have reached a point where one error in this work makes us more miserable than the thought of delightful hours that, if spent together, would have been so beautiful, so beautiful . . . [.][1]

Helene Bresslau arrived at this perspective nine years after she met Albert Schweitzer at the wedding of a mutual friend and five years after their pivotal pact of friendship. Just what was said on March 22, 1902, as they stood at their special place along the Rhine River is unknown. What we do know is that words of deep affection were spoken by Albert and misunderstood by Helene. "You have been good for me and at the same time you have injured me," she wrote six weeks later.[2] She was referring to Albert's firm resistance to the notion of marriage, which he continued to express two years later despite the adoration: "When, in any kind of struggle, one has the possibility of taking refuge in a being with ideas as pure as yours, a being who encourages and consoles you from a distance, then it is easier to live and move forward with one's head held high."[3]

On the edge of a new century, both were careful about their promises to one another from the beginning, and young Bery often stressed the importance of remaining *wunschlos* (free of expectations). He would remind her, more than once, of the promise made in 1902, "when you suffered and yet where you nevertheless understood me. My promise to call you when and where I need you."[4] Helene's open-ended understanding was just what he needed, and in a sense it liberated her as well. By 1907, not only was she *wunschlos*, but she was also immersed in her work as the first woman inspector of Strasbourg's City Orphan Administration and busy developing the Strassburger Mütterheim, a home for unwed mothers that would open in November.[5]

Helene's accomplishments in the autumn of 1907 seemed to excite Albert to new heights of emotion. His rare love letter written "toward midnight" on the last day of the year is unusually focused on its recipient rather than on his own busy schedule: "What a year's end for us, a dream! You seated at my table in Gunsbach in the silence and peace of our house. . . . It seems to me that we have found our direction and that we are navigating from the mouth of a great river into the open sea." This is Schweitzer at his poetic best, and yet this beautiful image of two souls in motion is also colored by a cautionary note in the same letter that reveals his understanding of Helene's personality: "My friend, it is difficult, this life I demand of you. I often wonder if it won't consume and weaken you." And yet "[y]ou have offered it to me and I accept and I know that we are profoundly happy, that no other happiness could make us any happier."[6]

His expressive mood continued throughout the winter: "When I think of you, it's like a dream."[7] But the first available response from Helene had little to do with romance. Their mutual friend Elsa Polczek-Gütschow, the first female student to enter what is today the University of Strasbourg, had given birth to a dead child and would lose her own life within a few days. Helene was understandably shocked and upset as she wrote to Albert, though at the end of her note she reassured him of her affection. "I thought so much about you all day . . . [.]"[8]

By her thirty-first birthday in 1910, Helene was clear-eyed about the future and did her best to convince Albert of her resolve: "We know that our life, however difficult, will be so much more worthy for having been lived and that it is in our shared work that we will find happiness. Next to that, ordinary things don't count. . . . Oh, my great one, don't worry so much about me and do not doubt me—things will work, I am not afraid."[9]

☙

Nearly thirty-seven years after writing those lines, Helene sat in her cottage in the Black Forest, surrounded by boxes of letters, journals, large brown envelopes, folders, and drafts of Albert's manuscripts tied together with string. In 1947, the time had come to sort through papers accumulated in the decades since those early days when everything was new and full of promise. She wanted to preserve what was important, or necessary, and to eliminate excess.

Among the papers were studio portraits of herself in various fashions and postures. She must have studied the soft gaze of herself as a young, obedient nurse wearing a heavy cape and starched cap, perfectly set. It was in Frankfurt during that pivotal year of 1911 that she became "Sister Helene," in German medical parlance. This was far more than she had expected of herself seven years earlier during her first nursing course in Stettin, Germany, when the time away from Strasbourg felt like a mere experiment in independence. Her letters from Stettin reveal the deeper thoughts she shared with her "*ami*" at the time: "I am very, very happy here and I'm even free of suffering from the physical fatigue that I felt at the beginning. Nevertheless, I will not remain forever, even if I had—but I would never have—my parents' permission. Why? Because I am too egotistical, too individualistic, and I do not want to give up my individual life once and for all. Here the work takes everything, both physical and psychic strength."[10]

Another photographic portrait explains why the children at the old vicarage in Gunsbach called her "Auntie Etiquette" behind her back.[11] In this image, she posed for the photographer in a large hat made for city streets. Hats and gloves, cameos and hairpins, lockets and lace, beaded bags—there was a time when all of that had mattered to her. Then, suddenly, it ceased to matter as a new kind of femininity became synonymous with useful work and simplicity of style.

We have a glimpse of Helene's modern femininity in the full-length portrait taken around 1906 among the props of a photographer's studio: faux brick wall, fragile trellis, painted sky. The long dress with chevrons darting across the bodice could be mistaken for a mourning dress with its tight cuffs and high neck. Or it might be viewed as sober elegance. This vertical portrait of Helene Bresslau seems to demonstrate her motto in those years: "I want to be an individual." What determination it took, what courage in those days, for a girl to even think such things, much less carve out a life around her own ambitions.

Albert accepted her as she was because independence was part of the pact they shared—to put the power of a hard-won individuality to the service of others, whatever such ideals might require. "More uncertainty, more struggles, more difficult decisions, only one must learn to wait, to look in front of your feet and not always to impatiently scrutinize the horizon. For myself, I have learned to wait, but for you, it's more difficult," he wrote.[12] Clearly, Albert Schweitzer liked to see himself as the more measured of the two, despite his driving energy and often chaotic emotions. But a common desire united them: both wanted to act out of faith in the world yet to come.

☙

Helene Bresslau and Albert Schweitzer met "by chance" on August 6, 1898, at the wedding of Lina Haas and Willibald Conrad. Lina's and Albert's fathers had known each other for years, and both Helene and her brother Ernst were friends of the bride. In the Bresslau home, the occasion was felt as a perfect opportunity to present their only daughter to the best of Strasbourg society. Essential to this social stratum was the community of German birth that now constituted city leaders active in Strasbourg's ambitious expansion as well as the most successful professors and promising students from the university.

Influential Germans had been present everywhere since the Treaty of Frankfurt signed on May 10, 1871. With that document, France changed shape when the French provinces of Alsace and Lorraine were annexed to the German Empire. What had been a part of France for the previous two centuries suddenly became part of a powerful *Reichsland* controlled by Kaiser Wilhelm I's (r. 1861–1888) iron hand.[13] As for the French who lived in what were commonly described as the "amputated" provinces, they were given the option to retain their nationality by settling elsewhere in France. Although the statistics have remained almost impossible to verify, it appears that during 1871–72 approximately 360,000 people "opted" to leave Alsace-Lorraine and move to some other region of what was left of France, and 26,000 chose to relocate in foreign countries.[14] Meanwhile, Germans poured into Germany's newest region along the Rhine River.

People such as Albert's parents, Pastor Louis and Adèle Schweitzer-Schillinger, were at an age and stage of life when it was possible to adapt to such dramatic changes. They did so far from Strasbourg in the Alsatian villages of Kaysersberg and Gunsbach, eventually raising a family of five children. Had their second child and first son been born on January 14, 1871, instead of January 14, 1875, he would have been born French. Instead, Albert Schweitzer was among the youngest Alsatian citizens in what historian François Igersheim describes as a "quasi-state" of the German *Reichsland*, consisting of Upper and Lower Alsace, the province of Lorraine, and the region of Moselle.[15]

Helene was born in Berlin in 1879, the same year a parliament was established in the still "new" German Alsace, although the first elections by universal suffrage had already taken place there in 1874.[16] Knowing chances for professional advancement would always be limited in increasingly anti-Semitic Berlin, Helene's Jewish parents moved their family to Strasbourg in 1890. Like the Schweitzer family in the Münster Valley, Harry and Cary Bresslau-Isay were at an age and stage of life when adaptation was possible and even welcome.

As both families grew, tensions in the Alsace seemed to lessen, and rules originally imposed on French citizens were relaxed. Meanwhile, Germanic efficiency translated into social gains and economic progress. A turning point came in 1903 when the new leaders elected were those favorable to developing the Constitution of Alsace-Lorraine, which was finally adopted in 1911. Although the official language of the region remained German, and despite Kaiser Wilhelm II's control of all railroad systems, this document included some surprisingly "democratic" provisions. Among them, "The number of members appointed by the Emperor must not exceed that of the other members." And the Lower House was to be elected for five-year terms by "general and direct" elections.[17]

Strasbourg was, from all appearances, one of Europe's most modern, progressive cities, strengthened—not weakened—by a blend of cultures, at least until World War I broke out in the summer of 1914. At that moment, emotions erupted along the lines of long-buried nationalism in the formerly French Alsace. Nearly forty years later Helene's German friend Elly Heuss-Knapp, also a professor's daughter raised in Strasbourg, wrote that "[i]n a moment we were separated from our Alsatian home. A wall stood between us."[18] Meanwhile, France wasted no time in establishing internment camps as a means of isolating "undesirable" German-speaking Alsatians from the enemy's border. Tensions between France and Germany would take yet another war to resolve, and once again—in 1940—the French citizens of the Alsace would find themselves invaded and occupied by German troops.

☙

In 1898, however, at the Haas–Conrad wedding, the world was in full flower, as was the gracious nineteen-year-old daughter of Herr and Frau Professor Bresslau-Isay. With romance in the air, someone took care to seat Helene next to Albert Schweitzer, then twenty-three years old and well known for his organ performances at St. William's Church (where Helene sang in the choir), for his sermons at St. Nicolas, and for his recent success in passing the state exam in theology. He was handsome, charming, and sparkling with intelligence but decidedly outside the elite social circle this wedding represented. This blunt reality was made clear when Helene teased him that day about his Alsatian dialect. Little did she know at the time that her urge to refine his linguistic "imperfections" would come to occupy years of her life as the research assistant, editor, proofreader, and—effectively—publications manager of the man sitting next to her.

By 1905, Helene was deeply engaged in Albert Schweitzer's first big book, which attempted to review the scholarly history of Jesus

Christ as a living being, *The Quest for the Historical Jesus* (*Geschichte der Leben-Jesu-Forschung*).[19] This participation involved Helene's organization of hundreds of bibliographic references, to say nothing of her comments on structure and content: "I find that the last pages are not as clearly expressed as the rest. I know it must be terribly difficult to make all these thoughts clear, but I would have liked a more condensed text, it would have more impact. Pardon me! I want to finish reading it first."[20] She also developed the *Namen Register* (name index) for this work, as she did for Schweitzer's other works, including the German edition of *J. S. Bach*, which appeared in 1908.

Helene also contributed time and energy to *Kulturphilosophie*, the book that Albert Schweitzer promised to write in 1904 as a tribute to her, with the title *Wir Epigonen* (We, inheritors of the past; eventually translated as *Philosophy of Civilization*). The original title referred to their shared inheritance of a severely flawed civilization that he hoped to explain in terms of causes and consequences. As the manuscript collection in the Zurich Central Library demonstrates, Helene's multifaceted involvement in this work began in 1915 when Schweitzer returned to the project while under house arrest in Africa.[21]

With war raging in Europe, Schweitzer reframed the essential question to focus on individual responsibility. "What is civilization?" he asked himself. For Schweitzer, the answer was clear: "The essential element in civilization is the ethical perfecting of the individual as well as society." Further, "The only possible way out of chaos is for us to adopt a concept of the world based on the ideals of true civilization."[22] Over the next eight years—in Africa and in Europe—he would work on the exposition of these ideas with the aid of Helene's careful editing, which included commentaries, corrections, alterations of word choice, and careful hand-written copies of various chapters.[23]

But in the first decade of the twentieth century, all of that still lay ahead for these idealists, and the brutality and sorrow of a devastating war in Europe were beyond imagination. Rather, in those early years of Albert's friendship with Helene, we see the glow of youth. Albert Schweitzer looked surprisingly well dressed and leisurely, often enjoying bicycle excursions with Helene and her circle of friends. Behind the leisurely pose, he was hard at work, of course, completing a double doctorate in theology and philosophy at the University of Strasbourg by 1900 with a dissertation titled "The Religious Philosophy of Kant." This doctorate and his ordination as a pastor that year led to a position as *Privatdozent* in the university's Protestant Theology Faculty in 1902. A year later, in 1903, he was named principal of the Protestant Seminary, a post he held alongside his role as curate at Saint Nicolas, where he had delivered sermons since 1898.

Schweitzer's fascination with organs and eventually a crushing concert schedule were worked in on top of his academic life and popular sermons. As if all this were not enough, by January 14, 1905, he had formulated his intention to serve as a medical missionary, which meant he would begin medical school at the late age of thirty. Helene knew and understood his goal as well as the complexity of his personality. But when Schweitzer announced his alarming decision to others near and dear to him in letters sent from Paris, their frequent response was shock. By coincidence, he was in Paris to meet with the Paris Mission Society in 1905 just weeks after the state funeral honoring the African explorer and antislavery activist Savorgnan de Brazza, a pioneer in the Ogowe region.[24]

ஒ

With so many daily responsibilities and goals on the horizon in the decade before their marriage, Helene became a refuge for Albert Schweitzer. He wrote to her almost daily and sometimes more often than that. Perhaps her role as his private sounding board and muse explains his seemingly selfish desire to conceal their special friendship, their *amitié*, to protect it from social pressure and conventional speculation. Helene allowed the secrecy but took care to inform her parents "just enough for them to avoid erroneous conclusions."[25] Nearly three years after their pact of friendship in 1902, Albert wrote, "Have you now realized that not allowing our true friendship to be known is the right and only way?"[26] It is in this letter that he refers to Helene for the first time as his "comrade"—his "good and loyal comrade," to be precise—a phrase that anticipates his dedication in the second volume of *Kulturphilosophie* (1923) to "[m]y wife, my most loyal friend."[27]

Although this dedication may sound tepid to twenty-first-century ears, generations of Schweitzer scholars have turned to it as evidence of Albert Schweitzer's devotion to Helene. Verena Mühlstein notes the emancipating nuance of the German word *Kamerad* (comrade) in the years before 1914, and Schweitzer's use of the term seems to bear this out.[28] After all, the best English translation of "Meiner Frau, dem treuesten Kameraden" is that by Oxford don C. T. Campion: "[m]y wife—my most loyal friend," in which the equality of friendship rather than passionate romance is expressed. It is also noteworthy that when Schweitzer wrote to Helene on July 9, 1905, to inform her that he had offered himself to the Paris Mission Society with no particular thought of her joining him, he addressed her as "[m]y loyal comrade."[29]

Only when Albert and Helene's daughter, Rhena, discovered the early letters in the 1980s could this strenuously discrete friendship be understood as a kind of experiment in modernity as well as a deeply felt connection. "For me, these letters were a revelation," Rhena Schweitzer writes in her foreword to the first published selection.[30] They are a revelation of deep affection, to be sure. But they also reveal the turmoil that both Albert and Helene felt over the future of their relationship. At the core of this turmoil was the essential question of what marriage represented to each of these unconventional people for whom liberty (Albert) and individuality (Helene) required considerable determination and resistance to polite society's social norms.

Among the topics they explored was the matter of what constituted a woman's happiness at the dawn of the new century. Could a woman born in 1879 be happy without marriage and children? And if not, was Helene squandering her best years on a liaison fraught with limitations? One of her first letters after their pact of 1902 frames the question in poignant terms: "I have often asked myself: of the thousands of young girls who await their happiness are they really so much better than I? It seems to me that I am not so bad, even as I recognize that I have a number of faults." Here, she is grappling with Albert's clarity on the point that his feelings, however intense, should not be taken to imply marriage, home, and family. "Certainly," she goes on,

"I don't yet know what my path will be—it is easier for a man to know, for his profession opens the way. . . . When a woman does not possess special talents, it is difficult to carve out a path that is truly her own."[31]

By the autumn of the following year, her inner struggle had become almost unbearable and was, in fact, shared by Albert, who was beginning to feel like an obstacle in her life. The issue came to a head late in October 1903, five months after she first signed the guest book at the old vicarage in Gunsbach, where Albert grew up, during her first overnight visit there. Ever attached to her extended family in Germany, Helene had plans to spend two months in Berlin with her cousin Johanna prior to a three-month nursing program in the distant city of Stettin[32] and then to visit with Aunt Clara in Hamburg. In other words, she was facing months of separation from Albert.

His letter of October 27, 1903, makes it clear that she had spoken to him about her conflicts:

> Fundamentally, I have feared it, I have known, for a long time, that you too, you would search one day for "your life," "your happiness," but when you said so last night, so calmly in the shadows of your room, I was seized by it and I have been wondering ever since: did I have the right to take her off her path, her natural way, where she certainly would have found happiness like others? . . . You seem to me so great and strong and I was so proud to think of you as my "equal" that I wasn't able to express all that I was thinking. But an instant later, I felt fear once again when I told myself that it is because of me that you have arrived there.[33]

"There" was, effectively, a state of depression very likely made worse by Albert's long, introspective letter before her departure for Berlin, in which he turns to an almost biblical metaphor: "I am harvesting in a field that does not belong to me."[34] One can only wonder how Helene interpreted his words at the time. But as Mühlstein explains, this "identity crisis" among affluent young women of Helene's era was not so unusual and often found its resolution in social work. In citing the famous example of Bertha Pappenheim, who entered psychoanalytic literature as the anonymous "Anna O.," Mühlstein addresses the paradoxical belief among (primarily male) psychoanalysts at the beginning of the twentieth century that social work was a cause of, not a cure for, depression in bright young women from "good families."[35]

In retrospect, it is difficult to think of Pappenheim as a disintegrating personality. Among other things, she was elected as president of the first League of Jewish Women at an important meeting of the Council of Women in Berlin in 1904. It is quite possible that, although twenty years older than Helene, Pappenheim, like the trailblazing social worker Alice Salomon, served as a kind of public role model. It should also be noted that these powerful German women were, like Helene Bresslau, of Jewish origin. Surely these living examples of highly cultured, self-possessed women had an emancipating effect on Helene. A few years later, during her pioneering social work in Strasbourg, Helene wrote, "As I have seen it, it was my duty to prove that this sort of work was not reserved for ladies of good society, but that it carried a value in and of itself, and was able to bring satisfactions."[36]

While Helene was involved in nursing studies in Stettin, her father was appointed chancellor of the university in Strasbourg. Insofar as she identified with Harry Bresslau's social status and considerable intellect, it is probable that this honor contributed to her sense of possibility as the brilliant daughter of a brilliant man. Based on her letters to Albert written from Stettin, it becomes clear that her work as well as this time of separation from Albert helped Helene to clarify her needs and desires for herself. She became stronger in every way but remained at some distance from Schweitzer because the months away from Strasbourg were extended by a family vacation in Germany's Black Forest. It would be late summer 1904 before she returned to the Bresslau apartment on Strasbourg's Ruprechtsauerallee, ready for a fresh start. At the end of the year, in December, her first publication appeared—an article entitled "God" written anonymously by "A Seeker" for a German weekly.[37]

෨

A major shift occurred in Helene's world in the spring of 1905 when she was hired as the first female inspector in the City Orphan Administration. By then, Strasbourg had grown well beyond its medieval boundaries and tripled in size since the Bresslau family's arrival in 1890 with their eleven-year-old daughter and two young sons, Ernst and Hermann. Under the rising star of Rudolf Schwander, who was elected mayor in 1906, much of the poverty and misery of the previous century was literally swept away and replaced with decent living quarters, funds for the unemployed, greatly improved hygiene, and a new compassion for the poor.[38] Helene's work in the first decade of the twentieth century contributed to this spirit of renewal. She greatly appreciated Mayor Schwander's progressive spirit at the time and his kind words spoken years later: "Helene Bresslau understood how to make the reasons for monitoring children clear to the relatives of those children, so that their resistance could be overcome."[39]

Like many others, including her Bery, whose dream early in 1905 was a chance to "re-educate children in distress,"[40] Helene had wanted desperately to be a part of the exciting changes under way. But to play a role in social change of any kind was a challenge for a woman in those days, a challenge that could not be satisfied by teaching well-to-do girls, as Helene was qualified to do. Nor was it enough to enjoy leisurely travels or take sewing lessons. *Sewing lessons*! We can well imagine Helene cringing at this necessary skill. Not surprisingly, Helene found her university courses to be far more interesting, as Mathieu Arnold explains in his detailed summary of her university studies. She was allowed to take courses because the professors granted permission and because she had already earned a teaching certificate. Under these terms of engagement, Helene took her father's course in medieval history and studied art history and modern history at the university.[41] She also devoted two years to voice and piano lessons at the Strasbourg Music Conservatory, in which she excelled. In brief, she was never idle.

But how different it must have felt to be given an office, a part-time staff, and a chance to influence the lives of thousands of women and children. Albert was amazed at her accomplishment and wrote in April 1905 to tell her so in uncharacteristically competitive terms: "But there now, it is you who have won, happy to have found a task that will fill your life, and you've done it ahead of me!"[42] She kept that letter, even though it said too much about both of them. As any woman of her generation knew, ambition required ladylike discretion, even among good friends such as Marianne and Elly Knapp, Elsa Güt-schow, Helene Fehling, and Albert's three sisters, all of whom were fond of their brother's special "*amie*" in their own way.

Her work, however, was not easy. Writing to Albert Schweitzer from the Social Congress in Frankfurt of 1907, Helene expressed her surprise that others dared to complain of their workload with 80 to 120 orphans and eight to ten visits per day.[43] In contrast, Helene's office near the Strasbourg cathedral supervised 300 to 500 children at any given time and logged twenty-five to thirty visits per day with a similar number of staff. If Helene was especially good at her job, it was only because she believed that human points of connection were to be found in all circumstances, especially among women. This out-look opened the door to the other project that preoccupied her at the time, the home for unwed mothers that she cofounded with Helene Fehling. After a long meeting in October 1907, it was decided that her friend Ella Schmalz would be director and Luise Hoff, Helene's future sister-in-law, vice president. With this team of capable young women in place and with Mayor Schwander as their chief supporter and presi-dent of the organization, Helene was ready to persuade the people of Strasbourg to think differently about young mothers in distress.[44]

An article published in the winter of 1908 conveys Helene's invalu-able combination of compassion and resolve, perhaps intensified by the death following childbirth of her friend Elsa Polczek-Gütschow.[45] Indeed, this piece on the Strasbourg Mother's Home (Strassburger Mütterheim) in the *Blätter für das Strassburger Armenwesen* was writ-ten with a new authority that firmly placed her in the ranks of an expe-rienced social worker: "The girls are to be educated, not with words but, rather, with practical instruction through the example of every-day life," she wrote.[46] Indeed, she was opposed to moral instruction designed to demoralize young women. The Mother's Home would focus on the development of life skills necessary to coping with the burden of being alone and yet responsible for a child. Without such skills, she reasoned, there would only be more orphans. In its first year of operation, the Strassburger Mütterheim served eighty-five new mothers, of whom seventy-four were unmarried and fifty-four utterly destitute.[47]

In the retracing of Helene Bresslau's actions and words through the cycle of unwed motherhood, orphans, and threats to public health, it is apparent that she was a strategic and systemic thinker eager to solve social problems at the source. How could anyone argue with the importance of teaching girls to care for infants or learn the rudiments of light housekeeping so that "those who were previously pushed out of a house and have lost the feeling for simple, organized domesticity are able to take a new kind of pleasure in it and also discover a new courage"? In her view, mothers needed to develop a relationship with their children in hopes that "[t]hey can keep the precious stability of a sense of adult responsibility and know the feeling of motherlove." And so she stirred compassion for otherwise "immoral" and unfortunate girls by evoking the promise of maternal instinct. Meanwhile, Helene's approach promoted education and responsibility. She even dared to suggest that what we call "family planning" today should not be limited to unwed mothers but be encouraged among married women as well.[48]

☙

In late summer of 1905, six months after beginning her professional work in Strasbourg with the City Orphan Administration, Helene traveled to England, where she found herself to be the only woman in a room full of "terribly strange men" at a "Congo evening." Her letter to Albert explains how she gathered her courage "like a lion" to stand and ask if there were missionaries other than the British in the Congo.[49] Clearly, she was there to learn but was also fully aware of Albert's "Congo" intentions, for he had written to her in July that year to confirm his intentions of offering himself to the Paris Mission Society, before he told anyone else. Furthermore, it is abundantly clear in this letter written to "[m]y loyal comrade" that he envisioned going to Africa alone: "I am doing you harm without being able to show that I feel how much you will suffer to see me leave, how alone you will be. . . . Will we separate in order to find each other again?"[50]

By mid-1905, Helene understood herself as an independent woman determined to make the most of her skills, with or without Albert. But was she happy? Even her generous expression of affection in May that year resonates with a wistful sense of farewell. "Thank you for being all that you are for me, thank you for letting me be all that I am for you. Thank you. For everything."[51] She was clearly trying to prepare herself for the fine line between individuality and loneliness, for there can be no question that she loved Albert Schweitzer deeply. This explains why she could not tolerate his persistent suggestion that she find herself a husband when he saw her in a weary state after a long day, which he interpreted as the exhaustion brought on by her efforts to achieve "an individual life."

Helen's unusually strong letter of November 26, 1905, came after an unexpected confrontation at a party, and it reveals both her ongoing inner conflict as well as her firm resolve not to give up. "Any qualms I may have of this sort pass quickly and I am, basically, perfectly solid and lucid," she explains. Furthermore, "[n]othing I see is beyond my strength." And just in case her position is not clear, she drives the point home: "I beg of you, for the last time, not to speak to me again in that way because it makes me ill. . . . I know what awaits me: the complete destiny of a woman but in another sense than what is typically meant by that, and without the ordinary happiness that goes with it. One aspires and, at the same time, struggles constantly against this aspiration."[52]

As Helene's "destiny" became clear in her mind, she plunged into her job with the City Orphan Administration, a position she would hold for four years until spring 1909. She enjoyed the success of the Mother's Home, even as Albert's studies dragged on and Africa remained a distant dream. When a professor's wife known to Albert heard one of Helene's public talks about the Mother's Home, she asked him to pass along her compliments. His note to Helene is as decisive as it is glib. "You seem to be someone," he writes.[53] But, in fact, he was enthusiastic about the project and eager to help. When the Mother's Home opened and was filled to capacity within a few weeks, Albert Schweitzer donated time and medical services in perfect sync with Helene's goals.[54]

In this partnership of equals, Helene also donated her time and skill to Schweitzer's writings. Was it because of their desire for discretion that her contributions to these writings was not acknowledged publically until after their marriage in June 1912? Schweitzer's note at the end of the foreword to the second edition of *The Quest for the Historical Jesus* of 1913 reads like a sweeping attempt to set the record straight, one week before their departure for Lambarene: "Many thanks to my wife for the collaboration on my work on the first edition as well as this one. In the matter of corrections, I acknowledge my friend Pastor Karl Leyrer of (Lower Alsace) as well. May all help be hereby most gratefully acknowledged. Strasbourg, March 14, 1913, Albert Schweitzer."[55] The next public mention of Helene's early contributions to his work will not appear until 1931 in the retroactive note of appreciation included in his autobiography *Out of My Life and Thought*: "My wife had already been a valuable collaborator in completing manuscripts and correcting proofs before our marriage, and she was again a great help with all the work dealing with my publications that had to be completed before we started for Africa."[56]

There can be no doubt that Helene found satisfaction in doing this work, even if it came on top of the other work that filled her days. But contrary to the notion of Helene as a woman whose identity was shaped by and for Albert Schweitzer, her linguistic and intellectual gifts were offered as fully developed skills. Her German was excellent from an early age, and her capacity for detail was an invaluable dimension of her considerable intellect. Helene was not in any sense Albert's student in the process of editing and correcting his manuscripts. Even a passing glance at her notes, indexing, comments, and corrections in the Nachlass A. Schweitzer (A. Schweitzer Papers) of the Zurich Central Library demonstrates her significance as a collaborator in her seemingly endless work on books by Albert Schweitzer.

&

It is only with Helene's decision to enroll in a rigorous course of study in Frankfurt to become a certified nurse (1909–10) that we can begin to speak of her professional choices as determined by her relationship with Albert Schweitzer. Historian Matthieu Arnold pinpoints the moment with specificity: a Sunday evening in January 1909 in a train car traveling from Gunsbach to Strasbourg. That, he declares, is when and where the two made the decision to marry and go to Africa together.[57] But why would they decide to marry in January 1909 and then wait nearly three years to become engaged—on December 26, 1911—especially when an engagement of less than six months was embarrassingly brief by the standards of the day?

The timing of this decision to marry and whether it was merely a marriage of convenience to satisfy the rules of the Paris Mission Society or perhaps a more defensible *mariage de raison*[58] remain debatable themes in Schweitzer studies. In either case, it is clear that Helene's resignation from the City Orphan Administration and commitment to a higher level of professional nursing studies in the spring of 1909 mark the moment when she embraced Albert Schweitzer's plans as her own. In other words, prior to her thirtieth birthday on January 25, 1909, Helene's life can be read as a search for her own individual destiny, aside from the ideals and emotions she shared with Albert Schweitzer.

It is also with the decision to take on a grueling year of nursing school that the limits of her health entered their lives. Throughout the year in Frankfurt, Helene lived a tightly structured existence that included long hours of study, applied work, "night watch" duty, and rigorous exams. In April 1910, she was tempted to "return to Strasbourg and pass the exam as a nurse's aide."[59] In June, she was counting the days and weeks: "Still 14 weeks and 104 days, according to my father's calculations." This note, like many others, was hastily written: "Farewell, I don't have time. The chief is back, hours of revision begin Monday and at the same time hours of religion."[60] For religion, too, was part of the curriculum. Finally, in September, "I'm in my room to write clinical reports to prepare myself for the exam. . . . Tomorrow at eight I will have completed the practical work. . . . You can't imagine how my nerves are used up. Take care and excuse your friend whose head is empty of ideas, your G."[61]

Helene's head would soon recover, but her body would never be the same. Just before Christmas a small tumor was identified as the source of her back pain. Albert quickly reassured her that the tumor "presents nothing to be alarmed about."[62] In January 1911, he was pleased that her back pain had lessened but urged her to take more time before putting herself to the test: "Only when your health is truly restored will I be able to erase those terrible memories that remain with me of that day when I was invited to your home and placed across from you at the table, when I saw the suffering you endured."[63]

A month later Helene was in Switzerland, soaking up the sun on Lake Leman from Montreux's Grand Hotel Eden, a "getaway" that continued into March, when she traveled to Interlaken for continued rest, only to find a letter from Albert on arrival: "M.G. It's necessary that a note is waiting for you when you arrive in Interlaken with a painful back."[64] In May, she was in the Black Forest, a region of Germany known for its fresh air, clinics, spas, and curative ambience. From the Pension Waldeck in Königsfeld, she wrote optimistically: "You know, Bery, I only slept badly the first night, I only slightly feel the lumbago, I can stand up straight again and yesterday I walked easily for an hour and a half."[65]

What she did not mention in her optimistic letter was that her treatment in the Black Forest was aimed at a greater threat: tuberculosis, Europe's most deadly public-health catastrophe of the time, also known as the "white plague" and "consumption." Helene's first brush with the disease had been a case of pleurisy before the age of ten. By 1905, the microbe had been identified, and its discoverer awarded the Nobel Prize, but the path to cure was far from clear.[66] By the time a vaccine was successfully developed and used in a Parisian hospital in 1921, Helene would be in her forties.[67]

After visiting Helene in Königsfeld in 1911, Albert seems to have resigned himself to the challenges of her health, challenges that would rise and fall in the years ahead. Despite the uncertainty, they became engaged the day after Christmas in 1911. Meanwhile, between October 1911 and July 1912—a period that overlaps with Helene and Albert's wedding in Gunsbach on June 18, 1912—the Paris Mission Society board met fourteen times to discuss the "Schweitzer question." This phrase was a euphemism for concerns about his German citizenship and liberal theology, both of which were at odds with pre-vailing missionary zeal.[68] Frustrated and depressed by the delays, Schweitzer turned to Helene, who anchored their future with her natural optimism and the careful editing of his income-producing publications. She also took on the role of managing their accounts as donations came in for their "Congo project."[69] In the end, the extent of the Paris Mission Society's support for a strictly medical mission was understood to be a house on the riverbank and nothing more.

൭

Helene's early years in Strasbourg reveal the painful evolution of a modern woman in a perpetual state of becoming. It is, therefore, peculiar to encounter the commonplace notion that Helene Bresslau was, somehow, Albert Schweitzer's "creation." Even Professor Jean-Paul Sorg, whose tireless work over many years allows French-speaking researchers to read more than six hundred pre-Lambarene letters, has suggested that "Helene might have come to the point of succumbing to the manners of her era had Schweitzer not entered her life, had not pushed her to choose an occupation and, on this basis, emancipate herself."[70] But in retracing Helene's steps in these early years, one senses that she would have had no choice but to emancipate herself, with or without her special friend's encouragement. Indeed, she *did* emancipate herself, even if she could write a note like this just weeks after beginning her professional life as a social worker in Strasbourg in the spring of 1905: "You brought me such a feeling of peace, a calm interior, an assurance that makes me believe in myself and in life."[71]

As we look at early portraits of Helene Bresslau through the telescope of time, the full-length image captures her deep-set eyes set on a distant horizon. She tilts slightly forward, gently asserting herself, as she probably did at the Congo meeting in England, at the mayor's office in Strasbourg, and in her talks aimed at dignified solutions for unwed mothers. If the months in Stettin clarified her psychic need for individuality and her excellent work confirmed her skills, her social milieu provided a ready template for organizing a multifaceted life. Frequent travels, displacements, and separations had taught her how to manage on her own, how not to cling to routine. As for her innate gift of efficiency, that would smooth many aspects of Albert Schweitzer's life, including his relationship with his daughter.

Out of these Strasbourg years, Helene Bresslau's character emerges like wings opening slowly but fully. By 1907, she is a decidedly modern woman with work of her own. By 1909, she is prepared to cast her fate with Albert without fear or misgivings. Despite hard-earned skills and a spirit of adventure, she knows her destiny will not be easy.

3

· · ·

In and Out of Africa

Long before Helene and Albert Schweitzer arrived in Africa, the continent had become a frontier for pious, adventurous, or simply greedy citizens of the world's most powerful nations. Dr. Robert H. Nassau (1835–1921), an American Presbyterian missionary and medical doctor, was the first to establish a mission station on the Ogowe River in 1874, nearly twenty years before the French claimed the region as a colony.[1] French explorer Savorgnan de Brazza (1852–1905), for whom the capital city of the Republic of the Congo is named, came as a peacemaker opposed to slavery. The first non-African faces in the region also included some very independent women. Dr. Nassau's wife, Mary Foster Nassau, and his sister, Isabel, were the first white women to live in Gabon.

Mary Kingsley (1862–1900), a British explorer, shared Dr. Nassau's fascination with the study of ethnology—"fetishism," as she called it—but also enjoyed the challenge of dodging rapids and maneuvering a pirogue (dugout canoe) around Lambarene Island in 1895.[2] As a predecessor of Helene Schweitzer in the Ogowe region, Kingsley penned the now classic *Travels in West Africa*, which occasionally includes poetic meditations on the region's dazzling natural beauty. Here, she describes a sunset on the Ogowe River: "The day closed with magnificent dramatic beauty. Dead ahead of us, up through a bank of dun-colored mist rose the moon, a great orb of crimson, spreading down the oil-like, still river, a streak of blood-red reflection."[3]

Kingsley also records her impressions of Talagouga, a small island upriver from Lambarene, where the first gathering of Christian missionaries in the region was organized in 1893. At the turn of the twentieth century, the mission station at Talagouga was the pride of Edouard and Valentine Lantz, young Alsatians who died of Blackwater Fever in 1902 and 1906, respectively.[4] Albert and Helene Schweitzer visited the grave of Valentine Lantz in 1914, inspired by her valiant effort to establish a dispensary on her veranda. In the days following her death, fellow missionary Daniel Couve expressed his grief and fear in a long letter to the director of the Paris Mission Society: "Everything we have felt in these days of anguish and tears, you would feel it with us. We don't dare to think of the repercussions that such an ordeal will have on our work. For our Congo, the loss is irredeemable. After Mr. Junod, Mr. Chapuis; after Mr. Chapuis, Madame Lantz. Mail received speaks of the end of Madame Champel; all that in less than two years. And each of us wonders: Will my turn be next?"[5]

By the time the Paris Mission Society vigorously debated the "Schweitzer question" in 1912, Daniel Couve was a board member who understood all facets of the situation. Among other things, he knew that a doctor was desperately needed along the Ogowe. At the same time, the rapturous pietism driving the Mission Society—which even Couve seems to question in his 1906 letter to Paris—was decidedly at odds with Albert Schweitzer's approach to service in Africa. Above all, Schweitzer was motivated by a desire to "atone" for the sins of Europe and enact his belief that "missionary work in itself is not primarily a religious matter" but "first and foremost a duty to humanity."[6]

Helene's religious views were similarly down to earth, though she counted in the board's discussions only as a symbol of conventional moral underpinning. Had Albert Schweitzer been less determined— or perhaps as capable as Helene at working within institutional structures—we can imagine that both might have remained in Strasbourg and focused their careers on social work and public health. In the end, Albert Schweitzer was accepted as a medical missionary *only* and with a stern warning not to preach. Helene went with him because by then his life was hers. With an optimistic spirit and hard-won nursing credentials, she set out to become what Mary Kingsley describes as "one form of human being whose praise has never adequately been sung, namely, the missionary's wife."[7]

ॐ

After leaving the port of Paulliac near Bordeaux on March 26, 1913, the Schweitzers' first stop on the African coast was at Dakar, Senegal. There, on April 4, they changed into their white tropical clothes for the first time and sat in a café, laughing at each other's unusual appearance. A few days later, just past Conakry, Helene wrote in the diary she would keep until November 21, 1915, "We are truly in love with Africa."[8] This diary (*Tagebuch* in German) speaks of jungle vegetation as it comes into view, bright houses on the hillside, and an abundance of nature observed from the deck of the ship *Europa*: "This morning there were games of amusing schools of dolphins all around the boat in the foam of the waves. I saw flying fish, as well as a little bird who skimmed the water only to fly up and plunge in again with all its strength."[9]

In Libreville, the current-day capital of Gabon, the Schweitzers were greeted by E. A. Ford, an American missionary stationed just outside the city at Baraka, who persuaded them to join him for the end of the Sunday service.[10] They then made their way to Cap Lopez (now Port Gentil) and headed upstream on the riverboat *Alembé*. After two days on the Ogowe River, the river split to embrace Lambarene Island, then a center of trade and forestry operations. After a short crossing in a pirogue to a place called Andende, the couple climbed a hill late in the afternoon on April 16, 1913, surrounded by curious Africans and an abundance of orange, lemon, and palm trees as well as coffee and banana plants. Helene's next entry in her *Tagebuch* comes several days later as a breathless note dashed off in the midst of a hectic day: "Lambarene! Eight days since I've written here, but what an eventful week!" Following this sentence, her husband adds an ironic comment: "So 'Madame Albert' doesn't know where to begin. Oh well."[11]

After three weeks of leisurely travel in relative comfort, the Schweitzers were suddenly confronted with the reality of snakes, scorpions, stifling heat, and the urgent need to organize a house. Patients appeared almost immediately, informed through the age-old system of African drums. It would be two weeks before more than seventy cases of medications and supplies were delivered, each one bearing the initials "ASB" for "Albert Schweitzer Bresslau"—a monogram that would eventually become well known to customs officials and boat captains along the Lambarene route.

Helene and Albert went to work as soon as they could, organizing consultations outdoors while turning a derelict chicken coop next to their small house into an operating room.[12] In those early days and weeks, they became acquainted with the suffering they hoped to alleviate: strangulated hernias, elephantiasis, leprosy, malaria, sleeping sickness, and assorted skin infections. Helene quickly assumed the role of operating-room nurse and anesthetist. She was also responsible for the care and cleaning of surgical instruments, the preparation of bandages, and nutrition for those too ill to return to their villages, even developing what has been called a "homeopathic pharmacy" out of her garden of medicinal plants.[13] In their first nine months at Andende, Helene and Albert Schweitzer treated approximately two thousand patients with the help of a native nurse, Joseph Azowani.[14]

As usual, Helene adapted with optimism, filling her days with purposeful work and her diary with observations. However, although this document was written primarily by Helene, it was far from a private *journal intime*. Rather, a special notebook with carbonlike paper allowed each page to be made in five copies easily shared with friends and family back in Europe. Furthermore, both names are written at the top of the first page, meaning Albert was free to add his own entries. Their very different styles of handwriting—occasionally juxtaposed on the same page—announce two distinct personalities. Albert's small, wiry letters travel methodically across the page like careful embroidery, whereas Helene's firm, vertical strokes flow forward with astonishing energy.[15]

It is clear from this diary that both Albert and Helene valued careful documentation from the beginning of their adventure. In time, Albert would rely on Helene's *Tagebuch* as a rich source for his first books about life in Africa.[16] It lent itself to such use because Albert's contributions were as full of detail, wonder, and lyrical language as

Helene's. He was, for example, the first to describe the Ogowe River's luxuriant atmosphere in a particularly long, five-page entry shortly after their arrival, in which he concludes, "It all seemed so magical, just like in Robinson Crusoe!"[17] Indeed, the existence of this early written record might be credited as Albert Schweitzer's inspiration to set philosophy aside long enough to write what we now call "memoir" or "creative nonfiction."

However "unsung" Helene's wifely role might have been, we know from the *Tagebuch* and from their contemporaries, such as Marie Woytt-Secretan, Victor Nessmann, and Frédéric Trensz, that Helene plunged into her new life with vigor, efficiency, and even joy. Her capacity for hard work in a challenging environment can be read as proof that her independence earned in Strasbourg was now unshakeable. For the now thirty-four-year-old Helene Schweitzer, as for other European women who would follow in the long story of Lambarene, a life in Africa offered a chance to integrate multiple aspects of modern identity, perhaps even more freely and completely than would have been possible in Europe.

In this period, Helene is sociable, resourceful, and optimistic in the face of the unknown. The tone of her letters home and the sheer energy of the diary she kept for two years support her German biographer's view of this initial sojourn in Africa as "the happiest time of Helene Schweitzer's life."[18] The work was hard, but "Madame Docteur," as she was called by the native people, knew how to plant herself in foreign soil and grow, a trait that would prove to be essential in the difficult years ahead.

ରଙ

Wednesday, 5 VIII.14. I had sent Joseph to the Post Office to buy stamps and given him a note for Mr. Lager in order to learn when the *Anita Rose* would be leaving for Cap Lopez, for I wanted to send some bananas and vegetables to Mrs. Fournier. He comes back while we are still at the table and, overwhelmed, he tells us that all the Whites are at the administrative Post and gives the answer from Mr. Lager to Albert: that France had mobilized her troops on August 2, that they were waiting for their orders, that he would say his farewells now in case we should not see each other again . . . then Mr. Clasen, back from Samkita with a letter from Mrs. Morel, who is as ignorant as we are. In the chaos of thoughts that followed, when we were finally able to reflect on the situation after the wild anguish and mortal fear for our dear ones in Europe, the first thought that emerged: it is necessary to try to get to Cameroun. Mr. Ottmann goes to the Post for more details. Comes back with Mr. Clasen who explains to us that we are not authorized to leave: we are prisoners of war![19]

With this outpouring dashed off in her *Tagebuch*, Helene announced a new chapter for the Schweitzers and for Europe, though no one could have imagined on August 5, 1914, the life-altering destruction that lay ahead. The Schweitzers were clearly shocked to find themselves under house arrest as civil prisoners of war, suddenly guarded by a small group of Senegalese militia men. Dr. Schweitzer was initially ordered to stop practicing medicine, an order that was lifted in November once suspicions of espionage dissipated.[20] Nevertheless, as German citizens living and working in a French colony, Helene and Albert were suddenly implicated in a war that would kill nine million people in what Robert Minder aptly describes as a "mutual massacre."[21]

The reality of this brutal war radicalized Albert Schweitzer in ways that would become apparent only over time. To begin with, he returned to the book he had first imagined in 1904, *Wir Epigonen* (We, inheritors of the past), with a fresh resolve. As he wrote later in his autobiography, "At the beginning of the summer of 1915 I awoke from some kind of mental daze. Why only criticize civilization? Why limit myself to analyzing ourselves as *epigones*? Why not work on something more constructive?"[22] This defining moment in his fortieth year was further shaped by the horrifying scope of the conflict and eventually by his and Helene's personal experience of internment as civil prisoners of war. Their daily deprivations and witness to injustice account for the "thread of compassionate indignation" I speak of in the preface to this book.

In a sense, this thread became a kind of lifeline that allowed Schweitzer, at age forty-three, to pull himself up to higher moral ground as his youthful disdain for European culture was confirmed. His memorable sermons delivered in Strasbourg as early as October and November 1918 confronted the horror of war head on.[23] And as early as 1920, he formed a conscious intention to return to Africa, where he could live in accordance with Reverence for Life. Developed as a philosophy along the Ogowe in the midst of human suffering and teeming nature, the ethical system behind those words—"Ehrfurcht vor dem Leben" in German, a phrase that encompasses both awe and fear—became the cornerstone of Schweitzer's mature work. In addition, the publication of the first volume of *Kulturphilosophie* in 1923 marked a turning point when his writings seemed to "take on the world," no longer driven by academic achievement or theology alone, but by concern for human suffering in a real world created by deeply flawed individuals. Theology, from this point on, was an instrument of his action, not an intellectual pursuit.

It is significant that throughout the war Schweitzer maintained a supportive and slightly subversive correspondence with the outspoken French pacifist and presumed traitor Romain Rolland, then living in Switzerland.[24] Helene was included in this correspondence as a like-minded spirit. In fact, she had known Rolland for years, as a letter she wrote to Albert in 1907 makes clear.[25] Perhaps this connection accounts for a remark by Schweitzer's mentor, Parisian organist Charles-Marie Widor, who later suggested that it was German-born Helene whose "indiscretions" were of concern to the authorities during the war.[26] Her chief "indiscretion," of course, was that she was indisputably German and therefore considered to be a natural enemy of France, unlike the Alsatians, whose status was more ambiguous. Although there is no basis for thinking of Helene as anyone's enemy, her 1918 journal includes the occasional use of the pronoun *we* with regard to German gains and losses.

In either case, the war made life in Africa more difficult than ever, and Helene and Albert Schweitzer suffered along with everyone else. Donations to their work rapidly decreased. Reserves of everything from flour to medications ran low. They added monkey flesh to their diet of bananas, manioc, fish, and fruit as a means of combating tropical anemia. And at the end of the year, the flames of Christmas candles were extinguished early to save them for next year, even if the thought of another Christmas in Africa was almost unthinkable to Helene.[27] Nearly two years in the tropics had taken a toll, and she longed to go home.

Among the difficulties, Helene's respiratory problems were increasingly aggravated by the hot, oppressive climate of Equatorial Africa.[28] In January 1915, she suffered an attack of phlebitis that required two weeks of bed rest.[29] In April, their nurse, Joseph, left, unwilling to work for wages cut in half.[30] Although suffering from a painful boil on her foot that spring, Helene continued to stand for long hours to assist with operations. In addition to the physical strain, we can only imagine the psychological strain of being cut off from loved ones close to the front. Though they had no definitive knowledge of it for months, Albert's mother, Adèle Schweitzer-Schillinger, was killed in July 1916 by a soldier's runaway horse while she was out walking with her husband.

Before and after that tragedy, Albert and Helene coped with their new reality by spending months by the sea in a cabin at Cap Lopez, sometimes in the company of Alsatian missionary friends Georgette and Léon Morel. There, they enjoyed fishing, reading, and taking in the fresh air, and they even had the use of a sailboat. Meanwhile, somewhat to his surprise, Albert found the energy to work on his book-in-progress, *Kulturphilosophie*.[31] "My mental freshness I have, strange to say, preserved almost completely in spite of anemia and fatigue."[32] During this rare interlude of sea breezes and shared tranquility, Helene was happily engaged in Albert's philosophical work. In a letter to her father sent from Cap Lopez at the end of May 1917, she wrote, "I have started with the copying of the text and I hope to be able to work at it efficiently. L."[33] The evidence of her efficiency is now preserved on fragile, brown sheets of paper in the Zurich Central Library.[34]

Helene remained optimistic, perhaps because the alternative was too difficult to contemplate. One of her last letters in 1917 anticipated another "vacation" by the sea in October. Writing to her sister-in-law

Luise Bresslau-Hoff in a light-hearted woman-to-woman spirit, Helene reflected on the possibility of the war still going on in the spring of 1918. If that turned out to be the case, "In the dry season we will take one of the pensions now freed by the absent families of missionaries & I will have a little break—after living through a total of five years of housekeeping at the Equator!"[35]

Unfortunately, a "little break" in the spring of 1918 was not meant to be. In November 1917, the Schweitzers received orders to leave Africa for France, where they would be interned in an ancient monastery, Notre Dame de Garaison. There, in the mountainous region of the Hautes Pyrénées at Monléon-Magnoac, a chapel had been built in the sixteenth century, inspired by a young girl's visions of the Virgin Mary.[36] Three centuries later this once-popular pilgrimage site became a Camp de Concentration Austro-Allemand (Austro-German Concentration Camp), where a diverse society of more than two thousand people—including Helene and Albert Schweitzer—would endure periods of internment between September 1914 and December 1919.[37]

Oddly enough, the French initially used the term *concentration camp* to describe "free camps" where innocent civilians were "concentrated" but at liberty to come and go. Those at the old monastery in the mountains were drawn from a mixed population of Austro-Germans, Alsatians, Poles, Czechs, Jews, Gypsies, and "foreigners" from French colonies. The goal of this camp—one of seventy established throughout southern and western France as well as in coastal regions such as Brittany—was the sequestering of "undesirables" and "suspects" in facilities variously referred to as free depots, refugee depots, internment camps, work camps, colonies, and, of course, concentration camps. Hervé Mauran and Jean-Marie Ehret, two of the first historians to explore this troublesome period in French history, explain that the practice was widely viewed as a "barbaric regression in the heart of a civilized world," regardless of the context of war.[38]

ᠺᠣ

Forty-three years after the Franco-Prussian War, there were reasons to approach the population of Alsace-Lorraine as potentially sympathetic to the German cause. According to Mauran and Ehret, "We must, first of all, remember that Alsace, in 1914, was 90 percent German speaking." Included in this percentage were speakers of the Alsatian dialect because "High German had always been the written German expression of those who spoke the dialect."[39] Furthermore, regardless of language, those younger than forty were surely "germanized" in terms of culture thanks to the social and political power of German-born "elites" such as Helene's family and friends. As deadly battles began in the Vosges Mountains in the first months of World War I, reconquering the two "lost provinces" of Alsace and Lorraine was understood to be an essential component of French victory.[40]

As early as September 1, 1914, the minister of the interior in France mandated that "Austro-German subjects must be lodged in local collectives where they might submit to effective surveillance."[41] This directive led to a process riddled with human error as layers of French bureaucracy attempted to assign "evacuees" to requisitioned facilities based on their perceived loyalty to France. Mauran and Ehret estimate the number of those "evacuated" from Alsace and put through this process by the French army between 1914 and 1919 at no fewer than fifteen thousand.[42] Other prisoners came from Paris. And still others, such as Helene and Albert Schweitzer, came from the colonies with their status clearly defined. A telegram sent on November 16, 1917, from Bordeaux to the prefect in Tarbes announced the arrival of the "German Schweitzer couple" who are "considered as suspects to be interned."[43]

In 1916, the population at Garaison exceeded one thousand. But it was not until a few months before the Schweitzers' arrival in late 1917 that the facility encompassed practical amenities such as a butcher, a large garden, adequate water, and a school for the more than five hundred youths sixteen and younger who inhabited this camp during the war years. But even with these improvements, there were severe deprivations of freedom. Those interned were allowed to take walks during limited hours within a distance of one kilometer beyond the barbed-wire perimeter. Resources available—from food and clothing to heat and light—were not distributed equally, which naturally led to resentment among the inmates. Correspondence was censored and limited to thirty-two lines. For those who did not write in German or French, letters could not be censored and therefore were not sent.[44]

Helene and Albert Schweitzer arrived in Garaison in a weakened state via Bordeaux after weeks at sea, confined to their stifling hot cabin below deck most of the time and forbidden to speak with anyone else on board. Helene collapsed on the sidewalk in Bordeaux when they were forced to cross the city on foot, taunted as spies as they carried their own bags to the temporary barracks they would inhabit for three weeks.[45] There, Helene's health worsened, and Albert developed a severe case of dysentery.[46]

As if to clarify their solidarity with the French, one of Albert Schweitzer's first acts at Garaison was to write a long letter to the camp director on November 25, 1917, in which he names relatives and friends in Paris who could vouch for him and his wife. In this letter, he defends the work accomplished in French Equatorial Africa as a contribution to the French nation: "I was the only doctor in an immense territory ravaged by sleeping sickness. All the French who were ill and needed to be hospitalized were received at our place as guests, without any obligation to pay for their stay. In the same fashion we accepted European ladies who came to us to give birth." In closing, Schweitzer pleaded with the camp director to use his influence to keep them in Garaison because "[w]e need this climate at a moderate altitude to overcome severe anemia."[47]

Indeed, the refreshing mountain air of the Hautes Pyrénées restored their health to some extent. Another advantage was the frequent and efficient postal service, even if it came with constant monitoring. By keeping her written words cheerful, Helene was particularly successful at acquiring the censor's stamp *"Geprüft"* (proofed). The postcard sent to her father for his seventieth birthday in February 1918 reads almost like an ode to spring: "My dear Parents, Hopefully, with you both, everything is going along well! With us, things are quite orderly and we are enjoying the wonderful weather. It is just like spring, with most of the trees beginning to bloom, so one can sit at the open window until five o'clock in the afternoon. Can you imagine how good this fresh air and the fragrance of linden trees are for us. If only no more frost takes over, but that seems hardly possible in this season. Much love to all! With all my heart, Lene."[48]

As the only doctor in the camp, Albert was able to work, and both he and Helene enjoyed the multitude of talents, languages, and cultures around them. Helene found a seamstress to sew her a woolen suit, and Albert located a carpenter to build a table. On this, he drew a keyboard and played his "blind organ" with the music set before his eyes and the sound of Bach in his head. It is likely that copies of chapters in *Kulturphilosophie* were also made at this table, even if parts of the manuscript had been left behind in Africa. Furthermore, they had three-dozen books with them, including many philosophical and theological texts, which allowed their reading and intellectual work to go on.[49]

In other words, they continued to live in a private world of shared purpose. And when a group of Gypsy musicians "evacuated" from Parisian cafés recognized Albert, Helene's thirty-ninth birthday on January 25, 1918, was celebrated with a serenade under her window— the waltz from Jacques Offenbach's *Tales of Hoffmann*.[50] It is not diffi- cult to imagine music cutting through the silence of a winter night and a gentle waltz around their small room. In a letter sent to Königsfeld six years later, Albert's closing lines evoke the memory of that evening serenade: "In a hurry now, send many kisses. I thought of your birth- day in Garaison and also last year. From my heart, Albert."[51] Even in 1936, as Albert Schweitzer spent the last days of the year alone in Strasbourg, his thoughts turned back to that bittersweet time: "From 11 pm until midnight I will be sitting in silence, thinking of you and of those, beloved ones, who have left us, and of Garaison . . . [.]"[52]

ॐ

Helene and Albert Schweitzer were transferred against their will to another camp located outside the Provençal village of Saint-Rémy- de-Provence at the end of March 1918. In this remote, windy village, the former monastery of St. Paul-de-Mausole had found a new pur- pose in April 1915, as did many monasteries and factories through- out southern France. With its walled courtyard, thirteenth-century church, carpentry workshop, and numerous cell-like rooms, St. Paul was an ideal facility for the "Austro-German depot of Saint-Rémy-de-Provence." Furthermore, it was conveniently located outside the village adjacent to a former mental asylum that featured a pleasant garden and large fountain.[53] For France's wartime purposes, the old, stone complex was categorized as a *dépôt surveillé* (guarded depot) housing an exclusively Alsace-Lorraine population. As in Garaison, the rooms were locked at night, the food mediocre, and freedom to leave the grounds limited to certain days of the week and only with an escort.

It seems the mayor of Saint-Rémy would have preferred a more hospitable solution. As early as March 1915, a series of letters from the mayor's office informed the population of the imminent arrival of "a certain number of civil French prisoners, liberated from Germany, among which women and children are the great majority."[54] The mayor did his best to reassure the Saint-Rémois that these people were "not German prisoners, contrary to certain rumors, and should not be looked upon in a negative way."[55] He even urged his villagers to consider taking some of these "refugees" into their homes as temporary residents, recommending "kind hospitality."[56]

In the end, however, this rural population with fathers, husbands, sons, and brothers fighting and dying in the trenches of northern France did not feel disposed to offer any sort of hospitality to German-speaking people.[57] Rather, their presence created social tensions, especially because the internees typically came into the village in groups. If some of the younger men drank too much while their guard looked the other way, they might break into song in German or, worse yet, in their incomprehensible Alsatian dialect. The villagers were known to spit at the refugees, shake their fists, or yell "Boches!" ("Filthy Germans!").[58] Female prisoners could expect to be called "Cow!" or "Bitch!" if they showed their faces in town.[59] Perhaps because of the mayor's compassion and resolve, to say nothing of camp director Jean Bagnaud's calm demeanor, a suggestion published in a regional newspaper that the municipal council "limit the rights of movement in the city" of these "arrogant Boches" was not pursued.[60]

Meanwhile, inside the walls a cultural life had developed among a prison population that shared a language, a culture, and a history. As in most of the camps, an internee was found to serve as liaison with the authorities. At Saint-Rémy in June 1917, this person was a Mr. Xavier Schlienger, who wrote a gracious letter in impeccable penmanship directly to "Your Excellency, Minister of the Interior," with a brief list of requests before he signed off with a flourish, "In the name of the internees, the delegate, Schlienger." His demands were far from extreme: "1. Two or three regular weekly outings without escort in the region of Saint-Rémy. 2. The authorization to form a choir to sing songs in German, with the understanding that these songs would not be patriotic in nature, so not to cause offense. 3. Permission to form a small musical group consisting of eight to ten violins, accompanied by a piano, as are found in all the depots, in the French camps as well as the German ones."[61]

ౚ

A few months before Mr. Schlienger's humble requests, Helene and Albert had traveled to Saint-Rémy-de-Provence in a double-decker train car from Tarascon, arriving four days before Easter on March 27, 1918. At that time of year, they would have passed through miles of leafless plane trees with bare branches rising in black-fisted clusters. In the distance, they would have seen sage-colored hills, red-tiled rooflines broken by ornate stone church spires, and the occasional ruins of an ancient castle. It was probably a damp, windy day with flashes of sunlight when they climbed into the horse-drawn wagon waiting at the now vanished Saint-Rémy train station. Despite his fatigue, Albert surely kept an eye on their two trunks and hand baggage during the last leg of their journey up the slope to St. Paul-de-Mausole. We know from eyewitnesses that word of the Schweitzers' arrival created a wave of excitement among the eighty internees, all of whom came out to greet them, led by Jean Iltis, Albert's former classmate and more recently a schoolmaster in Gunsbach. Pastor Liebrich, the camp's chosen spiritual leader, had been Albert's student at the Protestant Seminary in Strasbourg. Suddenly Albert and Helene were among old friends.[62]

Unfortunately, the warm welcome did not relieve the physical challenges of life in Saint-Rémy. When they reached their room, they found cold floors, stone walls, and a window offering views of eerie black-green Cyprus trees dancing in the wind. Helene was very weak, and Albert was not much better. "Ever since my attack of dysentery in Bordeaux I had been aware of a continually increasing weariness, which I tried in vain to master," he wrote later. General exhaustion made it impossible for them "to join in the walks the camp inmates were allowed on certain days, escorted by the guards" because "the walks were always at a rapid pace." Furthermore, "[m]y wife's health had improved considerably in the mountain climate of Garaison, but now she suffered from the harsh winds of Provence. She could not get used to the stone floors."[63]

In retrospect, Helene Schweitzer Bresslau was the least likely of all the inmates to feel at ease among this small society of school teachers, railway employees, and forestry workers from small Alsatian villages.[64] The evidence of her "difference" can be seen in a group photo taken outdoors by a guard on April 28, 1918, a photocopy of which is the only reminder of the internment camp on display at St. Paul-de-Mausole today. Such photographs were common in the camps, and this one shows a striking similarity of appearance among the internees, including hats, hairstyles, clothing, and gestures—with the exception of Helene Schweitzer. She sits on the front row as one of eleven women in the photograph, but she is the only one wearing a tailored suit rather than a floral-print blouse or lace collar. She is also the only woman wearing a hat. Unlike the others, her hands are in her pockets, perhaps still unaccustomed to the cold.

Though generally known to be a private person, Helene was surprisingly open during her first days in Saint-Rémy, as we learn from a man who would become her husband's colleague, Dr. Jacques Scheib. His late-in-life memories recalled Albert Schweitzer's Good Friday sermon on March 29, 1918, in the austere St. Paul-de-Mausole chapel. After describing this sermon as "so simple, so profound, so moving that all those assembled were fascinated and had difficulty holding back their tears," Dr. Scheib goes on to recall the tragedy of that day when a German missile hit the roof of Saint-Gervais in Paris during the Good Friday service, killing more than eighty worshippers. "A.S. did not come back to us the rest of that day," Scheib writes. "He withdrew to his room and forbid anyone to come in, even his wife, who told us that he had wept like a child."[65]

Another internee, Anne Wersinger-Liller, was only twenty-four in 1918 but had already spent three years as an "Austro-German" prisoner of war. At the age of seventy-nine, she helped to commemorate Albert Schweitzer's one hundredth birthday by recalling the discomfort of the iron beds and straw mattresses, the guards posted at the gate, and the bad food. She writes of sitting in the garden mending clothes and reading books that the Red Cross had made available to women. (Men had the option of language instruction in German, French, English, and Latin or made wood carvings.) Wersinger-Liller also writes of "a feverish activity when the news was leaked that Albert and Helene Schweitzer were coming." She helped the others make garlands to decorate the gate and the room selected by Mr. Schlienger. "It was really an event for all of us and the doctor and Madame Schweitzer did not hide their joy in finding so many friends."[66]

Wersinger-Liller goes on to describe both Schweitzers' visible exhaustion, especially Helene's. "We were devastated to see her in that state." In an effort to help, a fellow inmate, Mr. Angelade, took over the daily task of making the Schweitzers' bed because Helene was simply not strong enough to do it. Meanwhile, "[t]he doctor was always working, reading, or writing." He also continued to play his "blind organ," using the volumes of Bach, Mendelssohn, Franck, Widor, and others he had with him in a trunk. When Dr. Scheib was transferred to another camp in June 1918, Albert Schweitzer took his place as chief physician, working for no compensation and promising to stay until the last convoy of prisoners was repatriated. "When I remember this time," writes Wersinger-Liller, "I must say that with the arrival of Mr. and Mrs. Schweitzer, life at the camp changed; it became less difficult, they brought us hope."[67]

Schweitzer also brought hope to the villagers, who, in addition to the deprivations of war, were living through the reality of what came to

known as the Spanish flu pandemic.[68] When Madame Simon Roumanille's particularly dire case worsened in the night, and the only local
doctors were either quite old or mobilized for war, her family decided
to call at the gate of the refugee camp, where both Dr. Scheib and Dr.
Schweitzer were interned at the time. As it happened, the guard at the
camp knocked on the door of Room 49. Schweitzer, upon hearing a
summary of symptoms, grabbed his bag and hurried down the slope to
the village with an agitated Mr. Roumanille at his heels.

The Roumanilles' daughter was only twelve at the time, but writing under a pseudonym years later as a regionally recognized novelist,
Marie Mauron published her account of Dr. Schweitzer's dramatic
appearance in her home. She also described Schweitzer's reassuring
words in the shadows of the sick room: "What will happen between
now and dawn . . . I don't know. But I will be here to the end." As she
recalled these words on Albert Schweitzer's eightieth birthday, Mauron wrote that "[a]n energy, a new cool composure, came to me in his
presence. These moments taught me the meaning of brotherhood."
At daybreak, light filtered into the room, and her mother's jagged
breathing evened out, as if she were "a drowned woman emerging
into life." Schweitzer beamed, triumphant, and hugged an elderly relative as the day unfolded full of hope. "Late in the day, when he left
us, more certain of his victory, this Foreigner had become one of us,
and the most precious one of all."[69]

Marie Mauron goes on to explain that when her father asked what
he could do to repay Dr. Schweitzer, the reply was a simple one: "My
wife is suffering by living as a prisoner, locked in at dusk. Would you,
by speaking on our behalf, be able to obtain permission to come and
visit now and then, both of us, to share a bowl of soup and spend the
evening here, to take some fresh air, to chat, free like honest people,
in other words, to find ourselves part of a family?" And so Albert and
Helene came to the village from time to time, sharing the table at the
Roumanilles' home. When news of Rhena's birth reached Saint-Rémy
the following winter, "[t]he tiny Alsatian girl was a little 'Helene' for
everyone," wrote Marie Mauron in 1955. "We felt a tenderness toward
her mother."[70]

☙

Marie Mauron's adolescent memories make for a touching narrative, but one that Robert Minder assesses as "rather novelistic."[71] Minder also quotes a cousin of Marie Mauron, who carves a sharp edge on Mauron's sentimental version of events: "The birth of little Rhena in 1919 did not bring the Saint-Rémois to the boiling point of excitement," said Marie Roumanille-Blanc, "and no one contributed money to send gifts for the simple reason that all of us were unaware of her existence at the time." This daughter of Barthélemy Roumanille was twenty-three in 1918 and probably more conscious of social tensions in her community. Somewhat reluctantly, she acknowledges that Dr. Schweitzer treated her relatives and engaged in casual conversations with her father. Her observations also confirm that Schweitzer was occasionally accompanied by Helene in the village. "The Doctor had a very good attitude, he was strong; I learned later that he was less so than we thought. By contrast, Madame Schweitzer was very pale with an air of fatigue, but drank a lot of hot beverages. She spoke very little, while the Doctor told us a lot of anecdotes that were funny or painful or sad."[72]

Clearly, Schweitzer's role as a doctor allowed him and Helene a level of mobility and hospitality that their fellow internees did not enjoy. That said, it is probable that either because of her limited strength or because of her innate sense of privacy Helene preferred to remain behind the walls of St. Paul-de-Mausole. In contrast to Marie Roumanille-Blanc's image of a reticent Helene, however, Wersinger-Liller's vivid memories offer a portrait of a far more sociable woman who enjoyed sharing stories of her life in Africa.

> She often enchanted us with stories of her work in Africa about the hospital she had founded with her husband, of the native people she had been forced to leave and with whom she remained connected in spirit.
>
> She also spoke of her experiences before her marriage and of her travels in England and Russia. Sometimes, she recalled their voyage back to Europe, when they had a small cabin at the back of the ship, which only added to the tropical heat. The Schweitzers were only

allowed to walk on the deck for an hour each day under military surveillance without the right to speak to anyone. She was so overwhelmed by her memories that her entire body trembled.[73]

Here we have a poignant image of Helene reflecting on her adventurous life in Africa and her dramatic experience of deportation. We now know, however, that all of her thoughts were not focused on the past, for, as was her habit, Helene took care to document her life in Saint-Rémy in a private journal kept daily from March 27 to June 29, 1918. These pages capture a wide variety of interior thoughts and exterior events, from daily life in the camp to the international politics of a world at war.[74]

The surprise of this journal, however, is not its scope but its carefully constructed stanzas of rhyming German verse. Why did Helene choose this unusual form to document her life in this period? We can only speculate that the challenge of poetic form was a pleasant distraction from tedium or, perhaps, a liberating choice that allowed her to express herself more freely, with irony and humor, on an extraordinary variety of themes. Through meter and rhyme, Helene's voice remains steady as she juxtaposes ordinary activity—such as doing the laundry—with gratitude for American intervention in the war.[75] She also writes of the Provençal landscape with its olive, fig, and almond trees and the Roman ruins nearby that speak ominously of "past grandeur."[76] The next day she notes that "Liberia has been bombed."[77] Albert is mentioned, as are world leaders (Taft, Stalin), homesickness, and anti-American "propaganda" from Japan.[78]

This rapidly shifting overlay of preoccupations tells us how well informed the internees were, even as they sat confined to the garden, helpless to influence events outside the walls. Helene's Saint-Rémy journal is thus a remarkable inventory of the world she and other such civil prisoners of war inhabited during uncertain months and years of internment. If viewed as a coping strategy, this small volume documents Helene Schweitzer Bresslau's practical character. If read as wartime *poésie d'occasion* created to mark the moment rather than out of literary aspirations, it expresses how language helps human beings survive even in unspeakable situations.

ॐ

Fortunately for the Schweitzers and thousands of others, the Bern Accords governing the treatment and repatriation of civil prisoners of war were in force by the spring of 1918. On May 30, Albert Schweitzer evoked his and Helene's rights to protection with his hand-written "Declaration of Alsace-Lorraine," cosigned by the depot director Jean Bagnaud.[79] Although Helene probably didn't know it at the time, she had become pregnant in the weeks following their arrival in Saint-Rémy. Her life would soon be redefined by Rhena Fanny Suzanne Schweitzer, born in Strasbourg on her father's forty-fourth birthday, January 14, 1919. When the Schweitzers' repatriation order was executed on July 13, 1918, both were very likely aware of Helene's condition. Even if the years in Africa and the experience of internment had damaged her health, Helene now had a new reason to carry on with hope and determination.

The postwar challenges for Albert Schweitzer would be entirely different. In Rhena's first years of life, her father would work his way out of poor health, depression, debt, and professional uncertainty. Within a decade, he would publish wildly popular books, receive prizes and honorary doctorates, build a home for his family in Königsfeld, and rebuild his hospital on the riverbank. Out of the experience of war, Albert Schweitzer would become more committed than ever to Reverence for Life.

As for the camps at Garaison and Saint-Rémy, both would be liquidated by 1920, thanks to the work of Alsatian patriot Abbott Emile Wetterle (1861–1931). Some of the inmates remained in the regions where they were interned. Thousands of others were repatriated, formed associations, and demanded reparations for their indignities and economic losses. In time, the histories of the camps and those who endured them would drift into the archives and quietly undergo a process of erasure, at least until the mid-1990s, when research on them began to appear in France.[80]

When the train arrived in Constance, Germany, on July 18, 1918, Albert and Helene Schweitzer disembarked in a war-torn city among hundreds of people drawn from camps throughout southern France.[81] As the official intermediary, Switzerland facilitated this prisoner exchange, which involved a very long journey by train to the old city on the edge of Lake Constance.[82] Albert was surprised to be greeted by family and friends who had known of his imminent arrival for weeks.[83] Helene probably searched the crowd until she found her parents' eyes and felt their arms embracing her small frame. Harry and Cary Bresslau must have held her close for a long time—their only daughter, their beloved "Lene," who had gone to Africa in 1913 and come home to them at last.

1. Helene Bresslau, c. 1906. Copyright © Archives
Centrales Schweitzer Gunsbach.

2. Helene Bresslau on becoming a certified nurse in Frankfurt, Germany, 1910. Copyright © Archives Centrales Schweitzer Gunsbach.

3. Albert and Helene Schweitzer correcting printer's proofs together in 1912. Copyright © Archives Centrales Schweitzer Gunsbach.

4. An outing in a pirogue on the Ogowe River in French Equatorial Africa, 1913. Copyright © Archives Centrales Schweitzer Gunsbach.

5. Helene Schweitzer as a civil prisoner of war in Garaison, France, 1917. Copyright © Archives Centrales Schweitzer Gunsbach.

6. Albert Schweitzer as a civil prisoner of war in Garaison, France, 1917. Copyright © Archives Centrales Schweitzer Gunsbach.

7. Albert, Rhena, and Helene Schweitzer in Strasbourg shortly before his departure for more than three years in Africa, 1924. Copyright © Archives Centrales Schweitzer Gunsbach.

8. Albert and Helene Schweitzer at the front door of their home in Königsfeld, Germany, 1932. Copyright © Archives Centrales Schweitzer Gunsbach.

9. The cottage in Königsfeld today. Photograph by the author.

10. Helene Schweitzer, c. 1932.
Copyright © Archives Centrales
Schweitzer Gunsbach.

11. Albert and Helene Schweitzer at the Nobel Peace Prize ceremony in
Oslo, 1954. Copyright © Archives Centrales Schweitzer Gunsbach.

12. Helene Schweitzer's room as it looks today in the renovated Historic Zone of the Schweitzer Hospital built in Lambarene in 1927. Photograph courtesy of Roland Wolf.

13. Cemetery near the river at the Schweitzer Hospital, with Helene Schweitzer's tombstone in the foreground. Photograph by the author.

14. Helene Schweitzer's 1905 file of notes for her index of Albert Schweitzer's book *The Quest for the Historical Jesus*. Reprinted by permission of the Zentralbibliothek Zürich, Nachlass A. Schweitzer, Dossier 36D.

15. Helene Schweitzer's 1915 edits to *Wir Epigonen*, the book that eventually became *Kulturphilosophie* (*The Philosophy of Civilization*). The larger handwriting is Helene's, including the large looped E containing her thoughts on liberalism that expand on Albert's point of view. In the lower-right corner, she also makes a strong comment on the bracketed text: "Remove this. Bring it in later." Reprinted by permission of the Zentralbibliothek Zürich, Nachlass A. Schweitzer, Sac 1.a.5, leaf III/18.

(1) Map of the Ogowe River.

(Lambaréné is a familiar to all those who are interested in the work now being carried on there and to those who have read the books entitled "On the Edge of the Primeval Forest" and "The Forest Hospital of Lambaréné". For the information of those who may be hearing for the first time, I will limit myself

(1a) From Bordeaux to Port Gentil.

to saying that Lambaréné is situated in the Gabon Colony, in French Equatorial Africa. The port of sail is Bordeaux. The boat follows the Western Coast of Europe, Iberic Peninsula and the coast of Africa and after a voyage of three weeks reaches the first port South of the Equator, called Port Gentil.

(2) Port Gentil.

The steamer is too big to enter the harbour and has to anchor in the fairway, from where the passengers and their luggage are taken ashore in lighters.

The large logs, to be seen on the sands are of valuable wood such as mahogany and a kind of wood similar to mahogany which the natives call Okoumé. This wood which, in former days, went mainly to the making of cigar boxes, is now very greatly sought after by cabinet makers and builders. It comes straight from the Virgin Forest, which runs along the coast to a depth of about five hundred kilometres. It is transported on

16. First page of Helene Schweitzer's typescript with hand-written notes for her lecture delivered in America in 1937–38, "Dr. Schweitzer's Hospital Work in Lambarene." Courtesy of the Antje Bultmann Lemke Collection Relating to Albert Schweitzer, Special Collections Research Center, Syracuse University Libraries.

4

• • •

Divided Destinies

A Sacrifice Observed

Helene is writing to Albert from her parents' home in Heidelberg, where she is visiting with Rhena in August 1920. It is hot and still except for the soft zoom of bees weaving through a small garden. Mother clips her flowers and brings them to the table. Father reads the newspaper and tires easily. Helene is losing weight, though her health has improved since Rhena's birth. We can imagine her there, fanning herself with a sheet of letter paper, resigned to this necessary immersion in family life while Albert remains on the other side of the Rhine, writing his sermons, working at the Strasbourg Municipal Hospital, and assembling notes for a book of African memories to be published in Sweden next year. The book is important, and she knows he needs to write it. Thank God he has regained his strength after two operations for intestinal ulcers.[1] Thank God for the Lindblad Publishing firm in Uppsala, which has commissioned the book.[2] Thank God, too, for Richard Clasen, who has offered the use of the photographs he took along the Ogowe.[3]

Since the end of the war, the lives of old friends have changed. Georgette and Léon Morel have returned to Africa, where they will soon celebrate Albert's arrival as a desperately needed doctor;[4] Elly and Theodor Heuss-Knapp are living in Germany with pride; even Rudolf Schwander, Strasbourg's mayor, born in Colmar, has cast his fate as a German citizen. And Clasen, too, has made a fresh start. Clasen—the timber man from Hamburg who called Helene "a gracious woman" in the guest book in Lambarene.[5] Helene does not write to Albert of her parents' quiet suffering as loyal subjects of a defeated empire. Nor does her pen express relief at seeing her husband resume an active pace again after his spring lectures in Sweden. It was all so different a year ago and the year before that. After the shock of war, nothing is predictable anymore.

In the summer of 1920, Helene's mind must have been buzzing like the bees in her mother's garden, looping through past and present before turning to matters that must be communicated, negotiated, and clarified with Albert. She knows he is surrounded by his notes in their small apartment on Strasbourg's quai Saint-Nicolas. But Clasen's recent letter calls for a response because he is on his way to Paris and hopes to visit on his return to Germany, around August 20. Should he order books for Albert's Africa project? There is also the matter of Harry Bresslau's missing birth certificate, suddenly found.[6] And then there is a vacation to organize that Albert wants to spend in Gunsbach in early September, but not before. Helene writes forcefully in a combination of French and German to explain her perspective on the last of these themes, underlining particular sentences in hopes of capturing his attention:

> You are forgetting in the midst of your projects that I have engaged a maid for September 1 who has never been trained, which is to say it is important that she begins with an understanding of the rules and conditions [of employment]. This is why I do not want to bring her to Gunsb. and prefer to go there before the 1st. She has been waiting for this job for 4 or 5 months, this is why I would not wish to reschedule her beginning with us and perhaps, as a result spoil it. Once again I see what misery it is to be looking for maids and I would not want to start over. So, reflect on this if you cannot pull yourself away during the last week of August. Think also about the visit from Clasen at the beginning of September![7]

A few days later Helene continues in the same instructive tone when she sends her father's German birth certificate. Clearly, something must be done with it in the now French province of Alsace:

"Regarding other things you need to know about the arrival of this paper, I'll explain them to you later, it's not at all urgent. What is important for you to remember is especially that papa begs of you that you keep this document in your possession and that you return it or send back to him later and, if it is necessary to add one to the papers to be presented, that he begs you to make a certified copy."[8]

Helene is clearly managing details for her parents, her husband, her home, and her child. Her closing comments include a delighted—and prophetic—description of her daughter's personality: "Rhena is adorable and continues to make great progress, this will be a little independent person and I am content about that."[9] We should not be surprised if Helene is pleased to see a reflection of her own independence unfolding in her daughter. Perhaps she already senses that their "family pact" will soon be redefined as a mother-daughter alliance lived at some distance from a man with limited time for either of them.

Helene's voice is strong in these letters from the summer of 1920. We sense that her body must be strong too, all things considered, because she is thrilled with her husband's gift of a bicycle. She thanks him with great enthusiasm from Heidelberg. "Just a note to say thank you for yours and the enormous surprise of the bicycle. How kind you are! But you must have had to spare yourself a great deal in order to be able to pay for such a gift! Thank you again."[10] She had traveled by train to Heidelberg with a baby and baggage. She had been in Sweden earlier in the year with Albert at the home of Archbishop Nathan Söderblom. If in this period Helene is struggling with a weak heart,[11] is underweight and easily tired,[12] or is "going through a daily cycle of apprehension, alarm, hypertension, and then hours of perspiring and anxiety,"[13] there is no evidence in her letters from Heidelberg that these difficulties are threatening to overtake her life.

ᐦᐦ

Helene's health had been unpredictable for years, but in the 1920s—as her strength seems to deteriorate in direct proportion to Albert's increasing power—it became the public rationale for a shift in the Schweitzers' relationship. This partnership of equals, so fully lived in their Strasbourg years and during the first sojourn in Lambarene, will soon be redefined through the tropes of "feminine frailty" and "wifely sacrifice." Primarily framed by male writers, including Albert Schweitzer himself, these stereotypes would eventually shape the public persona best described as the somewhat distant "Madame Schweitzer." If we wish to know Helene Schweitzer Bresslau as the person her daughter wrote about, "a woman of achievement in her own right,"[14] it is important to untangle the strands of fact and fiction that shape her image.

Much of the truth rests on an accurate deconstruction of Albert Schweitzer's decision to return to Africa alone in 1924. However unfinished the work there may have felt, however blocked and uninspired he was in Europe, it is clear that Albert Schweitzer made a choice to return to his "Congo project" as early as the summer of 1920: "When in the middle of July I quitted Swedish soil on which my experience had been so happy, I had firmly made up my mind to resume my work again in Lambarene. Till then I had not ventured to think of it, but had instead considered the idea of returning to a university career."[15]

These words and their timing are at odds with George Marshall and David Poling's curious suggestion that in a conversation initiated by Helene in 1919, she very nearly "commanded" Albert to resume the work in Africa. In this (wholly?) imagined conversation, Helene is reported to have urged her husband to return despite the fact that "his concern for her health and the birth of Rhena had brought an indefinite postponement to any thoughts he had about a return to the work in Lambarene."[16] Not only does this gallant scenario omit the reality of Schweitzer's own compromised health in 1919, but it also disregards Marshall and Poling's earlier suggestion of a widening gulf between Helene and Albert, even before their repatriation in July 1918: "Among other things," these authors write in their biography, "[Schweitzer] thought the child might overcome the separation developing between Helene and himself."[17]

At least Marshal and Poling allow that Schweitzer was not somehow tricked into fatherhood while in a vulnerable state as a civil prisoner of war, as Schweitzer's musical colleague Edouard Nies-Berger insists. After blaming Helene's "suave and aggressive" personality for the Schweitzers' "disastrous marriage of convenience," Nies-Berger advances a peculiar theory to explain Helene's pregnancy: "The spiritual giant had succumbed to feminine pressure and slipped a notch or two from his pedestal of sexual celibacy. Helene tied herself to him as no other woman ever would: this was her triumph."[18] Perhaps Nies-Berger's indignation at this slippage can be explained by his firmly held belief that "Schweitzer is an illuminate in the image of Christ."[19]

A more recent example of imagination gone astray is the tirade by André Audoynaud. His text is an apparent outpouring of frustration from a French doctor who served as chief medical officer in a public hospital in the Middle Ogowe region during Schweitzer's last years. Quite apart from his evisceration of Schweitzer's life and work, Audoynaud pretends to settle the question of Albert and Helene's separation by naming Emmy Martin, Schweitzer's chief administrator in Europe, as the unquestioned source of the separate lives that evolve between them. Describing Martin as "the viper who guarded the doors of the palace" and "some sort of Schweitzer in a skirt," Audoynaud asserts that Martin "detested" Helene and drove her out of Gunsbach to live in Königsfeld, Germany.[20]

Although it might be true that Helene was never comfortable with Emmy Martin's authoritative presence in Gunsbach, the author of these statements forgets that Helene had never felt at home in the tiny village of Gunsbach to begin with and had many practical reasons to settle in Germany years before the Schweitzer House inhabited by Emmy Martin was built (1929–30). In either case, the only useful statement to be extracted from Audoynaud is that "Helene's tuberculosis and climate-related reasons were not sufficient arguments" to explain the separation that occurred in the early 1920s.[21]

Writing years before Marshall and Poling, Nies-Berger, and Audoynaud, George Seaver addressed the matter with practical, albeit patriarchal, prose in 1947: "That his wife should accompany him again was out of the question; her own health was not equal to the strain; besides, she had the care of their infant daughter."[22]

A twenty-first-century reading of Seaver's incidental "besides" reveals how Rhena's care was implicitly assigned to Helene by a social structure that enabled—and even ennobled—Albert's abdication of active parenting. And yet because Helene herself was part of that social system, it is unlikely that she viewed raising a daughter as bright and charming as "Rhenele" as any sort of sacrifice. After all, Helene had been an outspoken advocate of responsible motherhood since her Strasbourg days as city orphan inspector (1905–9) and cofounder of a home for unwed mothers (1907). In the context of Schweitzer's return to Africa in the 1920s, if Rhena's parental needs were viewed as a secondary rationale for Helene's inability to join him, it is perhaps because the rationale of feminine "frailty" provided a useful, multi-purpose explanation readily acceptable in patriarchal culture.

Schweitzer's memorable commentary on the subject in 1931 is a brilliant triple play. In asserting his own sacrifice-worthy purpose he fixes Helene in a state of poor health and, simultaneously, assumes the "manly" posture of paying tribute to the most famous "single mom" of the twentieth century. Only Albert Schweitzer could accomplish so much in one eloquent breath: "On February 14, 1924, I left Strasbourg. My wife could not go with me this time because of her poor health. I have never ceased to be grateful to her that, under these circumstances, she made the sacrifice of consenting to my resuming work at Lambarene."[23]

But if Helene's health was too poor for travel in 1924, how, then, did she manage to engage herself with the Hospital Aid Association in Basel in October 1924? Or enroll in a three-week course in tropical medicine at the Medical Missionary Institute of Tübingen, Germany, in August 1926? As Helene will repeatedly demonstrate, renunciation of an active role in Lambarene was never her intention, despite motherhood, periods of illness, and even world war. Furthermore, it should not be forgotten that the first signs of lower back pain and respiratory problems had been addressed in the Schweitzers' pre-Lambarene letters and did not prevent their initial voyage to French Equatorial Africa in 1913. Nor were her tireless, professional efforts in the "heroic years" of that first sojourn ever framed as a "sacrifice."

Through the lens of history, it seems unlikely that Schweitzer's decision to return to Lambarene required a stunning "sacrifice" on Helene's part in the sense that Schweitzer and his biographers have envisioned it: the noble self-devaluation of a woman too weak to be useful outside the domestic sphere. If her hand-written edit inserted in the typescript of her American lecture in 1937–38 is any indication, Helene viewed her inability to travel in 1924 as a practical matter rather than as a defining moment: "In 1924, the physicians not allowing me to return to the equator for reason of health, Dr. Schweitzer went back alone."[24]

Of what use, then, is this narrative of "sacrifice" unless it somehow serves to relieve Schweitzer's conscience by resolving an internal conflict? If his destiny had to be fulfilled at all costs, wouldn't it have been more honest to rationalize his determination within the context of *his* personality rather than *her body*? And wouldn't a clarification of facts pertinent to Helene's reluctant acceptance of a two-year separation have provided a more balanced view of their story? For one fact is indisputable: as the date of Albert's February 1924 departure drew near, Helene never agreed to a separation of three and a half years.[25]

By now, the legend of Helene's "sacrifice" is so deeply inscribed with gender assumptions that the details of how it came about may seem irrelevant except for the fact that over time those assumptions accumulated as truth and became absorbed into her public image. Indeed, her posthumous identity has been shaped with the imprimatur of Albert Schweitzer himself and fed by the caustic and/or misguided prose of men such as Marshal and Poling, Nies-Berger, and Audoynaud. If we focus strictly on the facts, it is not difficult to see that Helene's needs were sacrificed *by* her husband, not *for* him. And despite the existence of a small child whose joyful baptism in Gunsbach was captured in a photograph—in which Helene is standing upright and does not appear frail at all—she continued to view the work in Africa as a shared project to which she would eventually return; like women today, she would take a "time out" for family life and then resume her career.

In the summer of 1920, Helene wrote letters to Albert from Heidelberg. We can imagine her turning to the child stirring in her crib, an unfinished letter on the desk in her parents' parlor to be concluded the next day. We can also imagine a vague remembrance of one of Albert's sermons in her mind. "It is now up to those of us who have survived to determine if those lost to the development of mankind and the Kingdom of God have died in vain, or if their suffering and death will prove to have been a fruitful sacrifice."[26] Perhaps she viewed the work of mothering and caring for loved ones as a contribution to the future, her own "fruitful sacrifice." But if a new life is necessary and one has no choice but to live it, can it rightfully be called a "sacrifice"?

ॐ

The unexpected rupture of the Great War left a lavishly optimistic Belle Epoque behind, replacing it with a modern world steeped in anxiety. It would be naive to imagine that this rupture did not permeate the relationships of those who survived it because survival could only occur in an altered world. Insofar as Schweitzer studies have evolved as the province of Albert Schweitzer alone, one might argue that this is a natural point at which to set Helene aside as an ordinary woman living the conventional destiny of wife and mother. Alternatively, one might argue that Schweitzer studies have evolved as a story constructed to fulfill human needs—male and female—for heroic figures and tales of resurrection, especially in the wake of catastrophic war.

Albert Schweitzer's life lends itself to biblical metaphor when he fulfills the imagination of his generation as a real-world Lazarus raised from the dead. Just as Jesus spoke to Martha, the sister of Lazarus, we can almost imagine him speaking to Albert Schweitzer: "I am the resurrection, and I am life. If a man has faith in me, even though he die, he shall come to life. And no one who is alive and has faith shall ever die. Do you believe this?"[27] A prefiguration of this view of Albert Schweitzer comes from Helene's good friend Elly Heuss-Knapp, who at the outbreak of World War I in 1914 imagined Schweitzer far away in Africa as a modern-day prophet reminiscent of Jonah swallowed by the whale. "Would he ever come back to us and preach again?" she wondered.[28]

In light of Albert's personal drama in the early 1920s, the hope and promise of resurrection may have entered his mind as he experienced feelings of being lost, forgotten, and subsequently found. Schweitzer describes these feelings in his autobiography in terms of two worlds that resemble life and death—a dark inner world where he was invisible and the "outer world" into which he finally emerged: "In my isolation at Strasbourg, ever since the war I had felt rather like a coin that has rolled under a piece of furniture and has been forgotten there. Only once—in October, 1919—had I been in touch with the outer world. . . . I went to Barcelona to let my friends of the Orféo Català once more hear me play the organ."[29]

Meanwhile, Helene was wandering in another direction, a lingering echo of that foreign figure from the ancient Hebrew Book of Ruth who leaves her homeland Moab and pledges loyalty to the God of the Israelites. Ruth's famous words, spoken to her mother-in-law, Naomi, have come to exemplify the great virtue of feminine loyalty: "Where you go I will go, and where you stay I will stay. Your people will be my people and your God my God. Where you die I will die, and there I will be buried."[30] In a sense, Helene's baptism out of Judaism in 1886 and her coming of age in Alsace as part of the "Old German" community represent a similar dislocation that was, in fact, exacerbated by two world wars.

It is possible that Helene's Ruth-like willingness to cross borders and live as a foreigner, combined with her predominant characteristic of loyalty, were in Albert's mind when he dedicated the second volume of *Kulturphilosophie* to "[m]y wife—my most loyal friend." As mentioned earlier, these words have been quoted repeatedly in Schweitzer studies as a great tribute to Helene, even though the use and interpretation of the term *Kamerad* (comrade, friend) remains open to debate. Does Albert's careful word choice suggest an emancipated partnership, or does it imply something closer to Julia Kristeva's trenchant analysis of Ruth that probes the link between loyalty and heterosexual love?

The book of Ruth is a magisterial reflection on the alterity and strangeness of woman which one finds nowhere else. Ruth is a foreigner and yet she is the ancestor of the royal house of David. Thus, at the heart of sovereignty there is an inscription of a foreign femininity. . . . In the *Song of Songs* the amours relation is figured as a relation between a man and a woman who are strangers, travelers, destined to lose each other. Separation is thus placed at the heart of the relation of one to the other in the Bible.[31]

Already in the autumn of 1918 there was a sense of separation as Albert and Helene approached the future differently. Indeed, their return to Europe had placed them in a landscape of "strangers, travelers, destined to lose each other" as each struggled with different priorities and very different losses to mourn. After the war, given his Alsatian family history, Albert was granted French citizenship, offered a job at a clinic of the Municipal Hospital in Strasbourg, and appointed curate of a popular church. His first sermon was gratefully received as early as October 13, 1918, and his appointment came with lodgings on the quai Saint-Nicolas. Madeleine Horst, whose husband was pastor of Saint-Nicolas in 1919, shared her memories nearly fifty years later: "At the end of the First World War, the parish was only too happy to see the return of the *one* who had given his heart from 1900 to 1913 up to the time of *his* departure for Africa."[32]

By contrast, Helene's friends and family were either harshly expulsed from Alsace or chose to return to the defeated German Empire after World War I. In order to visit her parents, she had to cross the Rhine with a baby in tow. Meanwhile, her brother Ernst was not only living in Germany as an unemployed scientist but also living through a forced separation from his Alsatian wife, Luise, and their family.[33] As Helene's loved ones dispersed in the wake of war, Albert's family remained intact. The permanent loss he had to bear was the death of his mother, who was accidentally killed in 1916. But even without Adèle Schweitzer, Albert had his beloved Munster Valley, the old vicarage, and his childhood village, Gunsbach, to return to, where his father remained pastor until his death in 1925. He also had a circle of siblings, nieces, and nephews nearby. His physical health was restored by the time he performed that organ concert in Barcelona in October 1919. And yet he still felt depressed and cheated out of his rightful position in the world.

Robert Minder frames the critical turning point in Albert Schweitzer's postwar life in language that recalls the advent of Christ: "The light came from the North at the end of 1919."[34] Minder is referring to Archbishop Nathan Söderblom's invitation to Schweitzer to deliver a series of lectures after Easter 1920 for the Olaus-Petri Foundation at the University of Uppsala in Sweden.[35] By the end of 1923, Schweitzer will have returned to Scandinavia many times; paid off his debts; received his first honorary doctorate from the theology faculty of the University of Zurich; delivered lectures in Oxford, Cambridge, and Prague; and published a best seller, *On the Edge of the Primeval Forest*, in Swedish, German, French, and English.[36] The "lost coin" was found, along with a considerable number of Swedish Kronors. Furthermore, as mentioned earlier, his decision to return to Africa was already fixed in his mind.

In April 1921, Schweitzer quit both of his jobs in Strasbourg, one at the Municipal Hospital and the other at Saint-Nicolas,[37] to devote himself to writing and to his vision of a return to Africa. As often happened in his life, a wealthy widow materialized from outside his orbit to offer help in the form of a pied-à-terre in Strasbourg, which amounted to an attic room in the center of the city.[38] Energetic volunteers materialized too, including some who would remain reliable friends and supporters for decades—such as the young pastor's widow named Emmy Martin.

In those first years of the 1920s—as trunks, tins, and crates of supplies accumulated—a Mademoiselle Lami kindly offered a depot on the rue des Greniers.[39] Albert often slept at the depot after long days of supervising the packing and trunks, each one labeled with the hospital's signature "ASB" for "Albert Schweitzer Bresslau." If Helene traveled to the city from Gunsbach to share in the work, she stayed with friends at night, careful to preserve her own sense of comfort and perhaps to manage unwanted expectations of being perceived as a loyal wife and nothing more.

ᘒ

During the evening of Easter Sunday in 1923, Schweitzer wrote to Helene, "I've been longing for you all day. I wanted so much to be with you this Easter, but it did not work out. And now I see the moon casting its silver light over the vineyard as far as I can see from my window, and I ask myself if my Rhenele has also seen this glorious moon."[40] As ever, Albert's emotions were stirred by the sensation of Helene following his work from afar like a distant star that could always be located with a postage stamp. In 1921, he performed concerts in Switzerland, Germany, and Scandinavia, writing frequently from Stockholm, Malmö, Roskilde, Ringsted, and Helsinki. At one point, he wrote from Switzerland to arrange a few days with Helene and Rhena in a hotel in Karlsruhe, Germany.[41] At Christmastime, he was in Scandinavia again, writing only to say, "If I were not so tired, I would write to you every day. But the hand can do no more. I embrace you, you who is as good as the Earth."[42]

Such tender letters, written twenty years after their initial pact of friendship, confirm that Helene and Albert's relationship was far more than a calculated marriage of convenience. Despite the scarcity of similar writings from Helene, we can only assume that she enjoyed her husband's notes and letters. Otherwise, why would they have continued, and why would she have preserved them? From all available evidence, their mutual "profound affection," firmly "rooted in a singular history of loving friendship," as Jean-Paul Sorg writes in the introduction to his third volume of pre-Lambarene letters, seems to have lingered for decades, even as geographical separation became a way of life.[43]

It is because of this deep affection that Helene joined her husband whenever she could. She was with him in England in 1922, for example, for his theological lectures at Mansfield College in Oxford; at Selly Oaks College in Birmingham; in Cambridge; and in London, where he spoke at the Society for the Study of Science and Religion.[44]

When she returned home, he traveled on to Sweden for more public appearances and then, after a brief pause in Gunsbach, was off on another concert tour of Switzerland. As the religion journalist who served as Schweitzer's guide in London put it, "He sometimes forgets that other people are not quite so tireless as himself, and I've sometimes been quite sorry for dear Madame Schweitzer!"[45]

∽

There is no evidence that Helene felt sorry for herself, but her illness in Gunsbach in the spring of 1922—involving pain, fever, and the coughing up of blood—led to the diagnosis that both Albert and Helene had feared and assiduously avoided until now: tuberculosis. At the City Hospital of Bad Cannstatt near Stuttgart, professor of medicine Arnold Cahn discovered three caverns in Helene's lungs, which explained the pain in her chest in the area of her heart. As Mühlstein states clearly, "After this point in time it is clear that Helene Schweitzer is ill with a life-threatening case of tuberculosis."[46]

Given the stigma, isolation, and "kiss of death" that such a diagnosis implied at a time when no antibacterial drugs existed, it is no wonder that Helene chose not to share this information beyond her family circle. Indeed, it was a mark of her modernity that she viewed her body as a realm separate from her character and life's purpose. Helene Schweitzer's health might be a nuisance, a challenge, an agony, or an obstacle, but she would not allow it to define her.

As for Albert, the reality of tuberculosis stopped him in his tracks long enough to decide on the construction of the home they could now afford in Königsfeld, Germany. Situated in the Black Forest at a comfortable altitude of 2,500 feet above sea level, this town known for its emphasis on health and well-being was an ideal place for Helene and Rhena to live. Plans were drawn up and building began even as Schweitzer carried on with his intention to return to Africa. As for Rhena, he relieved Helene of the child's care by making arrangements for Rhena to stay with a family friend in Strasbourg.

Meanwhile, Helene remained in Bad Cannstatt, for in addition to the open tuberculosis confirmed by the discovery of three caverns in her lungs, Dr. Cahn also diagnosed larynx tuberculosis. He cautioned Helene to whisper rather than talk normally and prescribed painful oil injections into her larynx. By the end of 1922, to her great relief, she was able to live with Rhena again in a rented apartment in Königsfeld's Villa Mendelssohn-Bartholdy. There, she occupied herself by correcting printer's proofs for *Kulturphilosophie*, most often alone. Albert was, however, present for moving day on May 1, 1923, a dawn-to-dusk effort that sent Helene back to the hospital with a relapse marked by difficulty in swallowing. When she refused another separation from Rhena, a nurse was hired to care for her at home, and her cousin Johanna Engel came from Berlin to stay for three months.[47]

Nevertheless, as 1923 unfolded, Albert's planned departure for Africa early in 1924 remained firm, and his presence in Königsfeld became increasingly intermittent. Later on, when he came to Königsfeld to work in his office for weeks at a time, Rhena was glad to have this visitor in the house. But as she grew, his role in her life was fraught with ambiguity. "I really don't know if I loved my father as a child or not," she said when she was in her fifties. "I certainly was happy when he was with us but I also adjusted when he left. I accepted his absences as a normal thing in my life."[48] Brabazon is quick to point out that "Rhena's ability to adjust tells us a great deal about the atmosphere of equanimity that her mother must have created in the home and her acceptance that the demands of the hospital were supreme."[49]

☙

Helene may have accepted her husband's priorities in principle, but Albert's departure from Europe in mid-February 1924 threw her into a period of desperation. Despite the four letters Albert wrote between their emotional farewell at the train station in Strasbourg on February 14—in which he thanks her for being "so wonderful" and asks her to convey his greetings to Emmy Martin—and his February 20 missive "On Board the [ship] *Orestes*,"[50] Helene clearly felt abandoned. Even though she had agreed to his departure, her emotions could not be contained. "Never have the nights been as long as [they are] now," she wrote at four o'clock in the morning shortly after his departure. "My dear, you have never known how my life was bound with yours—not until now. But now I feel a wound in the depths out of which all strength slowly drains, and will it ever close?"[51]

Among other things, Helene's response to Albert's absence tells us that her emotions in this period were linked to her feelings for her husband, not to some vague sensation of rivalry with other women. After all, it would be July before Mathilde Kottmann joined Schweitzer and his student assistant Noel Gillespie in Andende and more than a year before Emma Haussknecht appeared in October 1925. Unfortunately, it is Albert himself who, before leaving the continent on Valentine's Day 1924, swiftly conjured the image of repressed envy linked to frailty that would become associated with Helene Schweitzer: "I can well imagine what it must be like for you to see others collaborating on the work that would be yours, if you had the strength for it."[52]

But on what basis was Albert Schweitzer in a position to imagine the "new normal" that would become Helene's life as he traveled his own path? Or the questions that filled her mind once he acquired the concession of more than two hundred acres upriver from Andende, thereby allowing him to build an expanded version of the hospital they had founded together? Did he pause to imagine that this acquisition would mean an extended separation? As Helene Schweitzer's life increasingly became a matter of Albert's imagination, let us assume that he imagined her presence at his father's funeral in Gunsbach in May 1925 and that of her own father the following autumn in Germany. Perhaps her feelings about his astonishingly brief three-day visit to Königsfeld in August 1927 after a prolonged absence of three and a half years cannot be described, at least not by anyone who did not endure the shock.

What we know is that in early October 1924 Helene attended a festive gathering in Basel in support of the hospital, though something about playing the symbolic role of "Madame Schweitzer" without Albert at her side felt sad and strained. The letter she wrote after that meeting expresses a moment of truth:

It is my fate that the work that was my happiness has been taken from me. . . . I try to make the best of it, but to repeatedly have to pull oneself together takes quite a lot of strength and the head always feels confused and dumb. Perhaps your friends from Switzerland and Alsace write that they have seen me and I am well. Physically, things are going along fine, but what is beneath the surface, no one knows and it takes a lot of strength to constantly conceal it. I must say it to you once, to You my Only One—perhaps you should not have left me so alone.[53]

To this Albert replied with a masterful nine-page letter that acknowledges his wife's "inner chaos," diagnoses "inner fatigue" as the cause of her "despair," affirms his love for her (more than once), and reminds her, "You have so much of what only a few women have, and for which some envy you." Nevertheless, the overarching purpose of this unusual, sermon-like letter—in which he quotes St. Paul—seems to justify his own incontrovertible decision: "I had to leave you alone because it is my profession to do the work that I do. It is tragic that you cannot be of help near to me in this work. But think again if I have left you so terribly alone. I [left] you with our beloved Rhena, that you should raise her for us."[54]

One wishes he had omitted the word *tragic* from his artful self-defense. Oddly enough, this makes Albert Schweitzer the first among many to describe Helene's life in this way. With this word choice, we see Schweitzer's complex and self-protective personality at work. He expresses love for Helene in his long letter from Lambarene in November 1924, and yet he also marks her with a sign of otherness that must have felt far from comforting as she read it in Königsfeld, half a world away. Life would go on, and their letters would continue. But it would be nearly three years before she saw him again.

※

It is the summer of 1928, and Albert has been back in Europe for a year, dividing his time between Königsfeld, Strasbourg, Colmar, and Gunsbach, where he has decided to build a house. The proceeds of his 1928 Goethe Prize from the City of Frankfurt will finance this project, made necessary now that the old vicarage is no longer his family home and Lambarene's doctors and nurses need a "headquarters" in Europe as they travel to and from Africa. He envisions visitors from all over Europe in this house that Emmy Martin will manage and inhabit.

Thinking in three dimensions has by now become a habit for him. As early as August 7, 1924, Schweitzer sent a sketch of improvements planned for Andende to Helene—a separate kitchen, a vast garden—but that was before it became clear how inadequate the site at the edge of the riverbank was going to be, considering the health-care needs in the region.[55] After his return to Europe in 1927, he might have shown Helene different sketches, of a hillside called "Adolinanongo" sloping toward the river and perhaps a rough map of where he chose to place the seven buildings he had already constructed with the assistance of the indomitable Mrs. C. E. B. (Lilian) Russell of Scotland. This particularly energetic woman, who also translated some of Schweitzer's early works into English, very likely exerted an influence on future staff selections with her exemplary talent for getting things done. "On the whole," he writes in his autobiography, "the authority of a white woman is more readily recognized by the Africans than that of us men."[56]

Apart from building projects under way in 1928, Helene follows the thread of Albert's fall concert schedule in Scandinavia, after which she travels with him to Prague at the end of the year where he receives another honorary doctorate. She is also corresponding with his Leipzig publisher, Breitkopf & Härtel, to clarify details related to early editions of *J. S. Bach* and to request a money order worked out to the last penny.[57] As Emmy Martin's role expands to encompass increasingly complex logistics, Helene continues to serve as editor, proofreader, and publications manager par excellence. After his fifty-fourth birthday in January 1929, Albert feels ready to write his autobiography. Helene surely smiles at the thought of such a project, knowing it will mean work for her. But there is more time for work now, with Rhena in school and her health more or less stable as spring blooms in Königsfeld.

Something inside feels different in the summer of 1929, a weakness that she tries to dismiss as Albert spends more time than usual in Königsfeld, working on his book on St. Paul. Time is running out before his return to Africa in December, but Helene is determined to return with him this time for a stay of six months or maybe a year. Arrangements have been made for Rhena to attend a boarding school in Königsfeld, with a friend taking care of her on weekends. And as an extra precaution, they agree to hire a nurse as Helene's travel companion, the young Marie Secretan.

The main point—the essential point as autumn approaches—is that Helene wants to return to Lambarene and see the "new hospital" more than anything else in the world. One senses that in these last months of 1929, Helene is at peace with her life and her marriage. Perhaps her thoughts even return to Albert's admonition, written five years earlier, of her enviable status. Rhena is a joy, and Helene's faith in the world, like Albert's, has proven to be unshakeable, despite the poverty and political upheavals going on in German society.

Then fate intervenes. In the autumn of 1929, Helene Schweitzer suffers an attack of pneumonia.[58] There is no "cure" for the damage in her lungs; they both know it. But why must she feel so exhausted again, so feverish and useless? Can she dare to contemplate a trip to Africa, much less spend a year in an oppressive climate? And if she cannot go? Given Helene's determination, this is a question to be avoided. Mercifully, the treatment she agrees to try in November brings relief, both to her and to Albert. He writes from the train on November 26, 1929, that "[t]he thought that I should have to go to Lambarene without you this time brought me so low that I had no more thoughts about anything. That was the last and hardest blow that I could have faced. That this sense of doom has passed is a ray of light in the darkness that surrounds me now."[59]

৯৵

A month later Mathilde Kottmann met Helene, Albert, Marie Secretan, and Dr. Anna Schmitz with a motorboat in Port Gentil, French Equatorial Africa, having arranged for 128 cases of supplies to clear customs and be transported separately to the hospital.[60] Kottmann's foresight allowed the party of four travelers to enjoy Christmas Day on the Ogowe River that year before their arrival on the afternoon of December 26, 1929. Albert and Helene Schweitzer disembarked together on the riverbank and walked up the slope through a corridor of welcoming smiles to the "new" hospital established in 1927. Writing soon after that for the *British Bulletin*, Helene recalled her memorable arrival as if it were happening in the moment: "There we can distinguish in the torchlight only a confused mass of human figures with joyful faces, all turned towards us." After dining in the new eating hall with fourteen people, they slept in the new house constructed according to Schweitzer's innovative architectural design, with open rafters for natural ventilation. "What overpowers us again is the impression of the amount that has been accomplished in the relatively short time," she wrote.[61]

Helene knew that others had worked tirelessly alongside her husband to achieve the new hospital compound, people such as Emma Haussknecht, with whom she toured the buildings and the vegetable gardens the next morning. But in her own mind she, too, had worked for this. It is telling to observe how she asserts herself as a full-fledged partner at the end of her article, noting that "inexhaustible patience, with unquenchable zeal for the great cause, is required of all who work with us."[62] But what would her work be now? That question must have been in her mind from the beginning of that journey, during the twenty-four-hour train trip from Strasbourg to Bordeaux and during the difficult weeks spent on board the ocean liner *Amérique*.

The first published accounts of this voyage appeared in the spring 1930 *British Bulletin* with articles written by Helene, Albert, and Marie Secretan. Albert's words describe a four-day storm in the Bay of Biscay, his grief at the death of a young Swiss doctor, and a reportage of logistics, staff resources, and the new water pump. Marie writes charmed descriptions of her boss's indefatigable work habits and seems enthralled with bird life on the Ogowe River. Helene's contribution, the shortest of all, speaks of a "sky brilliant with stars" once they reach that river where "nature seems to have returned to its primeval state." She feels at peace on the river: "It is like a dream to be gliding along once more so smoothly and quietly, without the noise and the restlessness of the big ship or the bustling open-air life of Port Gentil."[63]

But none of these chroniclers mentioned the harsh truth of that voyage: Helene's persistent fever and agonizing days spent reclining on deck, with Marie Secretan wiping sweat from her forehead. Nor was Albert's terrible indecision at the port of Abidjan, in current-day Côte d'Ivoire, a matter of public record in 1930. As we learned much later, he suffered through urgent hours on that voyage, seriously considering the option of sending Helene back to Europe on the next ship heading north. "What a difficult decision!" Helene's personal travel companion wrote years later. "We considered the problem from all angles and finally decided to do all that we could to bring this patient to Lambarene. The disappointment would have been too great for Madame Schweitzer; she had so ardently desired to see the hospital again."[64] These words, written long after Marie Secretan had married the Schweitzers' nephew Gustav Woytt—and after Helene's death—offer the truest image of Helene Schweitzer's second journey to Lambarene. That voyage undoubtedly took all of her strength, leaving her too exhausted to work and barely able to breathe in the suffocating heat.

After that magical arrival in the glow of torchlight, Helene's presence in Lambarene was problematic. She could not stay. She could not go. According to Woytt-Secretan, "She remained a great source of concern for her husband. She spent most of the day in a chaise lounge on the veranda where she was able to follow a large part of the life of the hospital and where Whites and Blacks came to see her. But her fever remained elevated. After three months, she had to return to Europe."[65] From that veranda, Helene must have experienced a gamut of emotions as she realized how impossible it was to compete with the active, independent young women now surrounding her husband as essential members of his team, at least in the equatorial climate.

If we try to fathom Helene's thoughts, the most that can be said is that there is no record of jealousy or hostility, but neither is there evidence of a true friendship with Emma Haussknecht, Mathilde Kottmann, Anna Schmitz, or any of the other remarkable women who contributed to the success of the Schweitzer Hospital in the 1920s and 1930s. Helene quite likely regarded these people as her husband's employees rather than as candidates for intimate conversation. But this did not keep her from admiring particular achievements. When she set about writing her American lecture "Dr. Schweitzer's Hospital Work in Lambarene" several years later, she mentioned two women, Emma Haussknecht and Dr. Ilse Schnabel, within the context of a successful five-hundred-mile "expedition" into the interior.[66] Even in top form, Helene would probably not have attempted such an adventure involving the provisioning of ten carriers, each with fifty-pound "rucksacks" made of boxes, bark, and a net of creeper stems. And with her own medical training behind her, she surely understood what it took for a woman to become a doctor. In either case, there were other roles to be fulfilled, and she would find them.

But first there was another voyage ahead and a lengthy stay in a sanatorium where she could be treated, even if no one really knew how to treat tuberculosis in 1930. To her relief, her old friend Georgette Morel was due for a trip home to Alsace, and she agreed to accompany Helene on what must have been one of the saddest journeys of her life. As Brabazon puts it, "Finally, to her bitter regret, she had to acknowledge defeat. She said good-bye to the hospital, her husband, and the brisk women who could work with him in that climate and set off on the long voyage to Europe, health, and loneliness."[67]

৩৶

It is tempting to accept Brabazon's grim prognosis, to view Helene's future through that telescopic moment of farewell when the riverbank receded in the jungle and life at the hospital went on without her like a silent film. By spring 1930, however, Helene was a problem solver of long standing who knew how to arrange her world with or without Albert. No sooner was she back in Germany than she decided on Dr. Max Gerson's clinic in Kassel, where the usual treatment of mind-numbing bed rest was combined with a principally vegetarian, salt-free diet and hormone therapy.[68] Though Helene was skeptical at first, her letter to Marie Secretan from the sanatorium in Kassel on July 14, 1930, was hopeful: "The success seems to be astonishing."[69]

Though still undergoing treatment in July, Helene's resumption of correspondence with Breitkopf & Härtel included a rare mention of her health: "Due to my great difficulty with the African climate and having had to return to Europe, I am once again in the position, as before, to be able to act as representative in my husband's affairs."[70] In the last weeks of her stay in Kassel, she devoted time to correcting the proofs of Albert's autobiography, *Out of My Life and Thought*, which he had been working on for the past year. Through these activities, Helene Schweitzer reclaimed a meaningful role for herself, a role that would expand in the years ahead to include public speaking and networking in the United States made possible by her fluency in English. Rumors of her struggle for health and the fact that she had been to Lambarene and seen the "new hospital" would add a note of moral authority to her presence and her words.

We have a glimpse of this outlook in a moving letter written in English to a Dr. Priestman, whose little boy died in 1930. Helene's compassion, as she writes from yet another clinic, is clearly founded on personal experience: "I can feel with you, because on my return in spring, I found my only daughter aged nearly 12 now, in a surgical clinic having undergone two days before an operation of appendicitis & I had lost a brother some years ago of that same operation. Most happily my girl recovered well, but ever since I have been in clinics & hospitals. Now I am much better & hope to be able to go to some southern place soon, to spend the rest of the winter there."[71]

In 1931, *Out of My Life and Thought* was published, and the building count in Lambarene reached thirty-two. For Helene, the voice that had once been reduced to a whisper was ready to speak publicly on behalf of the hospital. In Würzburg, Germany, a local newspaper reported on December 1 her powerful message to a standing-room-only crowd in the Alhambra Hall on the last day of November: "Those who have never been ill should not take it as something natural, a given, but understand it as a grace and bring a double offering of thanks, so that those who have not been granted their share of this grace may also be helped."[72]

In this way, Helene allowed herself to be seen as a member and interpreter of Albert Schweitzer's concept of the Fellowship of the Mark of Pain. She would further define this global "community" in her US lecture: "Those who have learnt by experience what physical pain and bodily anguish mean belong together all the world over; they are united by a secret bond."[73] In the end, it was her capacity for compassion rather than sacrifice that helped her to carve a path near to Albert Schweitzer, if not exactly with him. She came to know herself as a person who could not be defeated by distance or climate. Not even by tuberculosis. She also began to realize that her unexpected destiny held a quiet power of its own.

5

• • •

Against the Current

Near the equator, night falls in a flash. Helene traveled like a celestial navigator on the Ogowe River, heading downriver near midnight on August 2, 1941. She had fully expected this journey to take three months.[1] But only a few weeks after her departure from Lisbon on the neutral ship *Angola* and less than a week since her arrival in the bustling ports of Boma and Matadi at the mouth of the Congo River, her destination was near. She would always be grateful to the network of missionaries, colonial officials, and forestry entrepreneurs who had helped her through the Belgian Congo and into French Equatorial Africa at Brazzaville. Trains, transports, hotels, and border crossings had been relatively efficient. And, to her surprise, the road from Dolisie to Mouila was good enough for the van to travel at seventy kilometers per hour. On Friday, August 1, Helene expressed the challenge and relief of it all in her day book: "Arrived in Mouila very shaken and covered with a layer of red dust." Nevertheless, she continued on to Fougamou the same day as she made her way toward the Ngounie River. "Went to bed early, very tired after 13 hours of travel."[2]

At 9:00 a.m. the next day, she set off in a northerly direction for Sindara in the same small truck where she had stored her bags, courtesy of the Société du Haut Ogooué, a commercial trade association in French Equatorial Africa offering a variety of services to Europeans. After lunch and a visit to the Catholic Mission in Sindara, she was given passage on the riverboat owned by a Mr. Louvet-Jardin. As the sun set that night, she could be certain they would reach Lambarene within hours.

Helene must have smiled at the sounds around her—the slight breeze running through palm fronds, the ripple and splash of water, bats chattering high in the trees. African voices, too, calling to one another in cascading rhythms or softly hushed as they gathered around small fires in the jungle. *African voices.* What could be more comforting after the chaos of other voices in Lisbon, where she had spent weeks as one of forty thousand people trying to leave the Continent? *Do I have a chance tomorrow? Nothing certain. When will I know? Come back tomorrow. Did you get an exit visa? Not yet.* Such questions without answers formed the daily fabric of that "gateway to warring Europe,"[3] a port Arthur Koestler memorably described as "the last open gate of a concentration camp extending over the greater part of the continent's surface."[4]

After a year of uncertainty spent in France, Helene had traveled to Lisbon via Barcelona and Madrid, arriving there on June 10, 1941. She would always remember that city as a purgatory of sorts, where people wandered and waited in a collective state of quiet desperation. We learn from her journal that on June 25, 1941, she left the offices of the Colonial Navigation Company with the "half promise" of a place on a ship as long as she made a reservation by July 1. But first she would need an exit visa to leave Portugal, a process that was taking more time than expected, despite help from Mr. Dufournier. "Very depressed," she wrote in her day book on July 3. "Hope" was noted on July 7 after a telephone call with a Mr. Dufournier. A day later she felt low again: "Disappointment. More rounds without results."[5] But now, at last, she was gliding on the moonlit waters of the Ngounie that would carry her to the Ogowe River and her last six miles of a very long voyage.

Helene had fallen in love with Africa in 1913, even before she set foot on the continent.[6] Through the years, she had recorded her fascination with the Ogowe region in notes to family and friends, sometimes describing mesmerizing light effects on the water.[7] When she returned at the end of 1929, she was struck by the "sky brilliant with stars" and felt herself to be floating in a dreamlike state, "gliding along once more so smoothly and quietly."[8] Once again, in 1941, we can imagine that the fears she felt in Europe began to fall away as she floated downstream—fears for friends such as Bertha Lenel and for her daughter, Rhena; Rhena's husband, Jean Eckert; and the grandchildren she missed so much.[9] She surely thought about her elderly mother as well, Cary Bresslau, who felt farther away than ever after their farewell in Heidelberg two years earlier.

By 1941, at age sixty-two, Helene probably realized already that Germany would never feel like home again. She had moved to Lausanne with Rhena in 1933, six months after Adolf Hitler's rise to power in Germany, but a deeper sense of rupture occurred when she learned that the house in Königsfeld was inhabited by Nazi troops. "I am astonished again at how one learns to separate from those things that were so dear," she wrote to her sister-in-law Luise on November 18, 1940.[10] It was only after she mailed that letter to São Paulo, Brazil, that she wondered how her words might be received. After all, it was only a house. *Only a house.* Luise had lost so much more, widowed by Ernst's heart attack in 1935, arguably an early casualty of war hastened by the Nazi campaign against Jewish intellectuals. Broken careers. Book burnings. Confiscated assets. Like so many others, Ernst had no choice but to leave that world behind.[11]

Helene's last letter to Luise from Lisbon was written on July 9, 1941, two days before boarding a ship thirty minutes after her exit visa was granted.[12] If only she had known how soon it would happen, maybe she would not have shared her half-distraught thoughts with Luise: "Since it is now over a year since we have had an exchange of letters, and since he cannot leave the hospital as long as this war lasts, and no one can guess when it will end, in short his situation is unbearable, especially given his age and the length of time he has now been out there—six years!"[13] She was, of course, writing about Albert, but also about herself. Only when Europe disappeared could she breathe again and feel that familiar eagerness for Africa to appear on the horizon like a vast Garden of Eden.

ᘓ

Helene's journal reveals that her spirit was remarkably strong as she moved toward Africa, toward Albert, toward the place where she intended to be useful again. Her daily notations focus primarily on practical matters, from getting her hair done in São Tomé on July 26 to the quality of the Hôtel Métropole in Matadi on July 28, to her social interaction with customs officers, colonial officials, and missionaries. Regarding a dinner with "several guests" in Dolisie hosted by the regional director, Mr. Ciavaldini, on July 31, Helene writes that there was "[a] lively conversation on the Jewish question."[14] The absence of opinion, emotion, or elaboration in this notation tells us to what extent she was accustomed to keeping her thoughts to herself and her mind clear of turmoil. From all appearances, she remained grounded, rested, and practical as she moved toward Lambarene.

Behind her, beloved people and places would be marked forever by the brutality of war. Ahead of her was another universe, a place devoted to Albert's philosophy of Reverence for Life conceived as a kind of resistance against European greed, materialism, and so-called progress. Ever since he had felt the fullness of life as the right of all living things and written the phrase "Ehrfurcht vor dem Leben" (Reverence for Life) on a piece of paper in 1915, both had believed that this simple idea was like a star-studded night, ready to shine its distant light on the darkness of so-called civilization.

In their youth, neither Albert nor Helene—nor millions of others—could have imagined that the value of humanity itself would be called into question in their lifetime on European soil. Or that the age-old "Jewish question" would be reconfigured as a stain on German identity by 1930. When German soldiers marched into Paris a decade later, in June 1940, Helene Schweitzer found herself to be one among three hundred thousand "wandering Jews" in France whose lives were now in danger. Of all the journeys in her life, this inner journey from insider to outsider must surely be counted as one of the most difficult—a journey that, perhaps, puts all others into perspective as mere logistics.

Helene's small 1941 journal records her nocturnal arrival in Lambarene. Owing to the dry season, the riverboat captain knew they would not get close enough to the river's northern shore to disembark there. Instead, he would anchor the boat on a sandbank in front of the

Catholic Mission on Lambarene Island. Helene would have guessed, by then, that Dr. Schweitzer was aware of her imminent arrival, news of her journey having traveled to Lambarene by the highly efficient system of African drums, the *télégraphe de brousse* (telegraph in the bush), as well as by her own telegram sent from Brazzaville four days earlier. Indeed, African men were waiting in their pirogues, ready to announce Helene's arrival to Dr. Schweitzer by sounding a trumpet crafted of animal horn.[15]

In one of the innumerable notebooks where Schweitzer recorded all manner of day-to-day information, his notes on this event betray no emotion, although he had not seen his wife since her brief visit in May 1939.[16] "Arrival of Helene on Saturday, August 2 at midnight, coming from the southern arm [of the river]. She came with the boat of Louvet-Jardin. I had ordered people at the passage between the big river and its little arm, because the motorboat couldn't pass there, because of the sand. They had a canoe to ride from there to here. With a trumpet they announced the arrival of the motorboat and they were glad to be on guard only up to midnight instead of the whole night."[17]

Helene's notes in her own *cahier* (notebook) are even more concise and to the point: "Meeting on the sand bank in front of the Cath. Miss. [Catholic Mission]. Albert's men took me to the Hospital that they informed with the horn trumpet. Received by Albert and Miss Emma and Elsa [*sic*]."[18]

Schweitzer's public report from Lambarene sent to the United States after the war made far more of this remarkable moment, describing Helene's arrival "as if it were a miracle."[19] It was, indeed, a kind of miracle, but one aided and abetted by Helene Schweitzer Bresslau's determination. The true "miracle," however, was not that she escaped Nazi Europe and appeared in Lambarene near midnight on an August night but that throughout World War II she was able to withstand the equatorial climate and work as a nurse with no health crisis to slow her down. Only occasionally would she take a break at the Catholic Mission in Dolisie. There, the Alsatian director, Father Bromberg, was always pleased to welcome her.[20] Best of all, because her tuberculosis was by this time cured, she was able to remain in Africa throughout the war and witness the outcome of her own successful efforts to inspire support for Lambarene beyond the confines of Europe.

ॐ

Helene's decision to move to New York with Rhena in the fall of 1937 had been motivated by both Albert and Helene's desire for Rhena to perfect her English and develop her skills far from the growing dangers of Europe. But it seems clear that Helene also saw the opportunity for widening Lambarene's circle of friends and supporters, thanks to her command of the English language and numerous contacts. Indeed, because a number of friends and relatives had already immigrated to the United States, she had a ready-made network to smooth the way and open doors. Shortly after arriving at their apartment on Riverside Drive in New York in October 1937, Helene set to work lining up venues for the highly detailed, thirty-two-page slide lecture she delivered throughout the winter of 1937–38, beginning with an appearance at the nearby Riverside Church in New York City on December 10, 1937.[21]

With an ambitious schedule of public lectures, often delivered in nearly flawless English, she inspired audiences in the Northeast through mid-March 1938 and then—after Easter Paris and four months in Lambarene—resumed her talks later in the year when she traveled as far as St. Louis.[22] American friends who had met the Schweitzers in Africa or in Gunsbach assisted with these travels along the eastern seaboard: missionary Emory Ross; Middlebury College professor Everett Skillings; and Edward Hume, secretary of the Christian Medical Council for Overseas Work.[23] But Helene also traveled as far as Chicago, Minneapolis, and the University of St. Louis, where her cousin Dr. Leo Loeb was teaching in 1938. After two days with Leo and Georgina Loeb, she headed off to her last talk in Greencastle, Indiana, before returning "home" to New York City in time for Christmas.[24]

Apart from a new life in America and the rigors of work, the first weeks of November 1938 were marked with the horrors of what was then called Kristallnacht (Night of Broken Glass) in Germany on November 9–10.[25] For the first time, Jews were deported by the thousands to concentration camps such as Buchenwald or Sachsen-hausen. Surely Helene was aware of this pogrom and may even have seen the supersize headlines in the *New York Times* on November 10: "NAZIS SMASH, BURN AND LOOT JEWISH SHOPS AND TEMPLES UNTIL GOEBBELS CALLS HALT."[26] Schweitzer, too, must have heard of Kristallnacht via radio contact established in Lambarene in 1938, but his letter to New York a month later avoids the matter, focusing instead on Helene's tireless work: "Mg. I've just got your short note written between two night rides on the train. So often I imagine, when you travel long distances in trains, all that you have to endure, and everything that a lecturer has to take on in such situations."[27]

Schweitzer understood what her days and nights were like because her tour to promote the hospital in the United States was modeled after his own exhausting concert and lecture tours. And like his own talks and performances before World War I, Helene's American slide lectures paid off with funds for the hospital and a new network of friends. Furthermore, in May 1942 cases stamped "ASB" filled with medications, rubber gloves, and even cooking utensils arrived at the four-hundred-bed hospital on the riverbank. "The new drugs came in the nick of time, for our supply was nearly used up," Schweitzer wrote in a pamphlet published by the Albert Schweitzer Fellowship.[28] This organization—still active today, though with a redefined mission—grew out of the nucleus of friends Helene made in Boston and New York and was originally known as the Schweitzer Committee of the USA.[29]

Perhaps the confidence Helene derived from her time in America made the hardships of wartime easier to bear. She quickly found a footing in Lambarene in 1941, just as she had in 1913. Indeed, with the exception of her difficult sojourn in 1930 cut short by poor health,[30] whenever she arrived in Lambarene, she felt instantly at home. And from 1941 to 1946, she was strong enough to perform the duties of an operating-room nurse and relieve other nurses weary from years in the jungle climate. More nutrition conscious than ever since the benefits of Dr. Max Gerson's treatment plan—largely based on a low-salt, vegetarian diet—Helene planted a garden to support her own health. Albert worked all day and played his piano late at night. As photographs attest, they shared picnics on sandbanks as well as work. Helene also helped with Albert's perpetual correspondence with friends, relatives, and supporters throughout the world.

The great difference from the early days, apart from an increasing load of correspondence, was the harsh reality of war in their lives, with its inevitable waves of grief. Ever since World War I, both had endured the displacements and losses that war inevitably inflicts on noncombatants. Both had experienced the isolation of internment.[31] And both had felt the losses of friends and family in the 1920s, especially after the disintegration of the Weimar Republic created a power vacuum. It was then that the popularity of Hitler's Nationalsozialistische Deutsche Arbeiterpartei (Nazi Party) began to gather support like a dark cloud over a German population desperate for relief from social and economic upheaval. Even before January 1933, when Hitler was elected chancellor of Germany, this party's extreme politics were evident in all facets of German life. By 1941, Nazi extremism had replaced rational society.

Like everyone else, the Schweitzers lived with anxiety and loss as they learned of deportations, torture, violent death, and suicides of beloved friends and relatives.[32] Even their daughter and son-in-law, Rhena and Jean Eckert, were placed on a list to be deported to Auschwitz with their three small children, precipitating their dramatic border crossing into Switzerland.[33] "We are haunted by the thought of those poor deported ones," Helene wrote to her sister-in-law in November 1943. "I don't know anyone who has ever heard from them again."[34]

No grief, however private, was felt apart from the world at war. Two months after her arrival in Lambarene in 1941, Helene recorded her mother's death in her day book with a Christian cross and a small rectangle drawn around the German word for "grandma" (*Oma*).[35] The quiet restraint of this notation expresses the loneliness Helene felt in the wake of Cary Bresslau's death in Heidelberg at age eighty-eight. Months later she wrote to Luise, "I am grateful that the end was gentle and without suffering, and that the anguish of the world cannot reach her. As for the reasons behind the anguish that remains, for me, related to her fate, I will never get over it."[36]

⁂

The "anguish of the world" that Helene referred to had intensified throughout the 1930s, especially after Albert's return to Europe in the winter of 1932. For both him and Helene, his keynote address in Frankfurt on the one hundredth anniversary of Johann Wolfgang Goethe's death marked a turning point. After all, March 22, 1932, stood for other important anniversaries as well: thirty years to the day since their pact of friendship along the Rhine and nineteen years since their first departure for Africa. Perhaps Schweitzer felt inspired, even emboldened, by these memories as he stood to speak of Goethe's ideals, the fear palpable in the air that Hitler's Sturmabteilung, or SA soldiers, might storm the Frankfurt Opera House. Helene and thirteen-year-old Rhena joined Schweitzer on this trip, with Marie Secretan coming along as a nanny. In an article published fifty years later, Secretan recalled Schweitzer's mood as apprehensive: "I am so fearful for the future," he told her.[37] And yet his talk conveyed no fear at all.

After speaking eloquently of Goethe's profound connection to nature and the meaning of Goethe in his own life, Albert Schweitzer seized this opportunity to deliver an urgent message to hundreds of people listening in utter silence, rapt in their ominous historic moment: "What is Goethe's word to us, to us human beings plunged as we are in terrible need?" he asked. His answer was gripping: "Society is something temporal and ephemeral; man, however, is always man. So Goethe's message to the men of today is the same as to the men of his own time and to the men of all times: 'Strive for true humanity! Become, yourself, a man who is true to his inner nature, a man whose deed is in tune with his character.'"[38]

He then transformed the theme of the day from ethical to political by posing another question with reference to Goethe's classic work of a man who enters into a pact with the devil: "What is now taking place in this terrible epoch of ours except a gigantic repetition of the drama of Faust on the stage of the world? . . . In deeds of violence and murders a thousand fold, a brutalized humanity plays its cruel game!"

Positioning Goethe as one who understood the "great problem" that would face humanity in the future—"how the individual can assert himself in the face of the multitude"—Schweitzer stated flatly that "the material and spiritual independence of the individual, so far as it is not already destroyed, is most seriously threatened." He spoke of "the frightful drama being enacted" and evoked Goethe's voice: "Do not abandon the idea of personality, even when it runs counter to developing circumstances. . . . Remain men in possession of your own souls!" For Albert Schweitzer, this "ideal of human personality" was so precious that "[i]f it is given up, then the human spirit will be destroyed, which will mean the end of civilization, and even humanity."[39] In this way, Schweitzer's tribute to Goethe laid bare his opposition to Adolf Hitler, to authoritarian government in all its forms, and to the Nazi Party's already evident inhumanity that would eventually lead to the Holocaust.[40]

As Helene sat listening, most likely with a calm expression, and then accompanied her husband to the evening reception, dinner, and concert, there could be no doubt that she was firmly allied with Schweitzer's worldview. Indeed, she had probably discussed the speech with Albert in advance, offering edits and suggestions as she had done so many times before. The Goethe speech undoubtedly increased the risks for both of them, but especially for Helene, whose Jewish origins were no secret. Her German bank account was frozen later that year. So be it. She was only waiting for the end of the 1932–33 school year to emigrate with her daughter from Germany to Switzerland.

ॐ

There is much to say about the nuanced way in which both Schweitzers handled themselves during those years of pressure and outright terror. We must inevitably confront the persistent critique of passivity at this time owing to Albert's presence in Lambarene from 1937 to 1948, with the exception of a brief visit to Gunsbach in 1939, and Helene's return to Africa in 1941 for a sojourn of five years. In approaching this critique, however, we must bear in mind that the traditional dates for the "war years," 1939 to 1945, are deceptively brief.[41] Indeed, these dates assigned by historians encompass only part of the story of Nazi Germany. Among other things, they omit years of political struggle throughout the 1920s and 1930s and set aside powerful ideas such as those voiced by Schweitzer in the Goethe speech in 1932.

In a recent study of Schweitzer's politics, *Albert Schweitzer als "homo politicus"* (Albert Schweitzer as "homo politicus"), Thomas Suermann tends to underestimate Schweitzer's political role in World War II by interpreting the 1932 Goethe speech as an isolated incident. In Suermann's words, this speech was "the only moment when Schweitzer took a public position pertaining to the political and social situation."[42] Unfortunately, this perspective overlooks numerous other speeches and statements. It also assumes an indifference that Suermann supports with references to Schweitzer's well-known refusal to sign anti-Nazi petitions or to play an active political role, as some of his influential friends urged him to do.[43]

However, an alternative reading of Schweitzer's acts and words across several decades before and after the outbreak of World War II offers a more expansive and ultimately more accurate picture of Schweitzer's approach to the politics of war. Taken together as a consistent body of thought, Albert Schweitzer's political action might be understood to encompass his furious antiwar sermons in November 1918, his years of work on *The Philosophy of Civilization* (*Kulturphilosophie*), his commitment to developing the hospital throughout the 1920s in the spirit of Reverence for Life, his public lectures in Great Britain in the 1930s, and even his provocative 1962 preface to the American edition of Rolf Hochhuth's *The Deputy*, which he wrote at the age of eighty-eight.[44]

These works and actions form a fabric of opposition to everything Hitler stood for even as Schweitzer includes himself, according to *The Deputy* preface, as one who could have done more: "Our failure made us all participants in the guilt of those days." But this statement is more rhetorical than confessional. The larger point of the preface is clear: "To stay on the right path of history we must become aware of the great aberration of those days, and must remain aware of it, so as not to stumble further into inhumanity."[45] Ideas like this consistently articulated over half a century make Albert Schweitzer, and Helene by association, more politically relevant than they may have appeared as Hitler's machine rolled over Europe.

Schweitzer's autobiography, which Helene carefully proofed during her stay at Max Gerson's clinic in 1930–31, leaves no doubt about the political views that she helped her husband formulate in eloquent German: "The man of today is forced into skepticism about his own thinking, so that he may become repetitive to what he receives from authority." Drawing inspiration from the "inalienable human rights proclaimed in the eighteenth century," Schweitzer took a firm position in his widely read book: "I declare myself to be one who places all his confidence in rational thinking," he stated flatly. It is in this context that one of Schweitzer's most quotable quotes occurs: "Verzicht auf Denken ist geistige Bankrotterklärung" ("To renounce thinking is to declare spiritual bankruptcy").[46] If the 1932 Goethe speech carried extra weight because it took place at an ominous moment in the heart of Frankfurt, Germany, it was far from Schweitzer's first, only, or last public warning expressed before the outbreak of World War II in 1939.

In fact, these themes of ethical thinking as a shield against "spiritual bankruptcy" and the value of "irreplaceable life" as the basis of humanity run through Schweitzer's life and work like a warning call to his generation. As for his distrust of German expansion, he expressed the first signs of it privately to Helene as early as 1911 when he was thirty-six years old. In a letter sent to her during her treatment in Bad Schwartau, where saltwater baths relieved her respiratory problems, he predicted war within a year or two and outlined the probable causes as Germany's desire to weaken England and claim an Atlantic port in northern Africa. As for Germany's touting of "honesty, morality, rectitude, etc.," Schweitzer dismissed these claims as nothing more than a show of "empty concepts" driven by "a madness unworthy of its people."[47]

Helene was interested in global politics from an early age and enjoyed political debates with Albert, as is evident in a letter from her that inspired his prophetic words quoted here. As a German-born citizen with great admiration for her country and its culture—at least in 1911—Helene asked and answered a provocative question: "Who is out to conquer territory? It's the French who are not satisfied with what has been conceded to them at the Algesiras conference[48] and who believe themselves able to impose their will of [further] expansion because they sense the support of an England jealous of Germany."[49] Although this exchange of views took place within the context of a larger question—whether the region they called "our Congo" might become German territory or not and how such a turn of events might influence their plans—Schweitzer remained firm in his wariness of German nationalism and, in fact, of all forms of nationalism as a substitute for humanity. In the same letter quoted here, Helene correctly interpreted one of his primary motives for going to Africa as a chance "to prove by example that humanitarian work can and must transcend separations attributable to national differences."[50]

More than twenty years later, with Helene at his side, Schweitzer delivered the Hibbert Lectures in Oxford, in October 1934, followed by the prestigious Gifford Lectures in Edinburgh. Like the 1932 Goethe Speech in Frankfurt, these lectures in Great Britain demonstrate once again how Schweitzer's words carried meaning on more than one level, in this case both theological and political. In the opening paragraph of a widely read summary of his Gifford Lectures, "Religion in Modern Civilization," Schweitzer plunged in with a blunt reference to World War I: "There is a longing for religion among many who no longer belong to the churches. . . . And yet we must hold fast to the fact that religion is not a force. The proof? The war!"[51] In this lecture, Schweitzer warned against authoritarian leadership and then returned to the theme of *thinking* as an essentially individual responsibility.[52] "In modern thinking, the same thing happens as in religion. Thinking drops the tiller from its hand in the middle of the storm. It renounces the idea of giving to human beings ideals by the help of which they can get on with reality. It leaves them to themselves, and that in a most terrible moment. For the present moment is terrible."[53]

Who had "dropped the tiller," if not Hitler's followers? And who, if not Adolf Hitler himself, did Schweitzer have in mind when he declared that "[t]oday there is an absence of thinking which is characterized by a contempt for life"? And just in case his intended connection between ethical thinking and the world situation was not crystal clear, he continued bluntly, "Let me give you a definition of ethics: It is good to maintain life and further life; it is bad to damage and destroy life."[54]

გა

The question of Schweitzer's wartime politics has remained unresolved or simply ignored owing to a curious reluctance to read his acts and words as a covert political strategy, despite an open invitation to do just that from his old friend Theodor Heuss in 1951. When Heuss, then president of Germany, addressed Schweitzer personally on the occasion of the 1951 Friedenspreis ceremony in Frankfurt,[55] he confronted the question of Schweitzer as a *"homo politicus"* without hesitation. "It is now quite noticeable that this Schweitzer is no politician," said Heuss, "but through his attitude that reaches beyond politics he has become a political event in and of himself."[56] This "reach[ing] beyond politics" to address the spiritual-ethical-political crisis of the 1920s and 1930s may explain Schweitzer's apparent desire to stand apart from the war despite friends' urging.

Among others, German Jewish physicist and Nobel laureate (1952) Max Born urged Albert Schweitzer to turn away from Lambarene and use his moral authority for the good of Europe.[57] That Schweitzer chose not to do so in an outspoken way only reveals what we already know—that Schweitzer was stubbornly independent in all aspects of his life. Meanwhile, his position on the current situation was so well known in Germany and throughout Europe that it actually required no public explanation or defense, despite pleas from friends. In other words, those who interrogate Schweitzer's words and actions in this period must inevitably grapple with a contradictory claim for two Albert Schweitzers: one whose position was widely understood and therefore of great value and another whose apparent reticence deprived the world of an asset it already possessed. In the end, we cannot have both.

Interestingly, history has since demonstrated that French Equatorial Africa's role in bolstering Charles de Gaulle's Free France beyond Europe was far from insignificant. Schweitzer himself explained how the region had been hotly contested at the beginning of the war: "In the fall of 1940, the troops of General de Gaulle and those of Vichy were engaged in fighting for the possession of Lambarene. . . . The crews of the aircraft on both sides were ordered by their leaders not to bomb the Hospital, so it escaped serious damage and became a haven or refuge for both white people and black."[58] As the most reliable hospital in an area of what historian Eric Jennings has referred to as "exterior resistance,"[59] the Schweitzer Hospital was not removed from the dangers and deprivations of World War II, as some have presumed.

Likewise, although living as exiles during most of the 1930s and 1940s, Helene and Albert Schweitzer were far from unscathed by the war. As early as 1942, they were treating an indigenous population depleted by the need to supply Free France with rubber, among other things, in order to lessen dependence on the Allies.[60] They mourned with millions of others as news of deaths and losses arrived, a painful solidarity made possible by radio and newspaper communication, to say nothing of letters from America, England, Brazil, and Switzerland.[61] We might surmise that, relying on the strongest argument they had, the symbolic meaning of the Schweitzer Hospital, both Albert and Helene envisioned their work as a living alternative to the spiritual void and unspeakable brutality of Europe. Theodor Heuss suggested as much in 1951 when he directed his remarks to Albert Schweitzer as the recipient of a prestigious prize: "Your name, indeed your way of being and the fact of your being in the world during the corrupted and condemnable years, was for countless persons a form of consolation and tranquility."[62]

Helene's invisibility in this eloquent tribute is unfortunate. Like Schweitzer's, Helene's "way of being" and the "fact of [her] being in the world" resulted in daily contributions to the maintenance and preservation of life in the Middle Ogowe region during those difficult years. Like Schweitzer, she spent the 1930s "on the road," traveling with her husband to Frankfurt (1932) and Great Britain (1934) before delivering her own lectures in America (1937–38), an effort that resulted in both material and spiritual support. Why did she push herself so hard for so little recognition if not because of a commitment equal to that of her husband? Unless we are prepared to dismiss Helene's American "campaign," her voyage out of Europe in 1941, and her wartime work in Lambarene (1941–46) as wifely "women's work," she must be understood as a woman determined to make a difference in dark times. That her health was not always up to the challenge implies an even stronger determination to overcome obstacles.

On January 14, 1935, Schweitzer's sixtieth birthday was widely celebrated in Strasbourg and Switzerland before his February return to Lambarene. To mark this milestone, the Schweitzers spent a rare week together in Les Avants, a small village high above the "Swiss Riviera" city of Montreux. We can imagine their talks in that strangely peaceful setting where the French Alps rise in the distance on the opposite side of Lake Leman. Among other things, this was the season of Albert Schweitzer's presumed letter from Joseph Goebbels, supposedly written to lure Schweitzer back into a "pure German" musical culture where J. S. Bach held a special place of honor.[63] Goebbels's opportunistic letter is rumored to have closed with a favorite Nazi phrase banned after the war for its murderous associations: "With German Greetings."

As Theodor Heuss told the story in his 1951 Friedenspreis "Laudatio," Schweitzer flatly refused to be recruited and signed off briskly in a letter of his own: "With Central African Greetings."[64] This squaring off with Hitler's propaganda minister was tantamount to saying, "We live in different worlds, Mr. Goebbels, and the center of my universe is very far from yours." Schweitzer was in the room when Theodor Heuss told this story and did not deny its veracity because he knew perfectly well that, like a modern-day leak to the press, this anecdote made an important political point on his behalf. With or without archival documentation—and none has been produced in more than sixty years of Schweitzer studies—the alleged exchange of letters serves as a characteristically oblique but representative expression of Schweitzer's anti-Nazi politics.

ᏻ

This pause in the midpoint of the 1930s announces a turning point for Helene. Perhaps thoughts of her own future are working in the background as Albert finds his own stride between Africa and Europe. Her brother Ernst's sudden death in May 1935, only a year after moving to Brazil, surely comes as a shock and may serve as a reminder of her own mortality. In either case, there is a surge in Helene's independence in the 1930s, a new sense of confidence and openness to her own public persona. One small piece of evidence is the dignified photographic portrait made around 1932. From the photographs produced at this sitting, she chooses a sober, elegant view of herself that she will use for years as a thank you gift to visitors, which she often signs in white ink with a brief inscription or simply with her signature, "Helene Schweitzer." One can hardly imagine her asserting herself in this way a decade earlier.

In the winter of 1936, there seems to be tension over Albert's insistence on bringing Mathilde Kottmann along during his visits to Lausanne, where Helene is now living with teenage Rhena.[65] That residence, chosen for its proximity to the train station and for its uplifting views across the lake to the eternal snow of the French Alps, allows Helene to remove herself from Germany and provides excellent schooling for her daughter. In the summer, Helene's address shifts to the Ville d'Avray near Paris, France, a temporary move motivated by an extended treatment for Rhena's skin condition.[66] Meanwhile, Albert is performing throughout Europe, including twenty-one organ concerts in Switzerland in 1936. With some difficulty, the Schweitzer family manages to find two hours to spend together at the Strasbourg train station in the midst of a long day.[67] It is, at best, a hectic life in a world of uncertainty.

Helene's mind works as she travels, even if she seems only to gaze from the train at open fields and vineyards. Friends and family in America, including her cousin Johanna Engels's nephews, have invited her to travel across the Atlantic. Perhaps the time has come for Rhena's first trip to America and for Helene to put her English-language skills to use by speaking on behalf of the hospital. Perhaps she is also ready for a change of scenery, a wider world, and some relief from European politics. Albert supports the idea, and Helene sets off for New York City in November 1937, with Rhena fresh from her baccalaureate. Deep inside, Helene is ready to present herself as a voice of peace and freedom, to assert herself as a woman who understands the state of the world and wants to do something about it.

ଡ଼ଋ

As Helene approaches the hospital in Lambarene near midnight in August 2, 1941, the sound of water fills her mind like the nocturnes she used to play on the piano so many years ago. Before the wars. Before marriage and motherhood. Before her first glimpse of this river and a place called Lambarene. She is sixty-two now and growing accustomed to the way the past surfaces in her mind like fragments floating against the current of ordinary days: the crowded train station in Constance after months of internment in 1918, Albert's brave talk in Frankfurt in 1932, the echo of applause in Würzburg in 1931 and America in 1938. One can only wonder if she also returns to the memory of painful days when she was immobilized in Max Gerson's clinic or to the anxieties of Lisbon.

As she steps onto the sandbank, the dark shadows of pirogues slice across the southern arm of the Ogowe River, appearing suddenly like swift-moving alligators in the night. Metallic black faces glisten in moonlight—silver, gold, and bronze—before the raw sound of a trumpet cuts through the air. Helene is suddenly home again, home in Lambarene, gliding toward the riverbank where the hospital seems to light up the jungle. She is ready once again to claim that part of herself that belongs here and nowhere else.

The next morning is devoted to unpacking essentials and touring the hospital with Emma Haussknecht, who shows her a project she has supervised: the planting of two thousand palm oil trees and an abundance of fruit trees now considered "common property."[68] Clearly, "Miss Emma" has become indispensable.[69] Helene enjoys notes and flowers sent by missionaries nearby and an invitation to visit Mr. and

Mrs. Bourelli at the Protestant Mission in Andende as soon as possible. There are also predictable problems to deal with: the arrival of the mail boat without her trunks and the tedious necessity of repairing the seam of her mosquito net, which seems to have taken hours.[70] Patients, too, are waiting. As ever, there is a job to be done, a job that will continue for the days, weeks, months, and years of her longest sojourn in Lambarene.

ౚ

The war in Europe ended with the official German surrender at Reims, France, on May 7, 1945. It was nearly a year later, in January of 1946, before Schweitzer began to negotiate Helene's repatriation with officials in the colony's capital, Brazzaville. His first letter to the governor general of French Equatorial Africa was quickly acknowledged. In late April, the good news came that a *réquisition de passage* (requisitioned transportation) for Helene and her companion would be made available at no charge on demand.[71] Albert's letter to Governor General Soucadoux on October 3, 1946, expresses his profound gratitude: "Your generosity has rendered an even greater service, since the two travelers with their baggage had to travel to Libreville on the roads in order to embark, which meant considerable costs. Fortunately, when the *Felix Roussel* docked in Libreville a day late, this allowed them to arrive on time with the military convoy of [Officer?] Peignier. Otherwise, they would have had to come through dangerous zones, which would have required very high costs."[72]

Helene's journal notes her departure from Lambarene on Sunday, September 8, 1946. Once arrived in Libreville, she settled into a guest house. Two days later she dined with the governor of the colony after receiving a telegram from "Mademoiselle Emma," who was still in Lambarene making lists of Helene's baggage for the customs agent. Emma Haussknecht arrived in Libreville on September 11, "very tired" after a long day that included "new declarations to fill out."[73] Clearly, Emma Haussknecht supported Helene at times as well as the Schweitzer Hospital, both women fully aware of their different social positions. Nevertheless, on September 12, 1946, they set off together on the *Felix Roussel*, a ship recently returned to civilian service, en route to the Mediterranean port of Marseille via Pointe Noire, Dakar, and Casablanca.

In "Casa," Helene was greeted by Paul Ehretsmann, Albert's sister's son, who was living there at the time. She notes that they went to the market and had lunch at his home. Helene finally reached Marseille on October 4, 1946, after a rough night at sea. With assistance from the Red Cross, she then coped with long lines and paperwork before making her way to Strasbourg and the apartment of a cousin, "A. Biedermann," located a few steps from the train station. At this point, the language of Helene's journal shifts from French to German, as if she simply changed her coat.[74]

In a sense, Helene's trip *out* of Africa was almost as dramatic as her voyage *into* Africa five years earlier. However, by 1946 Helene Schweitzer was accustomed to unexpected routes as well as to unexpected kindness. In a letter written from Lambarene to British biographer George Seaver dated March 24, 1945, she acknowledges the kindness and efficiency of those who had made her longest sojourn in Africa possible:

> I asked the Red Cross to supply me with the address of the office in London, stating as my reason the fact that I was the oldest of the nurses at Lambarene and might be of some use since no young nurses were available. They replied that . . . the reply might take a long time. It took a very long time. But then I had a wonderful surprise: a telegram, followed by a letter. . . . I was at liberty to proceed at once! Moreover, the competent authorities in London had given instructions that my journey should be facilitated as much as possible!

Her enthusiasm was tempered, however, by a delay of seven weeks before she could obtain permission to proceed from Bordeaux and leave France. Like thousands of others, she made her way via Spain to Lisbon, where she waited nearly a month for a place on a ship:

> In fact, I received my last permit just half an hour before the ship was to leave that port! . . . I had prepared myself, with some

apprehension, for a long and lonely journey of three months through the bush in unfamiliar territory, but found to my great relief that this was reduced to a week's drive by car on new roads, and finally to a cruise along the well-known river to the Hospital which I reached on August 2, 1941. . . .

Once again and with deep gratitude I would acknowledge my debt to that miraculous help which I have so often received in my life from strangers, which has made it easier to stand what would have otherwise have been sad and difficult.

The end of this letter includes a gentle reminder of her role in the life of the hospital and of her partnership with Albert Schweitzer: "We met with a mutual feeling of responsibility for all the good that we had received in our lives, and a sense of our duty to pay for it by helping others. It has been the joy and the pride of my life to follow and assist him in all his activities, and my one regret that failing strength prevented me from keeping pace with him."

Also at the end of this letter, we hear an echo of Helene's passionate public voice: "May the end of this catastrophic war be near, and allow for the dawn of more humane and worthier conditions for all mankind!"[75] It can be no surprise that she sounded less passionate in a private letter to her sister-in-law in Brazil a month later: "Now that the end of the war draws near . . . where is the immense joy with which one would like to greet this ending? Everyone is overwhelmed with too much sorrow."[76]

6

. . .

Madame Schweitzer
in the Age of Obscurity

Birdsong in Königsfeld. In the spring of 1947, Helene was in that place she knew so well, in the clear air of the Black Forest, in the cottage built in 1923 with its rooms full of memory, surrounded by the fresh sound of birds. She slept in the small room at the front of the house, where shadows took shape at dawn through a veil of violet light. Since her arrival the previous fall, boxes full of papers had been waiting patiently like animals resting in a jungle. But the jungle she knew was thousands of miles away, and everything here felt strange by comparison, especially at dawn. No drums. No bell. No deep-throated voices calling from the river. No echo of Albert's footsteps on wooden planks as he set off to begin another day of work. Alone in Königsfeld, Helene would awaken to what had become a necessity at the age of sixty-eight, her sorting through letters, notebooks, files, and photographs. Quite apart from the paperwork of recovering their house from military requisition status imposed during the war, it was time to bring order to the past she had now shared with Albert Schweitzer for forty-five years.

It remained unclear in the spring of 1947 when Albert would return to Europe. He seemed to have no desire to do so after spending more than a decade in Lambarene.[1] Helene had become the one who migrated back and forth to Africa like a bird, traveling thousands of miles farther than she would have thought possible in her youth. If a hint of girlish adventure were still alive inside her, Helene knew very

117

well what others saw in her outward appearance: drifts of thin white hair, tired eyes, pale skin, and deep wrinkles. She had never dwelled on her image in the mirror, even if her well-cut clothes revealed a taste for fashion. But the physical changes of recent years were undeniable. Her face had become a mask of someone she remembered, like those heavy-lidded African masks she had always admired. Masks full of spirit, simultaneously concealing and revealing something beyond physical reality.

Helene had tried to express this paradox of body and spirit to her sister-in-law a few years earlier when she wrote that "I am preparing everyone who has known me as much as I can to be ready to see me as an old, bent, wrinkled grandmother. Just as when I arrived here [in Lambarene in 1941] I had to force myself to see myself clearly as an old woman, because I only feel my age in certain moments of weariness, but I am now old, old, old, and so tired . . . [.]"[2] Old, perhaps, but not too old to travel. Never too old to travel.

With the arrival of the first springtime Helene had spent in Germany since the end of World War II, she knew she would see Lambarene again before Albert would return to Gunsbach. She already had plans to fly to Lambarene in May for her own sense of peace.[3] She would take along photographs of the four grandchildren now living in Switzerland whom Albert had never seen, most certainly reminding him that their baptisms had been postponed until Grandfather could be there to mark a cross on each small forehead.[4] After so many years in Africa, she knew he would return to Europe only when he was ready. And as soon as he felt the hospital had gone too long without him, he would go back. There was no point in wishing it could be otherwise.

Albert must have been much in Helene's thoughts as she spent hours that spring re-reading their private letters, some written more than forty years ago. She made a project of it, waking each morning to relive those years, determined to make order out of decades of correspondence, day books, journals, photos, documents, and manuscripts. After her return to Europe in October 1946 from a sojourn of more than five years in Africa, her first priorities had been recovery from exhaustion and a long-awaited reunion with Rhena's family near Zurich. Now she was in Königsfeld again, alone in the house where she had raised her daughter throughout the 1920s. Germany would never be the same, but there was some comfort in returning to the refreshing air of the Black Forest.

Helene's priority was clear—to confront the task that had been waiting for years "because, in the end, I don't want to leave things in such chaos."[5] As her niece Carolina Bresslau confirmed years later, Helene wanted to avoid any possible misunderstanding of her role in Albert Schweitzer's work. She knew she had played a significant role, and she wanted it to be part of the record left behind. However self-effacing she might be in public, however gracious and grateful for the life they had shared, it was important to Helene to be understood as a full partner.[6] The documents, she knew, would tell the story.

◌৵

It could not have been easy to know where to begin, although their early love letters would come first if she approached the task chronologically. *Love letters*. What else could they be called, these unbridled confessions of admiration, encouragement, trust, and need—this voluminous record of youthful ideals? And yet she must have realized as she read the fragile pages that Bery had not used the word *love* in the beginning, as she had. He had addressed her as "My great one" or simply "Mg," but never as "my love."

She must have re-read some of his letters again and again as if she were encountering her seventy-two-year-old husband for the first time. Of course, he had expressed love as well as any young man ever could in the pure sincerity of his letters. In words dashed off late at night from his room in Strasbourg a few days before Christmas 1904, he wrote: "It will soon be eleven o'clock. The fire is extinguished and I no longer smell the odor of pine branches in my room. You spent a beautiful hour of my life with me, one of those hours that makes one shiver because one sees such a wide horizon of happiness ahead."[7] And on New Year's Eve that year, as church bells rang in the first moments of 1905: "I ended the year thinking of you and I begin the New Year thinking of you. You are what is most precious to me on earth . . . the person I adore the most and who has the greatest power over me."[8]

Happiness. Yes, they had known happiness as well as ambition and desire. And yet her letters written in the first years of friendship were full of the pressure of pleasing others, of mundane details, of worries and weariness, even of veiled recrimination because—she must have seen it clearly now—she had not yet achieved her goal of independence before the age of twenty-five. And so we might understand her urge to destroy the evidence of naïveté and confusion or perhaps what she felt to be too private for other eyes. But was it fair to keep all of his letters and none of hers? To make a mystery of herself or, worse yet, to leave the impression of coy reticence? How much did posterity deserve to know of personal matters behind the greater story of all that had been accomplished?

Given her innate sense of propriety, such questions must have entered Helene's mind as she walked slowly to the green, tree-lined center of Königsfeld, leaning on the cane that had become part of her appearance. She must have reasoned that the only letters she had the right to destroy were her own. This can be deduced because her responses to Albert's missives are often the missing pieces of their story.[9] But it is also clear that she decided to destroy selectively, leaving enough behind for their early years to be known—for Rhena, perhaps, who had suffered from knowing so little of her father as a young man.

The work on manuscripts that began with *Von Reimarus zu Wrede: Eine Geschichte der Jesu-Leben-Forschung* and *Wir Epigonen* (*Kulturphilosophie*) raised entirely different questions.[10] These writings, like all the books she had worked on beginning with *J. S. Bach* in 1905, were far less personal and, in the end, not hers—even if she had been responsible for the prodigious work of research, indexing, editing, copying, and proofreading, to say nothing of the endless conversations about the structure and content of Albert's arguments. Someday a scholar or pastor or one of the grandchildren or perhaps even a great-grandchild might like to see with their own eyes how Albert's ideas had come together—with her help.[11]

The documents that unquestionably belonged to her alone were her private journals and day books: seemingly endless pocket-size records of travels, visits, concerts, events, birthdays, and people she had encountered along the way. During those early spring days in 1947, Helene might have been surprised to realize how many journals she had kept through the years and from such an early age, though many of her girlhood friends had done the same.[12] The 320-page *Tagebuch*, written from 1913 to 1915, was another sort of journal openly shared with Albert to capture their early observations of life in Africa. Perhaps she re-read her own description of that first voyage out, recalling the exhilarating days at sea and the joy of climbing the hill at Andende with its abundance of palms, fruit trees, and coffee plants to reach the place where everything felt so new and untainted.

Somewhere in the box of journals were the two tiny black volumes of her Saint-Rémy journal, written so carefully during their internment in 1918. These nearly weightless booklets once carried in her skirt pocket were heavy with bittersweet memories from that troubled time. Each page triggered the memory of meeting the challenge she had set for herself: to record each day in two stanzas of rhyming German verse. Though far from a literary accomplishment, marking time within the framework of poetry must have helped to occupy her mind, especially when a stiff wind howled outside. If in 1947 she opened the small booklet to the first page, she would have been reminded of her sense of isolation at the old monastery outside the village of Saint-Rémy-de-Provence:

Unable to work I sit and weep
Till kind souls bestow compassion
Working for us unfortunates with passion
Alone in the park I rest, my dreams mine to keep.[13]

The journal kept in 1930 would have had similar effect on her spirits, taking her back to a difficult time marked by isolation and illness. In retrospect, her early return from Lambarene that spring could have been foreseen, considering her collapse a month or so before departure and the difficult weeks on board ship. How grateful they were for that Christmastime on the Ogowe and the joy of arrival that glittered in memory. For Helene, such days were enough to justify whatever suffering she had endured. After all, her first instinct had always been to resist being ruled by illness or obstacle.

The calendar books she kept throughout the 1940s demonstrate the same perseverance. At a glance, these miniature records might easily be mistaken for clutter. But woven into Helene's daily notations and often compressed or abbreviated penmanship is a personal history of names, places, impressions, travel itineraries, packing lists, doctor appointments, meetings, dinners, and hotel addresses as well as an ongoing record of correspondence received and sent. So many people had passed through her life in those years when the world started to twist and turn and break apart. Alone with the evidence of her journey from the "safe harbor" of Königsfeld, Helene could now recall the difficult months of 1941 spent in small apartments and hotels in Châtel-Guyon, Riom, Vichy, Bordeaux, Barcelona, Madrid, and Lisbon. The waiting had tried her patience, to be sure. But, looking back, she must have smiled as she re-read her notes dashed off en route to Lambarene, beginning with the day she boarded the *Angola* and settled into a shared cabin. Later that day her attention for detail extended to noting the names of the three children of Emile Kaltenrieder, a missionary traveling to Mozambique.[14]

Now that we, too, are able to read her day book from 1941, it is possible to follow each step of her determined return to Lambarene. Helene filled her tiny pages with excellent French, sometimes turning the journal upside down or sideways to take advantage of every fragment of space. She was in touch with a remarkable range of friends on her journey. Among them: Professor Everett Skillings of Middlebury College in Vermont, whose help had been indispensable in America in 1938, and Bertha Lenel, a dear friend from youth cruelly deported to Gurs during the war. Rhena and Luise appear numerous times in these pages, as do the names of efficient women who worked for the International Red Cross in London and Geneva, such as the ever-reliable Madame Schlumberger. It is also clear that the leader of the

Swiss delegation in France, Walter Otto Stucki, made time to meet with Helene in Vichy more than once, always reassuring her that an exit visa from France would come. It did come, though everything took longer than imagined at the beginning of 1941.

Helene recorded daily details with care, just as she recorded her mother's death on September 30, 1941. Through the telescope of time, that page looked strangely empty compared to other pages from 1941. Her thoughts were literally squeezed into the margins on the journey from Lisbon to the port of Soyo, then through the Belgian Congo by train, and, finally, into French Equatorial Africa at Brazzaville. So many people had helped at every step, in every port, in every imaginable way. Albert called her arrival in Lambarene a "miracle." But this "miracle" was made possible by Helene's determination and the kindness of fellow travelers in her own private history. In the end, Helene Schweitzer's private journals constitute a book of evidence intentionally preserved.

ᘛ

It is difficult to pinpoint when Helene's active life entered the age of obscurity, for she continued to travel, observe, think, write, and manage correspondence well into the 1950s. Nevertheless, something shifted in October 1947 when the widely read American weekly *LIFE* magazine proposed that Albert Schweitzer be anointed "the greatest man in the world." At least the unnamed author of this brief piece of photojournalism included a mention of Helene, although the adjective chosen to describe her is telling of the times: "A Christian shame for the white man's treatment of the Negro drove Schweitzer to go to Africa with his Jewish wife and set up a medical mission for the natives."[15] Oddly enough, another important boost to Schweitzer's American fame had appeared a month earlier in a special edition of the Unitarian Universalist *Christian Register* with the same eye-catching headline: "'The Greatest Man in the World': That Is What Some People Call Albert Schweitzer, Jungle Philosopher."[16]

This repetitious "billboard" effect had come about thanks to two enthusiastic Schweitzer supporters deeply connected to the Unitarian Church, Melvin Arnold and the Reverend Charles R. Joy. In his

September 1947 *Christian Register* article, the influential Arnold stated his intention—as editor and publisher of his Unitarian publishing house, Beacon Press—to create "a long-term publishing program seeking to make America as familiar with the work of Albert Schweitzer as is Europe."[17] A few months earlier he had traveled to Lambarene with Reverend Joy, at a time when both Helene and Albert were there, to deliver a desperately needed four-thousand-dollar donation.[18] Thanks to the Melvin Arnold Papers at the Harvard Divinity School, we know that Joy corresponded with Albert Schweitzer as early as May 1945 and occasionally with Helene Schweitzer before and after she traveled to America with her husband in 1949.[19]

Oddly enough, we have no evidence that Helene Schweitzer was in touch with either Arnold or Joy at an earlier date, though their paths came close to crossing. For instance, Joy was stationed in Lisbon with the Unitarian Service Committee in 1940 to help Americans flee Nazi Europe. And it's quite possible that Arnold might have heard Helene talk on behalf of the Schweitzer Hospital at the First Congregational Church in Cambridge, Massachusetts, on January 17, 1938.[20] More often, however, her lectures were in Baptist, Methodist, or Presbyterian churches.

These various American "denominations" must have felt a bit foreign to Helene, for whom a more generalized European Protestantism rooted in the Reformation was her frame of reference. Her 1948 contribution of an article to the *Christian Century* was written in this spirit. There, she asserted her Christian identity as she spoke almost autobiographically of personal struggles from her practical understanding of missionary work. "The missionary as a rule does not consider that he is making sacrifices. He feels joy in his work, and the consciousness that he is obeying Christ's command to teach all the nations gives him strength." And yet "[i]t is only when ill-health intervenes to separate man and wife who have been laboring together in the Lord's vineyard that the missionary feels he has chosen a hard life. The one who remains is anxious whether his fellow worker's health can be restored in a better climate, and the one who goes suffers as much from the knowledge that the whole burden now falls on the other as from his own physical insufficiency."[21] This measured, slightly distant, third-person tone exemplifies Helene's public voice as "Madame Schweitzer" even as it conveys a sense of personal isolation.

As this era of Albert Schweitzer's fame took flight late in 1947, Helene also confronted misperceptions forced upon her by his sudden celebrity. Quite apart from enthusiastic American assistance, Schweitzer's image was enlarged for the second time in his life as a symbol of humanity in the wake of a catastrophic war. He was forty-three when he returned to Europe from Lambarene in 1918, via internment in southern France, and seventy-three when he returned to Europe in 1948 in the aftermath of World War II. In both periods, he fulfilled a collective hunger for symbols of hope and survival.

If this hunger appeared to be more ravenous in the American imaginary after World War II, we might attribute it to an explosion of visual media that included the onset of television, newsreels in movie houses, and the postwar wave of popularity for large-format, image-driven weekly magazines such as *LIFE* and *Saturday Review*.[22] Among those inspired by images of Albert Schweitzer in such publications, Gwen and Larry Mellon, cofounders of the Albert Schweitzer Hospital in Haiti's Artibonite Valley, considered the October 6, 1947, issue of *LIFE* to be a turning point in their own commitment to humanitarian work.[23] They wanted to replicate the Schweitzer spirit in the most desperate place they could find. Their remarkable health-care organization in Haiti celebrated a half-century of operations in 2006, a fact that affirms the positive potential of mass media.

But just as we should not trivialize the power of the media in the mid–twentieth century, however "quaint" it may appear to us now, we should also take care not to minimize the significance of the seeds Helene planted in 1937–38. Her lecture tour was effectively the first "publicity campaign" in the United States on behalf of the Schweitzer Hospital. If by the early 1950s new technology, a new middle class, and a new cult of celebrity were in play, it should not be forgotten that many Americans first learned of the Schweitzer Hospital from Helene Schweitzer's English-language slide presentations in church halls. Insofar as publicity reflects culture, people such as publisher

Melvin Arnold, photographer-filmmaker Erica Anderson, and magazine editor Norman Cousins understood the "market value" of Albert
Schweitzer as a towering figure of resilience and compassion, but they
were not the first to bring his philosophy to America.

☙

When Helene Schweitzer accompanied her husband on his first and
last trip to the United States in July 1949, her exposure to aggressive
reporters and large-scale public events—including an American Wom-
en's Club luncheon in Chicago for seventeen hundred guests—often
placed her in the awkward position of being simultaneously applauded
and misunderstood. The object of this nonstop, three-week journey
was the Goethe Bicentennial (of his birth) in Aspen, Colorado, where
Schweitzer had agreed to deliver the keynote speech. If and when the
press took an interest in Helene, who had lived in New York and traveled much of the same ground more than a decade earlier, it was more
often to portray her as Schweitzer's loyal follower than to recognize
her own unique contributions.

In the *Woman Magazine*, Virginia Travers romanticized Helene's
gentility in an article entitled "Angel of the African Jungle." After
suggesting that Helene had lived most of the past thirty-eight years
in Africa, which she had not, Travers gushed that "[h]er story is one
of pure and selfless love." Later in the article, the journalist described
how "[s]hy, reticent Helene Schweitzer was noticeably appalled by the
many questions directed at her and the reporters' emphasis on 'the
woman's angle.'" There is no doubt that the "frail little woman, by
this time in her sixties," understood Travers's urge to label, frame, and
package her complexity in order to reach a prefabricated conclusion:
"Helene Schweitzer's life is the testimonial and the proof of her great
husband's precepts."[24] Having no more desire to be reduced to symbolic "proof" than she had to be ignored as a free-thinking individual,
it is no wonder Helene was "appalled."

Time magazine took a different, though commonplace, approach
in 1949, defining Helene in the shadow of her male relations as "the
daughter of a well-known Strasbourg historian."[25] This, if nothing else,
implied cultural refinement and some level of education but blatantly

ignored Helene's capacity for risk and hard work. Meanwhile, on June 30, 1949, the *Daily Boston Globe* acknowledged Helene's existence in an anecdotal moment that reveals the patriarchal culture of mid-twentieth-century America that Helene, standing on the sidelines as the potentially volatile (i.e., irrational) wife, had no choice but to endure: "A girl reporter told Dr. Schweitzer that he was the essence of civilized man, the epitome of genius, etc. 'How is it then,' she asked, 'that you could sacrifice your great works to live with the African natives?'" As if this fact might be too much for Helene to absorb, the article reported that Schweitzer played along with the mood of the moment, seemingly insensitive to the way in which it reflected on Helene's identity. "'Just a minute now, don't say that in front of my wife,' said Dr. Schweitzer good-naturedly."[26]

Such misinterpretations explain why Helene seized opportunities to clarify her perspective whenever she could, as she did with an unnamed *New York Times* reporter at a Christian faith gathering in New York in 1949.[27] In a July 19, 1949, article headlined "SCHWEITZER'S WIFE HONORED WITH HIM," Helene explained that "[i]t started over his manuscripts," referring to her involvement in Schweitzer's books, such as *J. S. Bach* and *The Quest for the Historical Jesus*. The reporter described her as "a tiny gray-haired woman leaning on her cane," noted her "good English," and stated that "[s]he not only read German manuscripts but read proofs for the French translations." Furthermore, there was time to explain that "[s]he took issue with such articles as 'God's Eager Fool' in a recent *Reader's Digest* and a current article in *Vogue* asserting she took up nursing to work with her husband. 'It was our common feeling,' she said, 'to find our own way, to take what was given and what we had learned and give it to others to help humanity,' she said. 'That brought us together.'"

Helene's point was clear: the ideals that led to Schweitzer's humanitarian work were shared between them from the beginning, not invented by "the greatest man in the world" and simply followed by his "frail little" wife. Even in her early years when her life's path was far from certain, Helene had thought of herself as an equal partner, never as a mere follower or an aimless young woman in search of a husband. As Schweitzer's fame threatened to swallow her reality, she wanted more than ever to assert the truth of her role in his public and private life as well as to claim her own measure of achievement.

An enormously successful talk at Freiburg University on June 14, 1952, marked another moment when Helene seized an opportunity to speak for herself. Invited to deliver a talk on "the land and the people of the Ogowe," she was astonished when eight hundred people filled every seat in the hall and spilled into the aisles. To accommodate the crowd, the doors were left open so that those unable to get into the hall could at least hear her words through a loudspeaker. A local newspaper, the *Badische Zeitung*, reported on June 15, 1952, the "intellectual vitality of the white-haired story-teller" and emphasized the great feeling with which she recounted her travels across land and sea to live and work in Africa's primeval forest.[28] One can imagine the satisfaction she felt, even if it was her last public speech and, in a sense, her final triumph.

இ

As if to set the record straight once and for all, Helene wrote her *Lebenslauf* (literally, "life run") in 1954.[29] Such a "summary of my life" in the German-speaking world can be long or short, according to individual choice. Helene's one-page document is noteworthy for its concise presentation of unadorned facts, for her particular selection of facts, and for its notable omissions. "Born in Berlin, I came to the Alsace when I was eleven years old, due to the appointment of my father to the University of Strasbourg (1890)," she begins. After stating how conscious she was of the enriching opportunity to be raised in two cultures, German and French, she turns to the matter of women's emancipation. "My youth fell into the period of the women's movement that, at the University of Strasbourg, led to the admission of women to the lectures, if the professors agreed, that our teacher exam was valid to participate." Thus, several semesters of university courses in history and especially art history were possible for "Fräulein Bresslau."

But the academic life was not her destiny. "An act of providence brought me into contact with the newly created social work in the city administration of Strasbourg. I could be active for four years as a city orphan inspector. In this time I was able to realize the foundation of a home for mothers." Of course, this "act of providence" had a great deal to do with her own considerable skill, alluded to as she describes her medical training: "When in the Alsace the state exam for nursing was established, I took up nursing again to learn more about it. Then I became a pupil in the Frankfurt Seminar of the Evangelical Deaconess Association, where I completed my training and passed the exam." Helene's emphasis is clearly on her professional accomplishments. There is no mention of youthful travels throughout Europe, of Rhena's birth, or of grandchildren. Likewise, there is no mention of her Jewish origins or of internment during the Great War or of the loss of friends and family before and during World War II. There is a paragraph about the hospital in Lambarene and a closing sentence: "Toward the end of this year, my husband and I have the intention to go back there."[30]

In reading this statement, one senses the seventy-five-year-old Helene's desire to announce the defining moments of her life. Perhaps she was weary of being viewed as a frail obligation or a maternal presence, as we see her in Erica Anderson's award-winning documentary *Albert Schweitzer*. Filmed in Europe, Africa, and en route to Africa in the first half of the 1950s, the documentary shows Helene as little more than a walk-on who smiles and waves from a window in Gunsbach and cuddles with her grandchildren on a bench beneath a tree. The script—which Albert Schweitzer authored and read in the German version of the film—mentions Helene's name once as a fact of his own life since she was the woman he married. Neither the German version nor the American version includes an image of Helene in Africa or any sort of commentary on her role as a capable nurse or cofounder of the Schweitzer Hospital. Ironically, the widely acclaimed film appeared in the year of her death, 1957.[31]

Did she, perhaps, agree to be invisible in this important film? If so, such a decision would have contradicted her postwar activities, beginning with her careful triage of papers to ensure posterity's accurate understanding of her role. Such a choice would also have contradicted the spirit of remarks quoted in the *New York Times* in 1949 and, more important, her 1954 *Lebenslauf*, in which she states that "[a]fter my marriage to Dr. Albert Schweitzer we traveled in 1913 to Lambarene, a mission-station in Equatorial Africa, because we had heard from missionaries, that they were in urgent need of a doctor. How *we* built *our* hospital and worked there, my husband has described in his book *On the Edge of the Primeval Forest*" (emphasis added). Throughout this period, Helene always employed the third-person plural *we* with reference to the work accomplished in Africa. Even as her ability to contribute physical labor declined, she maintained a keen sense of shared "ownership" and a desire for visibility in the long history of Lambarene.

༺

On November 4, 1954, Helene made her last international public appearance as "Madame Schweitzer" at Albert's rather strained Nobel Prize ceremony in Oslo, where seats had also been reserved for Emmy Martin and Erica Anderson. She sat quietly in the front row in a dark dress, hand on her cane, listening passively to a speech that, according to all accounts, was hard to hear and poorly delivered.[32] For Helene, the following evening was the better part of the celebration when she stood with Albert on the balcony of the Town Hall, smiling and waving to throngs of students who came to honor them both with a twinkling sea of hand-held candlelight. Albert Schweitzer returned to Lambarene before the end of the year, and Helene followed within a matter of weeks, determined to celebrate her husband's eightieth birthday with him.

We learn of her arrival in Lambarene in January 1955 from her niece Suzanne Oswald, who, as little "Susi" among the children in Gunsbach, had helped to invent the sobriquet "Auntie Etiquette" for Helene "because in her presence we felt obligated to behave correctly."[33] In January 1955, Oswald was a journalist writing for Switzerland's highly respected newspaper *Neue Zürcher Zeitung* and on a professional mission to cover her famous uncle's eightieth birthday. In addition to her newspaper coverage, she wrote a book that includes a portrait of Helene at the age of seventy-six: "Aunt Helene arrived three days before. The hospital bell rang out and soon everyone hurried down to the little dock to welcome her. Already in the distance we had heard the rowers chanting the news of *Madame Docteur's* arrival. Between two rows of black hands extended to greet her, the old woman climbed slowly and laboriously toward the top of the hill. Despite her immense physical fatigue, she did not want to miss being with her husband on this birthday."[34]

Within a few days of January 14, 1955, Helene was assisting Albert with his correspondence by writing to friends about his tireless work on the hospital's leprosy village: "Regarding health, we cannot complain, although my husband, who is now eighty years old, is tired and, as ever, has too much to do, working from early in the morning til late."[35]

Although her visit lasted nearly six months, and despite the positive comment regarding her health, Helene was no longer able to work effectively at the hospital. She spent most of her afternoon hours alone on the veranda of the Schweitzer house, watching life go on around her. From there, she could observe a new generation of purposeful women—including the ubiquitous Erica Anderson, who had been ever present in Europe and Africa since 1950, and the überefficient Ali Silver, who first arrived in Lambarene after the war in October 1947— moving at a pace Helene could only remember. If young nurses paused at the veranda to express false cheer or, worse yet, offer empathy that might be mistaken for charity, Helene was likely to react with visible irritation. As Mühlstein interprets Helene's state of mind at this time, her moodiness and irritability were due to an inability to accept her own "helplessness," which she experienced as a painful indignity.[36]

∽

Mühlstein's analysis aligns with Helene's lifelong desire to be both independent and useful. It is, in the end, a more valid perspective than those that tend to "freeze" Helene in a state of crass jealousy in her last years. We should keep in mind that the feminization of the Schweitzer Hospital had begun decades earlier, in the 1920s, when Mathilde Kottmann and Emma Haussknecht assumed roles that Helene herself had fulfilled in the beginning. Throughout many decades, she had seen, heard of, met, and worked with dozens of capable women who gave all or part of their lives to the Schweitzer Hospital. She had even expressed in writing her wish for the presence of such women, as in her 1930 *British Bulletin* article: "May still more helpers of both sexes be found, and in sufficient numbers, who will co-operate in the work in the same selfless and loyal spirit as their predecessors."[37] There is no question that Helene Schweitzer understood how essential competent women would be to the work that had to be done.

In other words, Helene's view of Schweitzer's numerous female coworkers and staff members was balanced by both reality and necessity, just as her view of his older women friends had been in the early years. We should also keep in mind that each woman who worked with Schweitzer—especially the long-standing devotees such as Martin, Kottmann, Haussknecht, and Silver—was a unique personality. It would be the worst sort of simplification to lump them together as a collective thorn in Helene Schweitzer's side, especially as she aged. Although a full exploration of these relationships is beyond the scope of this book, a few insights and observations can be helpful in understanding Helene's feelings toward Schweitzer's core *collaboratrices*.

From the impressive vegetable gardens noted at the end of 1929 to the "500-mile trek" mentioned in Helene's 1938 American lecture and to a journal entry of August 15, 1941, that records "a walk and picnic on a sandbank with *Doctoresse* and Miss Emma,"[38] it is clear that Helene Schweitzer admired Emma Haussknecht's energy and efficiency. We also know that when Helene returned to Europe in 1946, Haussknecht traveled with her and took responsibility for baggage, customs, and other logistical details, a role that implies considerable interaction between the two women as well as a mutual understanding of their different roles and social positions.

Naturally, tensions flared from time to time, especially in the first half of 1950, when Helene's heart problem became a factor in her daily life. This development most certainly added to her feelings of helplessness and consequently to her irritability. Her struggle against a sense of irrelevance could also be exacerbated by others, whose workload might explain their impatience with the old woman on the veranda. Schweitzer himself was entirely capable of impatience, to say nothing of unpredictable emotions, as he aged. Given the close quarters in which they all lived and the never-ending work of hospital life in a difficult climate, it comes as no surprise that Helene's last journals express more feelings of frustration than do earlier records of her life.[39]

And yet when Emma Haussknecht's ashes came back to Lambarene in August 1956, Helene was there to participate in the burial service at the cemetery where she and Albert envisioned their own tombstones. She had known "Miss Emma" for years in a variety of situations and very likely shared the sense of loss Albert Schweitzer expressed in a letter to Erica Anderson: "I can't imagine how Lambarene or the spirit of Lambarene can exist without her."[40] It is, incidentally, thanks to Emma Haussknecht that an impressive collection of African art and artifacts is now preserved in Gunsbach.

By contrast, Emmy Martin's proud nature and secure place in Gunsbach—where she enjoyed comfortable living accommodations at the Maison Schweitzer—was an unpleasant fact of Helene's life and over time a source of sadness and alienation. After all, Helene had never felt completely at home in Albert's childhood village. And once the Maison Schweitzer was built in 1929–30, Emmy Martin was placed in charge of what effectively became the European headquarters of the Schweitzer universe. At times, Martin allowed herself to be mistaken as the "first lady" in Schweitzer's world, traveling with him and posing for photographs in which she stands a bit too close to Dr. Schweitzer. Many people adored Emmy Martin, and her contributions were manifold, but Helene expected her own traditional notions of roles and boundaries to be respected. Martin's central position, obviously supported by Schweitzer himself, strained those expectations.

An example of the way in which Martin's presence could simply "erase" Helene's dignity is the tribute written by Friderike Zweig, the wife of the Austrian writer Stefan Zweig: "Madame Emmy Martin was his [Schweitzer's] greatest support for more than forty years." Recalling a time in 1932 when Martin accompanied Albert Schweitzer to the Zweig home in Salzburg, Mrs. Zweig goes on to declare that "Emmy Martin was a sturdy pillar in the towering edifice that was Albert Schweitzer's life and work."[41] Fortunately, this gushing praise was published in a limited edition of three hundred after Helene's death.

Of the quietly efficient Mathilde Kottmann, it is entirely possible that Helene viewed her as distant or even dull, despite her steady and efficient devotion to hospital work. It is telling that the introductory text to an exhibit honoring Kottmann in 2007 was entitled "To Serve with Discretion." In this context, Schweitzer's first impression of Kottmann is recorded: "There is a girl who knows how to keep silent. That's just what I need."[42] When Mathilde Kottmann returned to Lambarene at the end of World War II—after an absence of six years—Helene noted the "event" in her journal without emotion in four words: "Arrival of Mathilde Kottmann."[43]

Meanwhile, Ali Silver worked in her no-nonsense way to screen Schweitzer from tiring interruptions and continued to apply her skills to administrative and archival tasks in Gunsbach long after her Lambarene days. As a Dutch woman who spoke excellent English, Silver also handled a great deal of Schweitzer's English-language correspondence, as Helene had once done. It is possible that this may have contributed to Helene's heightened sensitivities in the 1950s, even if we have no record of resentment. Ali Silver eventually retired to a small house in Gunsbach, a house she called "akewa," from a word meaning "many thanks" in one of the African languages used in Gabon.

Another person who eventually retired to Gunsbach was a young nurse named Sonja Müller, who arrived in Lambarene in 1955 and, like many others, kept her distance from the old woman sitting alone on the veranda. That this particular nurse would eventually spend nearly twenty years of her life as director of the Maison Schweitzer in Gunsbach was unimaginable then, though she was already an astute observer of the Schweitzer world:

> Madame Schweitzer was not an easy person, and I would say there was some bitterness among some of the *collaboratrices* (female staff members) in their dealings with her. She complained a lot, but she had her back problem and her lungs. . . . It was not easy for her! So it was not easy for the others to be with her when they had so much of their own work to do. She was isolated and they could work with her husband. That must have been very difficult for her, a woman like

that, so brilliant, . . . cofounder of the hospital . . . one who worked on so many levels in the "heroic period."[44]

In the Schweitzer Hospital's centennial year, Sonja Müller Poteau expressed her abiding respect for Helene's role: "He [Albert Schweitzer] could not have done it without her."[45]

A similar image of Helene late in life comes down to us from Norman Cousins, who in addition to being a well-known magazine editor was an outspoken advocate of the human spirit's capacity to overcome illness.[46] Not surprisingly, he had several long conversations with Helene during his visit to Lambarene in March 1957, when she confided in him: "It makes me feel so foolish, this being so helpless. I ought to be working with the Doctor." Helene not only took an interest in photographs of Cousins's daughters but also wanted to discuss world affairs, the threat of communism,[47] US politics, and atomic energy, a topic of particular interest to the Schweitzers that spring when Albert Schweitzer was researching the topic of atomic weapons.[48] "You must understand that there aren't many visitors here from the United States," she told Cousins. "And those who come do not stay very long. They have urgent business, or so it seems, with the Doctor, and there isn't much opportunity to talk to them."[49]

Cousins's poignant portrait of Helene tells us a great deal about her state of mind a few months before her death. Regardless of fatigue, a weak heart, and other infirmities, she was well grounded in her sense of place and purpose. "We have been working here a long time, more than forty years," she told their famous American visitor. Once again, her choice of pronoun reveals her view of her role in the creation and development of the Schweitzer Hospital. When she came to Lambarene in her seventies, as she often did, she wanted to stay as long as possible. And when she was not in Lambarene, some part of her remained there, as if she had never left. One of the last entries in her last journal, written as Albert made his way back to Africa on November 23, 1951, says as much: "Departure Alb. from Bordeaux—such homesickness."[50]

Alert to this nuance, Cousins asked her where she felt most at home. Of course, there was no question for Helene that Lambarene was her home, regardless of the long periods of time she spent elsewhere. A year earlier she had been even more specific with Richard Kik, founder of the German Schweitzer Association in Frankfurt. She told Kik that the cool, screened corner of the dining hall with its distant view of palms and the river down below was "the most beautiful place in the entire hospital built by my husband."[51] In 1956, Helene liked to sit there with her coffee after lunch, chatting with Kik, who made notes in his diary from those pleasant hours. To his credit, he took time to remember her birthday and maintained a correspondence with her as if she, too, were a person of consequence.

Unfortunately, Helene could not remain in Lambarene indefinitely. By May 22, 1957, her final sojourn there, begun in January 1956, was coming to an end. Short of breath, blue-lipped, and almost too weak to walk, Helene flew back to Europe without her husband, accompanied by a devoted Dutch nurse, Tony Van Leer. When Rhena met the plane in Paris with a doctor at her side, her mother was beyond recovery. Helene was transferred via night train to a hospital in Zurich, where she died on June 1, 1957.

☙

A year before her death, German journalist Otto Schempp offered an astute observation of Helene Schweitzer Bresslau: "About herself Mrs. Schweitzer once said: 'I am not a person for public life. I only attend meetings reluctantly and only if there are unavoidable reasons to do so.'" Schempp also observed her with German president Theodor Heuss when she represented her husband at an outdoor event in southern Germany. Even though Heuss was an old friend and the husband of Helene's girlhood friend Elly Knapp, Schempp observed her as a reluctant guest at the party. "One sensed she preferred to be modest, inconspicuous, and to some extent incognito."[52]

This keen observation says a great deal about Helene. However, "incognito" is something other than "invisible," and serving as Schweitzer's emissary was never her preferred role. All along, she had maintained private friendships far from the glare of Albert's fame. For example, Winnifred Wirckau, a physical therapist who had rented a room from Helene in Königsfeld in the early 1950s, left warm memories of Helene's frequent postcards, invitations, and small gifts that often came on her day off from work.[53] Similarly, the Norwegian Tove Tau spared Helene an exhausting evening and another speech by Albert when she organized a small gathering in Oslo during the Nobel Peace Prize celebrations to honor the woman who, Tau explained, "believed in her husband before he was famous, served him before he was known."[54]

Helene was comfortable with these people, as she was with her eldest granddaughter Monique, who visited Königsfeld on summer vacations in the 1950s, often joined by her brother Philippe. True to her old habits, Helene required both of them to write weekly letters to their grandfather, which presented an ideal occasion for her to correct their German, just as she had done fifty years earlier with Albert. Indeed, it is only from a public perspective that Helene Schweitzer Bresslau seemed to drift into a kind of oblivion in the early 1950s, especially after poor health forced her to leave Lambarene in July 1950.[55]

When the Schweitzers' nephew Gustav Woytt stood to speak at his aunt's memorial service at the crematorium in Zurich on June 5, 1957, he emphasized her strength of character: "All too often one has only seen Helene Schweitzer Bresslau as a support figure to her famous husband. . . . She was, however, a bit too strong as an individual personality to live only in her husband's shadow."[56] Walter Munz, who arrived in Lambarene in 1961 and became Schweitzer's chosen successor in 1965, echoes this perspective. Dr. Munz knew and worked with those who had known Helene as a dignified woman with a mind of her own. "All who had met Madame Schweitzer were in total agreement that thanks to her strong personality she had always maintained, including with her great man of a husband, a beautiful spirit of independence."[57] Such statements strive to sum up a fully lived life in a few phrases, even as they take us into the realm of posthumous biography, that "afterlife" where the interests of the living and the dead often compete for truth.

Despite Helene's success at becoming what she wanted most in her youth—"to be an individual"—much of her life was spent defining herself in relation to her husband. After living the life of an exile for years—fluctuating between illness and health, stillness and movement, place and purpose—she watched "incognito" as Albert Schweitzer allowed himself to be transformed into a "myth." He did not seem to mind his larger-than-life public persona. He even constructed an efficient human-resources system dominated by a highly skilled court of men and women to support his goals with maximum devotion at minimal cost.

By contrast, Helene never quite trusted the entrapments of fame. Perhaps she sensed the danger of dehumanization lurking in the shadows of celebrity or the risk of humanitarian work being appropriated to serve the powerful instead of the poor. Perhaps she felt sufficient unto herself, at her best when unencumbered and unexposed. Perhaps she was secure in the knowledge that the truth that mattered was preserved in her private papers. The evidence of letters, journals, diaries, and day books waiting to be discovered must have brought her a measure of comfort, even as the airplane rose above the jungle forest and soared away from the river, leaving behind that place she called "home."

Five days after the memorial service in Zurich that Albert Schweitzer was unable to attend, he wrote to the woman who had infused his life with youthful energy since 1950. As the 450 letters he wrote in German to Erica Anderson (1914–1976) clearly document, this was a deep and important relationship for both.[58] It was also important for the "larger-than-life" image Albert Schweitzer attained in the 1950s, especially in the United States. Though never actually employed by Albert Schweitzer, Erica Anderson devoted years to documenting the Schweitzer Hospital, producing more than seven thousand color photographs and twenty-six thousand black-and-white images between 1950 and 1965. She, furthermore, continued to honor his legacy through her books and her Friendship House museum in Great Barrington, Massachusetts, until she, too, entered the cemetery in Lambarene in 1976.

It should come as no surprise that one of Albert Schweitzer's first announcements of Helene's death was written to Erica Anderson:

Deep in the Night

Dear Erica,

You have by now heard that my wife has passed away peacefully in Zurich. For the past three months her strength was failing visibly. I had not written to anybody about it, only to my daughter. In May my wife expressed that she could not stand the heat anymore and that she wanted to return to Europe. Also Tony [Van Leer] wanted to go back to Europe to see her terminally ill father once more. So my wife was taken care of on the flight . . . then in Switzerland her heart, which was already not functioning correctly, failed. She really didn't suffer during all this time. She just became weaker as time went along.[59]

Afterword

The Lasting Legacy of Helene Schweitzer Bresslau

"Without ever having turned back, she became part of a great adventure and the material of legend accompanying this giant; just as the photographers only ever saw her from behind, future generations would look at her likewise."[1] This picture of Helene Schweitzer Bresslau by the French writer Gilbert Cesbron may be coherent, but it does not describe the reality. Helene Schweitzer Bresslau was always aware of her own importance. She knew how she had influenced Albert Schweitzer and the important part she played in his work. That might have been her reason for keeping all the letters, journals, and day books that she did keep: to give future generations the opportunity to see her from the front. When in 1992 her daughter, Rhena Schweitzer Miller, published her parents' correspondence during the ten years before their marriage, the important and active role that Helene Bresslau played in her husband's life became obvious.

This correspondence is a rich source for the evaluation of the identity building of two young, intelligent people. It reveals as myth Albert Schweitzer's narrative about his decision to resign from a scientific career in favor of a life as a doctor in the tropical forest. The final decision to study medicine was not simply taken on a quiet evening after having read an article about the Protestant mission's need for medical help in the French Congo. Rather, it was a complex decision after nerve-racking months of emotional ups and downs during which Helene Bresslau's unconditional but never uncritical support was of invaluable importance. She was the first and for a long time the only person who understood and supported his plans. It is not an exaggeration to say that Albert Schweitzer would have never become the person he was without his close and trusting relationship to Helene Bresslau. In addition, these letters reveal both a well-educated woman looking for a purpose and an alternative to a life as a married housewife as well as how she achieved this goal.

Helene Schweitzer Bresslau was just as versatile as her husband. Not only was she the cofounder with Albert Schweitzer of the hospital in Lambarene, but she also supported the work with lectures and fund-raising. In the fifty-five years of their partnership, she was an indispensable help for all his philosophical and theological books. Yet how difficult it still was for a woman of her generation to become more visible in the public eye is demonstrated in Florian Illies's 2012 book *1913 Der Sommer des Jahrhunderts* (1913 the summer of the century). In the chapter "März" (March), he writes: "In March 1913, Albert Schweitzer received his doctoral degree. His dissertation, 'Die psychiatrische Beurteilung Jesu' irritated many but was well recognized. On the next day he sold his belongings. Then he took his wife Helene and, on 21 March, he travelled to Africa. In French Equatorial Africa on the Ogowe he founded the hospital in the tropical forest at Lambarene."[2] This little anecdote in which Helene Schweitzer Bresslau was taken to Lambarene like a suitcase has nothing to do with reality. It just proves that not only in the 1950s but still in the twenty-first century Helene Schweitzer Bresslau was and is remembered simply as the wife in the background of the famous Albert Schweitzer.

Patti Marxsen's book finally gives Helene the attention in America that she deserves not only as an equal partner to Albert Schweitzer but also as a unique and independent personality. She did not limit herself to the role expected of a woman at the beginning of the twentieth century. She saw herself as an independent modern woman with a full-time job. Even if Helene Schweitzer Bresslau was a great individualist, her life was paradigmatic for a young woman from the assimilated Jewish middle class at the turn of the twentieth century.

Helene's life reflects the history of this time and reveals the mental and social disputes and conflicts. Her life also reveals the shocking rupture in civilization that is so significant for the history of the twentieth century. The Bresslau family is a typical example of Jews who felt themselves to be completely German and whose world broke apart after 1933. Interned during World War I as a German in a French colony and then again in France, Helene Schweitzer Bresslau also had to flee from the German occupation of France in 1940. Even if she was the only member of the family who returned to Germany after the end of the war, she never again felt at home there.

Helene Bresslau grew up in an assimilated Jewish family where the education of girls was taken as seriously as the education of boys. Her father, the historian Harry Bresslau, was a great supporter of the education of women. Years before women were admitted to German universities, he gave public lectures in history for female audiences. Later, he was very proud that he had the first female student at the University of Strasbourg. He enabled his two younger sisters to become teachers, and it was taken for granted that his daughter Helene would attended the teachers' college as well.

When women with a teacher's certificate were allowed access to university, Helene Bresslau became one of the first female students at the University of Strasbourg. She always had role models of independent women in her family. Her aunts and their daughters were very strong personalities. In particular, her aunt Claire Heynssen was an engaged advocate for women rights and involved in the movement for women's suffrage. This large, liberal, and women-friendly family had an important impact on Helene Bresslau's modern self-image. During her entire life, her family remained her most important reference point, and she always had a very close relationship with all its members. Until the end of her life, her sister-in-law, Luise Bresslau-Hoff, was her closest confidante.

In Strasbourg, Helene Bresslau belonged to a circle of young, well-educated men and women from liberal German families. The women attended the teachers' college and many of them joined her as students at the university or worked as teachers. These bright young people discussed cultural topics, the rights of women, and other social questions.

The origin of Helene Bresslau's interest in social work was very likely her Jewish family. Baptized as a seven-year-old child, she had no "Jewish education" as such, but she lived in a "Jewish atmosphere," as evidenced by her parents deciding against baptism for themselves and the strong opposition to baptism expressed by her parents' siblings and their families. She might never have heard about the Jewish concept of *tikkun olam* (healing of the world), but the atmosphere in which she grew up made it clear that one of the most meaningful things in life is to make the world a better place. Her Jewish heritage brought with it the conviction that relationships between people require something more than just words: they require action, and we must commit ourselves to action beyond our words. This feeling of responsibility for others became the basis of Helene's partnership with Albert Schweitzer, as she explained to an English friend in March 1945: "It is now forty-three years since we became friends and started to work together. We met with a mutual feeling of responsibility for all the good that we had received in our lives, and a sense of our duty to pay for it by helping others."[3]

Her feeling of responsibility to others was also the reason why she decided to give up her studies of art history and history, regarding them as too theoretical and unworldly, in order to become a social worker looking after orphans, unwed mothers and their children, as well as foster children and their families in her home town, Strasbourg. As a full-time *Waiseninspektorin*, city orphan inspector, she was one of the first female employees in the community administration. She greatly appreciated the systemic approach of the public poor relief in Strasbourg, which included not only the orphans and half-orphans but also unwed mothers and the foster families. Her most important project was the foundation of a home where unwed mothers were admitted without regard for their religion or nationality. At the beginning of the twentieth century, it was absolutely revolutionary that unwed mothers were treated as human beings who needed help and understanding from the surrounding society. Even in progressive cities such as Leipzig, which cared for illegitimate infants, unwed mothers were at that time called "women without any moral feeling" who had to be sent to workhouses for "fallen girls."

Helene Bresslau strongly intended to demonstrate that this job was more than daily work; it was an interesting and challenging task for well-educated women. During the four years of her employment in the City Orphan Administration, the high infant mortality rate among illegitimate children decreased enormously, until it was no longer higher than the infant mortality of legitimate children. Her commitment and dedication to this work contributed significantly to the Strasbourg *Armenpflegesystem* (poor relief system) so that it became the most modern and successful social system in Germany and served as a model for social legislation in Germany after World War II. Even today it serves as a model for modern social welfare.

Helene Bresslau was proud of her achievements as a *Waiseninspektorin*, but later the center of her life was always the work in Lambarene. The first years in Lambarene were the happiest time of her life. Here she could develop and demonstrate all her abilities and skills. Even when her severe illness prevented her from being directly involved with the work in Africa, she supported Albert Schweitzer as a tireless promoter and avid fund-raiser for the hospital. Her multilingualism helped to internationalize their common work, and her promotional tour through the northeastern and midwestern United States in 1938 was crucial for the survival of the hospital during World War II.

The great tragedy of Helene Schweitzer Bresslau's life was tuberculosis, which she probably contracted as a child and which worsened to an open tuberculosis during her long stay in the tropics during World War I and the consequent internment in France. In a deeply tragic way, she had to learn the validity of Susan Sontag's statement: "Everyone who is born holds dual citizenship, in the kingdom of the well and in the kingdom of the sick."[4] She never came to terms with her fate. With a near-heroic will to survive, she took up the struggle against the disease and in the end even survived the life-threatening tuberculosis of the larynx. With an impressive attitude, she overcame the difficult years as a sick, single mother with a little child in a village where she felt isolated for reasons that went beyond her disease. During this time, her strong commitment to her own and her husband's work never ceased. When in the 1950s and 1960s the majority of those around Albert Schweitzer were full of uncritical admiration, she remained his critical counterpart.

During the difficult years in the search for a meaningful purpose in life, the exciting and exhausting years in Africa building the hospital under difficult conditions, the years enduring a life-threatening disease, all the long years of separation from her beloved husband—in threat and danger—until the end of her life, Helene always kept the "extraordinary dignity" that the historian Michael Meyer considers to be "a part of the legacy of the German Jews."[5]

Verena Mühlstein, M.D.

Chronology

◆

Notes

◆

Bibliography

◆

Index

Chronology

Helene Schweitzer Bresslau, 1879–1957

1879

Born in Berlin on January, 25, 1879, to Caroline Bresslau-Isay and Harry Bresslau as the second child and only daughter in a family of assimilated Jews.

1886

Baptism of Ernst, Helene, and Hermann Bresslau during their summer vacation by a German Lutheran pastor.

1889

Suffers her first serious illness, an inflammation in the lining of the lungs known as pleurisy.

1890

The family moves to Strasbourg when Harry Bresslau is appointed as regular professor of history at the Kaiser Wilhelm Universität (now University of Strasbourg.)

1894

Confirmation of "Fräulein Bresslau," a brilliant student at the private Lindner School for Girls in Strasbourg.

1895

Begins her teacher training in a program supported by the Lindner School.

1896

Completes her teacher training in one year instead of two and earns her credentials as a *Lehrerin für höhere Mädchenschulen*, a teacher in girls' schools.

1897–98
Studies at the Strasbourg Conservatory to develop her talents in piano and voice. Joins the choir established in 1884 by Ernst Münch at the Lutheran Church of St. Guillaume, where the choirmaster's accompanist on the organ is Albert Schweitzer. Also tutors girls at the Lindner School in French and takes sewing courses to please her mother, who is much focused on Helene's marriageability.

August 1898
Wedding of Lina Haas to Willibad Conrad in Strasbourg, where nineteen-year-old Helene is seated next to twenty-three-year-old Albert Schweitzer.

1899
Travels to Italy with her parents for six months.

1900
With permission from her father and Professor Georg Dehio, studies art history at the Kaiser Wilhelm Universität. Also takes Harry Bresslau's course in medieval history and Friedrich Meinecke's course in modern history. One of the first women to study at this institution.

1901
Establishes a bicycle club with friends Elly Knapp and Elsa and Fritz Haas. At Helene's suggestion, Albert Schweitzer is invited to join the group.

1902
Makes a bicycle excursion along the Rhine River with Albert Schweitzer on March 22, 1902. In a spot they will remember throughout their lives and never identify for others, they make a pact to be devoted friends forever. That autumn, Helene spends three months teaching music, French, and English at a girls' school in Brighton, England, and translates literary works from Russian to German as gifts for Albert. Explores social welfare needs of London and comes to know the social work of Dr. Thomas John Barnardo (1845–1905).

1903
Inspired by Barnardo's example, works as volunteer social worker in Strasbourg. Especially interested in the needs of infants and children born outside of marriage.

1904

Enrolls in a basic, three-month course at the nursing school in Stettin, Germany (now in Poland), where she meets Ella Schmalz. After this experience, visits Aunt Clara in Hamburg and joins her family for a summer vacation in the Black Forest. Her first published article, entitled "Gott" (God), is included in a weekly magazine aimed at liberal Protestants, the *Protestantenblatt*. The author's name appears only as "A Seeker." Meanwhile, Harry Bresslau is appointed chancellor of Kaiser Wilhelm Universität.

1905

Begins her professional life in April 1905 as the first woman inspector of the City Orphan Administration in Strasbourg. It is initially a part-time job, then becomes full-time, then varies over the four years that she holds this position.

Travels to England to attend lectures in the chapel of the Primitive Methodist Missionary Society. Attends a "Congo evening," where she listens intently to British missionaries, including Dr. Henry Grattan Guiness (1861–1915), a leader of the East London Training Institute for Home and Foreign Missions and a strong voice of concern about human rights abuses in the Belgian Congo.

1906

Rudolf Schwander (1868–1950) becomes mayor of Strasbourg in 1906. As Helene's boss, he greatly values her work, which involves supervising the care of approximately eight thousand children annually. He wishes her to work full-time, but she hesitates and even considers resigning owing to exhaustion. Schwander reduces her hours and brings in volunteer support.

Devotes time during the spring and summer to final edits of the manuscript that would become *Von Reimarus zu Wrede: Eine Geschichte der Leben-Jesu-Forschung*, Albert's exhaustive work published in 1906 and later translated into English as *The Quest for the Historical Jesus*.

1907

Attends a "Social Services Congress" in Frankfurt, Germany, in April, where many women social workers discuss their workload. Helene is surprised to hear that many feel they have too much to do in supervising the well-being of as many as 120 children and making eight to ten visits daily. Her office supervises 300 to 500 children at any given time and logs twenty-five to thirty visits per day with a similar number of staff.

In October, informs Albert of the official cofounding with Helene Fehling of her home for unwed mothers. The Strassburger Mütterheim (Strasbourg Mother's Home) opens on November 15, 1907, in the suburb of
Neudorf with room for eight mothers and their infants. Shortly after this
success, suffers a fracture of the spine in a snow-shoe accident. Feels the
impact of this event for the rest of her life.

1908

Publishes an article about the Strassburger Mütterheim in the magazine *Blätter für das Strassburger Armenwesen* (Publication for Strasbourg's poor relief
system). Also in this period, translates articles for a French Protestant weekly,
Le Messager. In August, travels to Holland with her cousin Johanna Engel,
who, as a single woman and an artist, provides a model of independence.

1909

Ends her four years of work as a city orphan inspector in Strasbourg in April,
satisfied that she has made a contribution. Travels to Russia with her friend
Lena in the summer. In October, begins a rigorous program in Frankfurt,
Germany, to become a certified nurse. By this time, shares Albert's vision of a
shared "Congo project" in Africa even though marriage remains undiscussed.

1910

Completes the nursing program in the autumn and passes the exam but
returns to Strasbourg exhausted and suffering from an attack of tuberculosis.
Fears she will not be able to go to Africa and realize her plan with "Bery,"
her nickname for Albert. In this period, Helene's health begins to become
an obstacle and a priority for both.

1911

Spends first four months of 1911 in treatment in a sanatorium in the Black
Forest and on the coast in northern Germany. Further convalescence continues in the summer in Königsfeld, Germany, before she travels to Bad
Schwartau, Hamburg, and Copenhagen, Denmark, for ongoing recupera-
tion. Meanwhile, Albert Schweitzer writes to "M. et Madame Professeur
Bresslau" to ask for Helene's hand in marriage. They become officially
engaged the day after Christmas, December 26, 1911.

1912

Takes a job at the Strasbourg Municipal Hospital as a nurse. Albert is studying tropical medicine, but his more difficult activity involves negotiations

with the Paris Mission Society over his desire to be assigned to French Equatorial Africa. Between October 1911 and July 1912, fourteen Mission Society board sessions in Paris focus on the "Schweitzer question."

In the end, Albert is accepted as a medical missionary at his own expense and warned not to preach his liberal theology in Africa. Furthermore, the Kaiser Wilhelm Universität does not accord him a two-year leave of absence, thereby forcing him to resign. Departure for the mission station at Andende is delayed until 1913 in part because of Albert's depression and a case of angina.

Civil marriage of Albert Schweitzer and Helene Bresslau in Strasbourg on June 15, 1912. A wedding ceremony in the church in Gunsbach follows three days later, when they are married by Pastor Albert Woytt, husband of Albert's sister Adèle. Many family members attend, including Cary and Harry Bresslau, recently retired from the university.

1913

Untimely death at age twenty-nine of Helene's beloved younger brother Hermann Bresslau (1883–1913) during an appendicitis operation. A few weeks later Helene and Albert Schweitzer depart from Gunsbach on March 21 and from Strasbourg on March 22, exactly eleven years after they made their pact along the Rhine. They leave from Bordeaux on the ship *Europa* on March 26 and arrive in Andende on the riverboat *Alembé* on April 16, to begin their first sojourn in Africa.

1914

On August 5, the Schweitzers learn that France has mobilized for war against Germany. They are placed under house arrest in Lambarene as civil prisoners of war. When this order is lifted in November, they return to their medical work.

1916

Albert's mother, Adèle Schweitzer Schillinger (1842–1916) dies on July 3 after being knocked over by a soldier's runaway horse while she is out walking with her husband.

1917

Albert and Helene Schweitzer are deported to France in October, traveling there on the steamboat *Afrique*. They arrive in Bordeaux in mid-November and are held for three weeks in a *caserne de passage* before being sent to a "concentration camp" in the ancient monastery of Notre Dame de Garaison par Monléon-Magnoac in the Hautes Pyrénées.

1918

The Schweitzers are transferred against their will to an exclusively Alsatian internment camp at the end of March, the Dépôt d'Austro-Allemands at the ancient monastery St. Paul-de-Mausole outside the village Saint-Rémy-de-Provence.

They are repatriated to Germany in July 1918 as part of a prisoner exchange facilitated by Switzerland. Helene is three months pregnant, and Albert requires emergency surgery within weeks of their return.

In the fall, Albert secures a one-year appointment as curate at St. Nicolas and begins to deliver sermons there in November. Also, with Mayor Rudolf Schwander's support, he is hired as a doctor at the Dermatology Clinic of the Strasbourg Municipal Hospital.

When the war ends with a victory for the French on November 11, 1918, Helene's parents are expelled from Strasbourg. As a historian much concerned with German identity, Harry Bresslau is viewed in France as a "militant pan-Germanist."

1919

Rhena Fanny Suzanne Schweitzer is born in Strasbourg on her father's forty-fourth birthday, January 14. Albert's health remains a concern, and a second surgery is performed to remove part of his intestines. In December 1919, an invitation comes from the Archbishop Nathan Söderblom of Sweden for Albert to deliver a series of lectures after Easter 1920 at the University of Uppsala.

1920

Helene travels with Albert to Uppsala in the spring, where they are guests in the home of Archbishop Söderblom and his wife. Helene also spends time with her parents in Heidelberg, Germany, that summer. Albert resolves to return to Africa.

1921

After resigning from his posts in Strasbourg in April, Albert moves with Helene and Rhena to the vicarage in Gunsbach, where his father remains pastor. Albert is away quite often, performing concerts throughout Switzerland.

On the Edge of the Primeval Forest is published in Swedish and then appears in German and English. It quickly becomes a best seller.

1920–1922

Albert is often away for concerts and lectures in Scandinavia, and his earnings allow the Schweitzers to repay their debts. Helene joins her husband in England in 1922 when he delivers lectures at Mansfield College, Oxford; Selly Oak College in Birmingham; Cambridge University; and the Society for the Study of Science and Religion in London.

In the spring of 1922, Helene suffers an attack of tuberculosis. A decision is made to build a house in Königsfeld, Germany, a place known for its high altitude and curative fresh air. Helene and Rhena move to an apartment in Königsfeld late in 1922 while the house is under construction.

1923

The Schweitzers move into their house in Königsfeld on May 1, 1923. Volume 1 of *Kulturphilosophie* is published earlier that winter, dedicated to "Annie Fischer with deep gratitude." The second part appears in July, dedicated to "[m]y wife—my most loyal friend."

1924

Albert departs with British medical student Noel Gillespie on February 14, 1924, to return to Africa and rebuild the hospital. Helene and Albert correspond frequently, but Helene feels abandoned and only gradually adapts to her life as a single mother.

1925

Albert's father, Louis Théophile Schweitzer (1846–1925), dies on May 5 in Gunsbach, France, where he had been pastor for fifty years.

1926

Helene's father, Harry Bresslau (1848–1926), dies on October 27 in Heidelberg, Germany.

1927

"Moving day," January 21, along the Ogowe River from the original Schweitzer Hospital in Andende to the new hospital upstream that has been constructed on a hill called "Adolinanongo." In August, Schweitzer returns to Europe after three-and-a-half years in Lambarene. He is soon traveling to raise money for the hospital by giving concerts and lectures in the Netherlands, England, and Scandinavia.

1928
Helene is living in Königsfeld with Rhena. She travels with her husband to Holland and England in the spring and is with him on August 28, when he is awarded the City of Frankfurt's Goethe Prize. They will spend the five-thousand-dollar prize on building a house in Gunsbach.

1929
Suffers a severe attack of tuberculosis or pneumonia as they prepare for their December departure for Lambarene. Her *second sojourn* begins in December, when she sets off with Albert, Dr. Anna Schmitz, and a private nurse, Marie Secretan. Helene's health is fragile during the voyage. The group arrives at the new Schweitzer Hospital on the day after Christmas, December 26.

1930
Albert, now age fifty-five, is working on his autobiography in Lambarene with Helene's assistance. In April, Helene's health becomes a serious problem in the oppressive climate, and she is forced to return to Europe in May. She enters a sanatorium in Kassel under the care of Dr. Max Gerson where she will remain for nine months. During her last weeks in Gerson's clinic, Helene corrects the final proofs of her husband's autobiography.

1931
Albert's autobiography, *Aus meinem Leben und Denken* (*Out of My Life and Thought*), is published, and his fame is assured. In November, Helene gives a talk in Würzburg to a standing-room-only crowd about working with Albert Schweitzer "in the primeval forest," a phrase that echoes the title of his 1921 best seller.

1932
Albert returns to his wife and daughter in Königsfeld after two years in Lambarene and finds Helene in relatively good health. They are together as a family when Schweitzer delivers the keynote address at the Goethe Centennial in Frankfurt on March 22, 1932. Soon afterward, Helene requires another round of treatment in the summer when it is discovered that one of the caverns in her lung has grown.

1933

The German National Socialist Worker's Party (Nationalsozialistische Deutsche Arbeiterpartei [Nazi]) assumes power in Germany with the election of Adolf Hitler as chancellor on January 30. With her bank account blocked by Nazi authorities and Albert in Africa, Helene resolves to leave Germany and move to Lausanne, Switzerland, with Rhena at the end of the school year.

1934

Albert returns to Europe and bases himself in Gunsbach. Helene occasionally visits him there, and he visits her in Lausanne. She also travels with him to England and Scotland.

1935

Albert's sixtieth birthday (January 14) is publicly commemorated in Strasbourg and Switzerland. Shortly afterward, Helene and Albert spend a week in a Swiss mountain village above Montreux, Les Avants, before his departure for a brief sojourn in Lambarene. At the end of the year, Helene travels with Albert to England.

Ernst Bresslau (1877–1935), Helene's older brother and a well-known zoologist, dies of a heart attack in São Paulo, Brazil.

1936

Albert's base of operations remains Gunsbach, where Emmy Martin works and lives upstairs in the Maison Schweitzer. Helene and Rhena continue to live in Lausanne, where Schweitzer occasionally visits his family, often accompanied by his secretary, Mathilde Kottmann. They usually arrive with sacks of correspondence requiring a response. Helene helps with this work.

1937

Helene is alone in Europe after Albert's February departure for Lambarene. He will remain in Lambarene until 1948 except for a hurried visit of less than two weeks in January 1939. On June 18, Helene celebrates her twenty-fifth wedding anniversary without Albert by visiting his family in Gunsbach.

In October, Helene and Rhena move from Switzerland to New York City. In December, Helene undertakes a lecture tour in the United States, beginning in New York and traveling to Baltimore, Philadelphia, Boston and Cambridge, and Washington, DC.

1938

Returns to Europe by ship in the spring, while nineteen-year-old Rhena remains in New York. Helene then travels on to Lambarene, arriving for her *third sojourn* on May 17, 1938. She is fifty-nine, and her health is better than it has been in years. With more than 370 patients under treatment at the Schweitzer Hospital, she makes the rounds twice a day with doctors and works in the nursery with babies and newborns. After returning to New York in September, Helene continues to deliver talks on the Schweitzer Hospital in the northeastern and midwestern United States, traveling as far as St. Louis, Missouri.

1939

Helene and Rhena return to Switzerland in mid-January, expecting to see Albert. They are shocked to learn that while en route to Europe, after hearing a radio broadcast of an ominous speech by Adolf Hitler, he booked a return ticket to Africa on the same ship, departing from Bordeaux ten days later.

In the spring, Helene visits her mother, Cary Bresslau, for the last time in Heidelberg, Germany. Her *fourth sojourn* in Lambarene begins when she sets sail from Bordeaux with Rhena in May for a visit of six weeks. Rhena experiences her father's work in Africa for the first time while Helene edits the manuscript of Albert's book *African Stories*.

World War II begins with the German invasion of Poland on September 1. The Schweitzers' first grandchild, Monique, is born at the end of the year.

1940

Helene's home base at this time is an apartment in Lausanne. But on June 14 she is visiting Paris to see Rhena and her husband, Jean Eckert, and their baby daughter, Monique. During her visit, German Nazi soldiers march into the city. Before the armistice is signed on June 22, nearly eight million French citizens take to the roads in a mass exodus toward the "Free Zone" in the South of France. Helene is among them, as are Rhena, Jean, and the baby. In autumn, Helene learns that Hitler's Third Reich has requisitioned her house in Königsfeld. Albert and Helene's second grandchild, Philippe-Emmanuel Eckert, is born on November 26.

1941

Helene's life is chaotic as she lives in small apartments and hotels in the Auvergne region of France, remaining in constant contact with the International Red

Cross to obtain copies of telegrams from Albert, who remains in Lambarene throughout World War II. She eventually escapes from Europe via Lisbon, the only way out of Nazi-occupied Europe at the time, by boarding a neutral Portuguese steamship on July 11. After changing ships in Soyo, Angola, she travels through the Belgian Congo with stops in Boma, Matadi, and Leopoldville before crossing into French Equatorial Africa at Brazzaville.

Helene's *fifth and longest sojourn* in Lambarene begins on August 2, when she appears just before midnight on a sandbank in the Ogowe River on a riverboat operated by Monsieur Louvet-Jardin. Albert later describes the event as a "miracle." Approximately two months later Helene's mother, Caroline Bresslau-Isay (1853–1941), dies in Germany.

1942

Wartime losses of family and friends accumulate. Among them, Helene's favorite cousin, Johanna Engel, commits suicide rather than allow herself to be deported to the German concentration camp at Theresienstadt. By autumn, German troops occupy all of France. Rhena and her family—which now includes Christiane, born on May 20—are at risk for deportation but succeed in a dramatic border crossing into Switzerland.

1944

The Schweitzers' fourth grandchild, Françoise Catherine, is born in Zürich on March 20.

1946

Departs Lambarene "completely exhausted" after her longest sojourn there, five years. Travels back to Europe with Emma Haussknecht, arriving in Marseille on October 4, 1946, then makes her way to Strasbourg.

1947

Returns to Königsfeld, in part to put her papers in order before returning to Lambarene in the spring for her *sixth sojourn*.

1948

Albert arrives in Europe in October. This marks the end of his longest sojourn in Africa, which began in February 1937, a period interrupted only by a hurried trip to Gunsbach in the winter of 1939. After a visit to Königsfeld, he meets his four grandchildren for the first time in Männedorf, Switzerland, and baptizes them in their living room.

1949

Helene and Albert travel to New York together en route to Aspen, Colorado. During this three-week visit, Albert delivers the keynote address at the Goethe Bicentennial in Aspen. This is his only trip to the United States in his life. They return to Europe in August and travel to Lambarene together in October.

1950

Helene's *seventh sojourn* is marked with tensions related to health difficulties that include an increasingly weak heart. She is under the care of her husband and a Dr. Percy. Her stay in Lambarene ends in July, when she returns to Europe in an exhausted state.

1951

Present when Albert is honored in Frankfurt in September with the German Booksellers Association's Friedenspreis. Guests for this event include her widowed sister-in-law, Luise Bresslau-Hoff, and old friends Elly and Theodor Heuss-Knapp. Theodor Heuss, then president of Germany, speaks at this event. Albert returns to Lambarene in November.

1952

More than eight hundred people attend Helene's last public talk on June 14 at Freiburg University on the "Land und Leute am Ogowe" (the land and people of the Ogowe).

1953

Rents a room in Königsfeld to Winnifred Wirckau, a young physical therapist who becomes a trusted friend. This connection as well as visits from her older grandchildren help to reduce Helene's increasing sense of loneliness.

1954

Present in Oslo to attend Albert's Nobel Peace Prize Ceremony on November 4, for the honor bestowed on him in 1952.

1955

Arrives in Lambarene on January 11 for Albert's eightieth birthday celebration on January 14. Her *eighth sojourn* lasts six months. Albert and Helene return to Europe together in July.

1956

Begins her *ninth and final sojourn* in Lambarene in January.

1957

Helps her husband prepare a speech entitled "Peace or Atomic War?" that is also known as Albert Schweitzer's "Declaration of Conscience." This powerful statement opposing atomic weapons is broadcast on Radio Oslo and throughout the world on April 23.

In May 1957, Helene leaves Lambarene in a fragile state of health, accompanied by the Dutch nurse Tony Van Leer. Rhena meets them in Paris and proceeds with her mother to Zurich. Helene Schweitzer Bresslau dies in Zurich, Switzerland, on June 1. A memorial service is held at the Zurich Crematorium on June 5. Albert remains in Lambarene until July, when he arrives in Europe for a stay of six months.

1958

On what would have been Helene's seventy-ninth birthday, her ashes are placed in the cemetery in Lambarene beneath a stone cross inscribed by Albert: "Ci gisent les cendres d'Hélène Schweitzer Bresslau née 25.1.1879. Mariée avec Albert Schweitzer 18.6.1912. Arrivée à Lambaréné 18.4.1913 pour fonder avec lui l'hôpital pour les indigènes. Décédée Zurich le 1.6.1957" (Here rest the ashes of Helene Schweitzer Bresslau, born 1.25.1879. Married to Albert Schweitzer 6.18.1912. Arrived in Lambarene 4.18.1913 to establish the hospital for the native people. Deceased in Zurich 6.1.1957.)

1959

Albert travels to Europe for the last time and returns to Lambarene at the end of the year. He will remain active at the Schweitzer Hospital until his death at the age of ninety on September 5, 1965. His tombstone is next to Helene Schweitzer Bresslau's in the small cemetery of the Historic Zone, an area central to the 1927 hospital recently restored to preserve the Schweitzer legacy. Meanwhile, half a mile uphill, the modern Schweitzer Hospital inaugurated in 1981 continues to function.

Notes

Abbreviations

AS-Gunsbach   Archives Centrales Schweitzer Gunsbach, France

Bonnet Collection   Collection Marcel Bonnet (1922–2007), Bibliothèque Municipale Joseph-Roumanille of Saint-Rémy-de-Provence, France

DASZ   Deutsches Albert Schweitzer Zentrum, Frankfurt am Main, Germany

SU-Lemke Collection   Antje Bultmann Lemke Collection Relating to Albert Schweitzer, Special Collections Research Center, Syracuse University Libraries

SU-Schweitzer Papers   Albert Schweitzer Papers, Special Collections Research Center, Syracuse University Libraries.

ZBZ   Zentralbibliothek Zürich

Preface

1. See *New York Times*, "Schweitzer's Wife Honored with Him."

2. *Badische Zeitung* "Frau Helene Schweitzer sprach in Freiburg."

3. Schempp, "Helene Schweitzer," n.p. All translations from French and German sources, including letters published in those languages, are mine unless otherwise noted.

4. Rinderknecht, "Helene Schweitzer," 14.

5. See Woytt, "Helene Bresslau."

6. The German title is *Helene Schweitzer: Einblick in das Leben einer Frau, der es gegeben war, sich selbstlos und aufopfernd einem grossen Werk der Nächstenliebe hinzugeben.*

7. Helene and Albert's daughter, Rhena, discovered the letters in the 1980s. The first published selection appeared in 1992 as Schweitzer and Bresslau, *Die Jahre*

vor Lambarene, edited by Rhena Schweitzer Miller and Gustav Woytt, and was translated as *The Albert Schweitzer–Helene Bresslau Letters* in 2003.

8. A. Schweitzer, *Out of My Life and Thought*, 86. Throughout this book, I cite the 1990 American English edition of Schweitzer's autobiography translated by Antje Bultmann Lemke unless otherwise noted.

9. This rank is similar to associate professor in current-day American higher-education hierarchy.

10. France lost this region in the Franco-Prussian War of 1871.

11. This teaching credential, the *Lehrerin für höhere Mädchenschulen*, qualified Helene to teach girls only.

12. Sorg, introduction to volume 1 of Schweitzer and Bresslau, *Albert Schweitzer et Hélène Bresslau: Correspondance, 1901–1912*, 1:17 (hereafter cited as *Correspondance, 1901–1912*).

13. Helene Schweitzer to Julius Bixler, Jan. 4, 1929, H. Schweitzer Papers, Colby College Special Collections, Waterville, ME. Julius Bixler eventually became president of Colby College in Maine from 1942 to 1960.

14. Most of these letters were written in German, though Albert and Helene also used French in their written communication.

15. Seaver, *Albert Schweitzer*.

1. In Search of Helene Schweitzer Bresslau

1. Albert Schweitzer was often called "le Grand Docteur" (the Great Doctor) by his African patients. This nickname has become widely used in French as a term of respect.

2. The commonplace form of a married woman's name in the Germanic world places her maiden name after her married name. Furthermore, a married man's "official" name traditionally includes his wife's maiden name. Helene Bresslau became "Helene Schweitzer Bresslau" when she married Albert Schweitzer in June 1912. At the same moment, Albert Schweitzer became "Albert Schweitzer Bresslau," thus his initials ASB.

3. "Ci gisent les cendres d'Hélène Schweitzer Bresslau née 25.1.1879. Mariée avec Albert Schweitzer 18.6.1912. Arrivée à Lambaréné 18.4.1913 pour fonder avec lui l'hôpital pour les indigènes. Décédée Zurich le 1.6.1957."

4. "Meiner Frau—meinem treuesten Kameraden" is the dedication in volume 2 of the larger work *Kulturphilosophie*, published in 1923. This multivolume book was translated into English as *The Philosophy of Civilization*.

5. Lee, *Virginia Woolf's Nose*, 8.

6. The name reverted to the French "Université de Strasbourg" (University of Strasbourg) after World War I. Note that this more familiar name is used frequently throughout this book with the understanding that the institution was named the Kaiser Wilhelm Universität from 1871 to the end of 1918.

7. Shifting nationalities in Alsace have required that formerly German street names be translated into French. The street where the Bresslaus lived when Harry Bresslau was chancellor of the University of Strasbourg, the Ruprechtsauerallee, is now the Allée de Robertsau. Note that all street signs in Strasbourg today are in two languages: French and Alsatian.

8. The home's cofounder would be her friend Helene Fehling, and the president of their organization would be none other than the mayor of Strasbourg, Rudolf Schwander.

9. This notion of colonization is open to debate. On the one hand, because the annexation of Alsace-Lorraine was imposed on the French people, the Germans who moved to the Alsace in the late nineteenth century might be viewed as colonizers. On the other hand, the French National Assembly acquiesced by voting in favor of annexation, albeit under duress. In either case, it is well known that Strasbourg benefited from the German Empire's development, which was the first expansion of Strasbourg since the fifteenth century.

10. H. Schweitzer, *Tagebuch* (diary), 1913–15 (kept from Mar. 26, 1913, to Nov. 26, 1915), private collection, Apr. 7, 1913, 13.

11. Helene Schweitzer (HS) to Cary and Harry Bresslau, July 18, 1913, quoted in Mühlstein, *Helene Schweitzer Bresslau*, 150 (the actual location of this letter is unknown). Note that for reasons mentioned earlier, Helene's initials ceased to be the "HB" of her early correspondence with Albert Schweitzer when they were married in June 1912. Although her "official" initials became "HSB," I use "HS" for letters cited after June 18, 1912, because most of her writings, journals, and many photographs were signed "Helene Schweitzer."

12. Cousins, *Dr. Schweitzer of Lambarene*, 110–12.

13. A. Schweitzer, *Out of My Life and Thought*, 210.

14. I am indebted to Verena Mühlstein for her explanation of the *Durchschreibehefte*, a notebook in which Helene wrote this early *Tagebuch* with the use of a special writing instrument called an *Achatstift*. In other words, Helene's 1913–15 diary was not written with pen and ink, as were most of her letters, day books, and journals, because it was never intended to be private.

15. W. Munz, *Albert Schweitzer dans la mémoire des Africains*, 153.

16. A. Schweitzer, *On the Edge of the Primeval Forest*, 121.

17. Ibid., 81.

18. Ibid., 56.

19. A. Schweitzer, *Out of My Life and Thought*, 139.

20. A. Schweitzer, *On the Edge of the Primeval Forest*, 103–4.

21. Ibid., 105.

22. Nessmann, *Avec Albert Schweitzer*, 74.

23. Trensz, "Témoignage," 209.

24. Woytt-Secretan, *Albert Schweitzer*, 66.

25. Rogers, "Madame Schweitzer," 35.

26. Brabazon, *Albert Schweitzer*, 155.

27. *Time* magazine, "Religion," 72.

28. Anderson, *The Schweitzer Album*, 14. It should be noted that the bride was thirty-four years old in 1912 and the groom thirty-eight.

29. Ibid., 112.

30. Rinderknecht, "Helene Schweitzer," 14.

31. Sieber, "Helene Schweitzer."

32. Cameron, *Points of Departure*, 156.

33. Cousins, *Dr. Schweitzer of Lambarene*, 110.

34. Urquhart, *With Doctor Schweitzer*, 25.

35. Schweitzer Miller, foreword to Schweitzer and Bresslau, *Die Jahre vor Lambarene*, 6.

36. See Schweitzer and Bresslau, *Correspondance 1901–1912*. It should be noted that Dr. Jean-Paul Sorg's French edition expands on earlier editions of the Schweitzers' pre-Lambarene correspondence consulted by James Brabazon and Verena Mühlstein for their biographical studies.

37. Albert Schweitzer (AS) to Helene Bresslau (HB), Sept. 25, 1903, in *Correspondance, 1901–1912*, 1:46.A.S. (In addition to the date, citations to letters in this collection include a volume number and a chronological numbering system, *not* page numbers, developed by editor-translator Jean-Paul Sorg for cataloging these letters across all three volumes; so "1:46.A.S." indicates volume 1, letter 46, and the sender's initials).

38. Nies-Berger, *Albert Schweitzer as I Knew Him*, 35.

39. See the website of the Association Internationale de Schweitzer de Lambaréné, http://www.schweitzer.org, for a detailed list of names and dates of those who have served at the Schweitzer Hospital.

40. Mühlstein, *Helene Schweitzer Bresslau*, 9.

41. Brabazon, *Albert Schweitzer*, 142.

42. HB to AS, May 5–6, 1902, in *Correspondance, 1901–1912*, 1:4.H.B.

43. Albert Schweitzer's father, Louis Théophile Schweitzer (1848–1926) was pastor in the parish of Gunsbach, Alsace, for fifty years.

44. See AS to HB, Apr. 11, 1910, in *Correspondance, 1901–1912*, 3:448.A.S.: "I am feeling troubled and emotionally shaken by Tata's farewell."

45. AS to HB, Mar. 18, 1912, in *Correspondance, 1901–1912*, 3:612.A.S.

46. The dedication reads: "Frau Annie Fischer in tiefer Dankbarkeit" (Mrs. Annie Fischer with profound gratitude).

47. Sorg, introduction to volume 3 of *Correspondance, 1901–1912*, 3:65.

48. HB to AS, Aug. 26, 1911, in *Correspondance, 1901–1912*, 3:558.H.B.

49. AS to HB, Jan. 22, 1903, in *Correspondance, 1901–1912*, 1:30.A.S.

50. HB to AS, July 22, 1904, in *Correspondance, 1901–1912*, 1:84.H.B.

51. AS to HB, n.d. (logically autumn 1904), in *Correspondance, 1901–1912*, 1:86.A.S.

52. AS to HB, n.d., in *Correspondance, 1901–1912*, 1:85.A.S.

53. See Nachlass A. Schweitzer (A. Schweitzer Papers), Sac 1.b.9. Beilage, Mar. 9, 1918, Zentralbibliothek Zürich (hereafter ZBZ). The first two volumes of the completed book appeared as *Kulturphilosophie* in 1923.

54. Nachlass A. Schweitzer, Dossier 36-D, Kleine Registrierzettel, Reimarus, II, Aufl, ZBZ. This is Helene's 1905 equivalent of an "index card file" of more than three hundred references to the work originally entitled *Von Reimarus zu Wrede: Eine Geschichte der Leben-Jesu-Forschung*. In English, this work is known as *The Quest for the Historical Jesus*, and in later editions of the work in German the main title is often omitted.

55. HB to AS, Nov. 25, 1911, in *Correspondance, 1901–1912*, 3:582.H.B.

56. Mühlstein, *Helene Schweitzer Bresslau*, 10.

57. HB to AS, Sept. 23, 1911, in *Correspondance, 1901–1912*, 3:574.H.B.

58. HB to AS, Apr. 2, 1912, in *Correspondance, 1901–1912*, 3:620.H.B.

59. Sorg, introduction to volume 3 of *Correspondance, 1901–1912*, 3:71.

60. Brabazon, *Albert Schweitzer*, 150.

61. Ibid., 149.

62. AS to HB, Jan. 13, 1903, in *Correspondance, 1901–1912*, 1:29.A.S.

63. AS to HB, Mar. 3, 1903, in *Correspondance, 1901–1912*, 1:31.A.S.

64. Note that Helene deliberately destroyed many of her letters later in life.

65. AS to HB, Dec. 17, 1905, in *Correspondance, 1901–1912*, 1:144.A.S.

66. HB to AS, Aug. 28, 1907, in *Correspondance, 1901–1912*, 2:247.H.B.

67. Sorg, introduction to volume 3 of *Correspondance, 1901–1912*, 3:23.

68. The fatal Blackwater Fever was so named because of the black urine it caused.

69. HB to AS, Feb. 9, 1911, in *Correspondance, 1901–1912*, 3:563.H.B.

70. AS to HB, Aug. 21, 1911, in *Correspondance, 1901–1912*, 3:555.A.S.

71. AS to HB, Feb. 8, 1911, in *Correspondance, 1901–1912*, 3:504.A.S.

72. Cousins, *Dr. Schweitzer of Lambarene*, 220.

73. From mid-February 1924 to August 1927.

2. "You Seem to Be Someone"

1. HB to AS, July 3, 1907, in *Correspondance, 1901–1912*, 2:236.H.B., suspension points in original.

2. HB to AS, May 5, 1902, in *Correspondance, 1901–1912*, 1:4.H.B.

3. AS to HB, May 29, 1904, in *Correspondance, 1901–1912*, 1:80.A.S.

4. AS to HB, June 1–2, 1905, in *Correspondance, 1901–1912*, 1:109.A.S.

5. The Strassburger Mütterheim (Strasbourg Mother's Home), opened on November 15, 1907, in the suburb of Neudorf, with room for eight women and their infants. Documents related to this project, including an "Aufruf zum Eintritt in den Verein des Mütterheims" (Appeal for support for the Mother's Home Organization), drafted by Albert Schweitzer and edited by Helene Bresslau, can be found in the Antje Bultmann Lemke Collection Relating to Albert Schweitzer, Special Collections Research Center, Syracuse University Libraries (hereafter SU-Lemke Collection).

6. AS to HB, Dec. 31, 1907, in *Correspondance, 1901–1912,* 2:274.A.S.

7. AS to HB, Feb. 10, 1908, in *Correspondance, 1901–1912,* 2:277.A.S.

8. HB to AS, Feb. 10, 1908, in *Correspondance, 1901–1912,* 2:279.H.B., suspension points in original.

9. HB to AS, Jan. 25, 1910, in *Correspondance, 1901–1912,* 3:432.H.B.

10. HB to AS, Feb. 2, 1904, in *Correspondance, 1901–1912,* 1:64.H.B.

11. Oswald, *Mon oncle Albert Schweitzer,* 62.

12. AS to HB, Dec. 31, 1907, in *Correspondance, 1901–1912,* 2:274.A.S.

13. Kaiser Wilhelm I died on March 9, 1888. After a brief succession by his only son, Friedrich III (r. Mar. 9–June 15, 1888), his grandson Wilhelm II became the last emperor the German Empire (r. June 15, 1888–Nov. 9, 1818).

14. Wahl, "Choisir la France," 49.

15. Igersheim, "Un tournant pour l'Alsace," 4.

16. Igersheim, "Le 'Reichsland,'" 32.

17. See Alsace-Lorraine Constitution of 1911.

18. Heuss-Knapp, *Ausblick vom Münsterturm,* 103.

19. The main German title, *Von Reimarus zu Wrede* (From Reimarus to Wrede), begins and ends with names of theological historians.

20. HB to AS, Mar. 10, 1906, in *Correspondance, 1901–1912,* 2:161.H.B.

21. A. Schweitzer, *Out of My Life and Thought,* 144.

22. Ibid., 148.

23. For examples of Helene's involvement with Albert Schweitzer's writings, see her notes on the introduction to *Wir Epigonen* dated September 27, 1915; corrections and notes to particular chapters (e.g., "Die Gründe des Niedergangs" and "Kulturstaaten und Kolonien"); and her hand-written copy made at Garaison, dated March 9, 1918, in Nachlass A. Schweitzer, ZBZ.

24. De Brazza died in Dakar on September 14, 1905, and was buried at Père Lachaise cemetery in Paris. His body has since been exhumed and placed in a mausoleum in Brazzaville, the capital city of the Republic of the Congo, named in his honor.

25. HB to AS, May 5, 1902, in *Correspondance, 1901–1912,* 1:4.H.B.

26. AS to HB, Dec. 5, 1904, in *Correspondance, 1901–1912,* 1:87.A.S.

27. The title of this second volume is *Kultur und Ethik* (*Culture and Ethics*). Note that *Kulturphilosophie* grew out of Schweitzer's original idea for *Wir Epigonen*.

28. Verena Mühlstein to the author, e-mail communication, Oct. 12, 2013.

29. AS to HB, July 9, 1905, in *Correspondance, 1901–1912*, 1:113.A.S.

30. Schweitzer Miller, foreword to *Die Jahre vor Lambarene*, 5.

31. HB to AS, May 5, 1902, in *Correspondance, 1901–1912*, 1:4.H.B.

32. The German city Stettin became the Polish city Szczecin in the aftermath of World War II.

33. AS to HB, Oct. 27, 1903, in *Correspondance, 1901–1912*, 1:49.A.S.

34. AS to HB, Oct. 31, 1903, in *Correspondance, 1901–1912*, 1:51.A.S.

35. Mühlstein, *Helene Schweitzer Bresslau*, 73–74.

36. HB to AS, Nov. 8, 1906, in *Correspondance, 1901–1912*, 2:198.H.B.

37. H. Bresslau, "Gott," n.p.

38. This enormous project, called the Grande Percée (Great Opening), reached its peak in 1910.

39. Quoted in Spear, "Helene Bresslau," 32; Spear cites Max Rehm, *Rudolf Schwander und Kurt Blum*, n.p., as the source of this quote.

40. AS to HB, Apr. 10, 1905, in *Correspondance, 1901–1912*, 1:98.A.S.

41. Arnold, *Albert Schweitzer*, 87.

42. AS to HB, Apr. 10, 1905, in *Correspondance, 1901–1912*, 1:98.A.S.

43. HB to AS, Apr. 27, 1907, in *Correspondance, 1901–1912*, 2:230.H.B.

44. See HB to AS, Oct. 4, 1907, in *Correspondance, 1901–1912*, 2:261.H.B. In this letter, Helene announces the official establishment of the Mütterheim to Albert Schweitzer and names the officers of the organization she has created.

45. See the letter dated February 10, 1908, cited in note 8.

46. H. Bresslau, "Strassburger Mütterheim," 15, quoted in Mühlstein, *Helene Schweitzer Bresslau*, 122.

47. Woytt, "Helene Bresslau," 24. This article also includes details related to the financing of the Mother's Home.

48. H. Bresslau, "Strassburger Mütterheim," 15, quoted in Mühlstein, *Helene Schweitzer Bresslau*, 122.

49. HB to AS, Aug. 28, 1905, in *Correspondance, 1901–1912*, 1:121.H.B.

50. AS to HB, Paris, July 9, 1905, in *Correspondance, 1901–1912*, 1:113.A.S.

51. HB to AS, May 6, 1905, in *Correspondance, 1901–1912*, 1:102.H.B.

52. HB to AS, Nov. 26, 1905, in *Correspondance, 1901–1912*, 1:142.H.B.

53. AS to HB, Jan. 29, 1907, in *Correspondance, 1901–1912*, 2:220.A.S.

54. Spear, "Helene Bresslau," 32.

55. A. Schweitzer, *Geschichte der Leben-Jesu-Forschung*, 29. Note that, regrettably, the full acknowledgment, mentioning Helene, does not appear in the John Bowden translation of this text included here in the bibliography.

56. A. Schweitzer, *Out of My Life and Thought*, 111.

57. Arnold, *Albert Schweitzer*, 197.

58. This French phrase implies a practical alliance grounded in fond feeling.

59. HB to AS, Frankfurt, Apr. 26, 1910, in *Correspondance, 1901–1912*, 3:452.H.B. The French category of this skill level below a fully qualified registered nurse was called an *externe*.

60. HB to AS, Frankfurt, June 19, 1910, in *Correspondance, 1901–1912*, 3:466.H.B.

61. HB to AS, Frankfurt, Sept. 19, 1910, in *Correspondance, 1901–1912*, 3:486.H.B.

62. AS to HB, Dec. 28, 1910, in *Correspondance, 1901–1912*, 3:494.A.S.

63. AS to HB, Jan. 5, 1911, in *Correspondance, 1901–1912*, 3:498.A.S.

64. AS to HB, Mar. 11, 1911, in *Correspondance, 1901–1912*, 3:508.A.S.

65. HB to AS, Königsfeld, May 30, 1911, in *Correspondance, 1901–1912*, 3:523.H.B.

66. Robert Koch of Berlin identified the *Mycobacterium tuberculosis* in 1882 and won the Nobel Prize in Medicine in 1905 for this discovery.

67. The Bacillus Calmette Guérin (BCG) Vaccine was named for two microbiologists at the Pasteur Institute in Paris.

68. See Wolf, "Albert Schweitzer im Jahr 1912," 55.

69. The name "Congo" was often used to refer to the vast region known politically as French Equatorial Africa prior to the independence movements of the 1960s. As the geopolitical boundaries and nomenclature of Africa changed, the name "Congo" came to refer to a separate nation.

70. Sorg, introduction to volume 1 of *Correspondance, 1901–1912*, 1:18.

71. HB to AS, May 6, 1905, in *Correspondance, 1901–1912*, 1:102.H.B.

3. In and Out of Africa

1. In 1893, the American Presbyterians transferred their mission stations to the Paris Evangelical Mission Society, the organization that granted Albert Schweitzer a place as a medical missionary.

2. See Othon Printz's book *Avant Schweitzer* for a thorough discussion of Schweitzer's predecessors in the region.

3. Kingsley, *Travels in West Africa*, 67.

4. See Bianquis, *In Memoriam*, on the Lantz mission in Talagouga.

5. Daniel Couve to Jean Bianquis, Talagouga, Easter Monday, Apr. 16, 1906, included in Bianquis, *In Memoriam*, 98–109.

6. See A. Schweitzer, *Albert Schweitzer—Essential Writings*, 75, for the sermon preached at St. Nicolas in Strasbourg on January 6, 1905, quoted here.

7. Kingsley, *Travels in West Africa*, 72.

8. H. Schweitzer, *Tagebuch*, 1913–15, Apr. 7, 13.

9. Ibid., Apr. 8, 1913, 14.

10. Ibid., Apr. 13, 1913, 16.

11. Ibid., Apr. 24, 1913, 20.

12. Later in 1913, Schweitzer built a corrugated iron building with palm leaves as a rooftop for this purpose.

13. Denzel and Naumann, "Jenseits in Afrika, Helene Schweitzer," 121.

14. A. Schweitzer, *On the Edge of the Primeval Forest*, 42.

15. The special writing instrument required to press through the five pages accounts, in part, for the bold impression of both Albert and Helene's writing in this document. But even if Helene's writing is distinctly larger and more energetic than Albert's, her style of German penmanship, called "*Kurrentschrift*," presents a challenge to modern eyes, even among native speakers of German.

16. *On the Edge of the Primeval Forest* (1921) and *More from the Primeval Forest* (1931).

17. A. Schweitzer in H. Schweitzer, *Tagebuch*, 1913–15, Apr. 24, 1913, 22.

18. Mühlstein, *Helene Schweitzer Bresslau*, 150.

19. H. Schweitzer, *Tagebuch*, 1913–15, Aug. 5, 1914, 244.

20. Minder, "Internement et retour en Alsace," 189.

21. Ibid., 197.

22. A. Schweitzer, *Out of My Life and Thought*, 147.

23. See Brabazon, *Albert Schweitzer*, 302–5, for an excellent summary of Schweitzer's direct approach to suffering in these sermons.

24. Rolland won the Nobel Prize in Literature in 1915, largely for his antiwar book *Au-dessus de la mêlée* (*Above the Battle*).

25. HB to AS, Aug. 30, 1907, in *Correspondance, 1901–1912*, 2:248.H.B. In this letter, Helene refers to meeting Romain Rolland and having her photograph taken with him during a few weeks with her parents in Trois-Epis.

26. Minder, "Internement et retour en Alsace," 190.

27. A. Schweitzer, *On the Edge of the Primeval Forest*, 99.

28. Note that the original plan was to establish an alternating pattern of two years in Africa followed by a full year in Europe. In March 1913, the Schweitzers left for Lambarene with just enough funding for a two-year sojourn.

29. Phlebitis is a painful inflammation of the veins in the legs that can lead to dangerous blood clots. See Mühlstein, *Helene Schweitzer Bresslau*, 170–71.

30. A. Schweitzer, *On the Edge of the Primeval Forest*, 145–46.

31. As mentioned earlier, years would pass before the first two parts of this book were published in 1923.

32. A. Schweitzer, *On the Edge of the Primeval Forest*, 107.

33. HS to Harry Bresslau, May 1917, unpublished letter, location unknown, quoted in Mühlstein, *Helene Schweitzer Bresslau*, 179.

34. See Nachlass A. Schweitzer, Sac 1.b.9, Beilage, Mar. 9, 1918, ZBZ, for original copies made by Helene Schweitzer.

35. HS to Luise Bresslau-Hoff, Sept. 9, 1917, unpublished letter, location unknown, quoted in Mühlstein, *Helene Schweitzer Bresslau*, 180. Note that Mühlstein had access to Helene Schweitzer Bresslau's private correspondence with Luise Bresslau-Hoff.

36. See Couturier de Chefdebois, "Notre-Dame de Garaison," for the history of this pilgrimage site.

37. Vimont, "Garaison," 1.

38. Mauran and Ehret, "Les camps d'évacués alsaciens," part 1, 117.

39. Ibid., part 2, 160.

40. Between 1871 and 1918, the French often referred to Alsace and Lorraine as *"les provinces perdues"* (the lost provinces) and described them as "amputated" from the French nation.

41. Quoted in Grandhomme, "Les Alsaciens-Lorrains dans les camps d'internement," 165.

42. Mauran and Ehret, "Les camps d'évacués alsaciens," part 1, 95.

43. Prefect of Bordeaux to prefect of Tarbes, telegram, Nov. 16, 1917, Archives départementales des Hautes-Pyrénées, 1917–18, 9 R 131.

44. Vimont, "Garaison," 7–8.

45. Woytt-Secretan, "Souvenirs d'une infirmière," 231.

46. A. Schweitzer, *Out of My Life and Thought*, 165. In his autobiography, Schweitzer identifies conditions at this *caserne de passage* as the source of his intestinal ulcers, which would require two surgeries at the end of 1918. It is also quite possible that his condition was the result of typhoid fever contracted in Africa.

47. A. Schweitzer to Garaison Camp Director, Nov. 25, 1917, 9 R 131, Archives départementales des Hautes-Pyrénées, Tarbes, France.

48. H. Schweitzer to her parents, postcard sent from Garaison, Feb. 10, 1918, Helene Schweitzer Korrespondenz, Deutsches Albert Schweitzer Zentrum (hereafter DASZ).

49. A. Schweitzer, "Deux caisses avec adresses et un paquet" (Statement of goods sequestered), Collection Marcel Bonnet (1922–2007), Bibliothèque Municipale Joseph-Roumanille of Saint-Rémy-de-Provence (hereafter the Bonnet Collection.) This document gives us remarkable insight into the library Albert and Helene carried, even as civil prisoners of war.

50. A. Schweitzer, *Out of My Life and Thought*, 167.

51. AS to HS, Jan. 26, 1924, Helene Schweitzer Bresslau Correspondence, 1919–1939, Albert Schweitzer Papers, Special Collections Research Center, Syracuse University Libraries (hereafter SU-Schweitzer Papers). Schweitzer's memory of Helene's previous birthday, January 1923, refers to a time when she was recovering from treatment following her diagnosis of open tuberculosis. See chapter 4.

52. AS to HS, Dec. 30, 1936, Helene Schweitzer Bresslau Correspondence, 1919–1939, suspension points in original.

53. Vincent Van Gogh spent most of 1899, the last year of his life, in this mental facility.

54. Mayor of Saint-Rémy to his citizens, Mar. 13, 1915, material related to Dr. Jacques Scheib, Dr. Albert Schweitzer, and the Dépôt d'Austro-Allemands de Saint-Rémy. Shelf M-261, Bonnet Collection.

55. Ibid., Apr. 24, 1915.

56. Ibid., Nov. 29, 1915.

57. More than 180 names of the war dead are carved in granite on the monument to the Great War on Saint-Rémy's Place de la République.

58. The derogatory word *Boche* is untranslatable. It combines resentment for Germanic power and visceral disgust.

59. Mauron, "Histoire de notre temps," 5.

60. *Petit Provençal*, Oct. 19, 1915, letter to the editor.

61. Xavier Schlienger, camp delegate, to Minister of the Interior, June 27, 1917, Bonnet Collection.

62. A. Schweitzer, *Out of My Life and Thought*, 172.

63. Ibid., 173.

64. See Wersinger-Liller, "Albert Schweitzer à St. Rémy," 203. When this observer arrived in the autumn of 1917, she counted eighty schoolteachers among the one hundred internees.

65. Scheib, "Mémoires d'un médecin," 33.

66. Wersinger-Liller, "Albert Schweitzer à St. Rémy," 204.

67. Ibid., 203–6.

68. Estimates place the worldwide death toll from Spanish Influenza at fifty to one hundred million people, with most deaths occurring in the last four months of 1918. See Barry, "The Site of Origin of the 1918 Influenza Pandemic."

69. Mauron, "Histoire de notre temps," 5.

70. Ibid.

71. Minder, "Internement et retour en Alsace," 192.

72. See Letters of Marie Roumanille-Blanc, Archives Centrales Schweitzer Gunsbach (hereafter AS-Gunsbach), quoted in Minder, "Internement et retour en Alsace," 192.

73. Wersinger-Liller, "Albert Schweitzer à St. Rémy," 204.

74. H. Schweitzer, "Journal, 1918," SU-Lemke Collection.

75. Ibid., Apr. 8, 1918.

76. Ibid., Apr. 14, 1918.

77. Ibid., Apr. 15, 1918.

78. Ibid., June 29, 1918.

79. A. Schweitzer, "Declaration of Alsace-Lorraine," May 30, 1918, Bonnet Collection.

80. See Grandhomme, "Les Alsaciens-Lorrains dans les camps d'internement"; Laurent, *1914–1918*; Mauran and Ehret, "Les camps d'évacués alsaciens"; and Vimont, "Garaison"—all pioneers in this relatively recent field of French history.

81. Note that what was then called "the Great War" did not end until the Armistice of November 11, 1918. Furthermore, Alsace and Lorraine were not officially reintegrated into the French nation until the signing of the Treaty of Versailles on June 28, 1919.

82. Using today's modern trains, it takes approximately ten hours to travel from Saint-Rémy via Avignon, Lyon, Geneva, Bern, and Zurich to Lake Constance, the body of water known in Europe as "the Bodensee."

83. A. Schweitzer, *Out of My Life and Thought*, 177.

4. Divided Destinies

1. A. Schweitzer, *Out of My Life and Thought*, 186.

2. Ibid., 189.

3. Richard Clasen's photographs illustrated the first edition of *On the Edge of the Primeval Forest*, which was first published in Swedish in 1921 as *Mellan urskog och watten*, translated from the German *Zwischen Wasser und Urwald* by Greta Lagerfelt.

4. See Morel, "Au Gabon avant l'arrivée du Docteur Schweitzer."

5. Quoted in Mühlstein, *Helene Schweitzer Bresslau*, 221.

6. The importance of this missing birth certificate is not clear, except that it apparently had to be presented in Strasbourg with some other documents. Could the issue relate to a bank account, perhaps, or Harry Bresslau's pension from the university?

7. HS to AS, Heidelberg, Aug. 5 and 6, 1920, Helene Schweitzer Bresslau Correspondence, 1919–1939, SU-Schweitzer Papers.

8. HS to AS, Heidelberg, n.d., Helene Schweitzer Bresslau Correspondence, 1919–1939. "Jeudi" (Thursday) is written at the top of first page, and because the letter continues to discuss an issue raised in the previous letter quoted, it is logical to assume the date to be the following Thursday: August 12, 1920.

9. Ibid.

10. HS to AS, Aug. 19, 1920 (postmark), Helene Schweitzer Bresslau Correspondence, 1919–1939, with "Jeudi" written at the top.

11. Brabazon, *Albert Schweitzer*, 324.

12. Mühlstein, *Helene Schweitzer Bresslau*, 189.

13. Marshall and Poling, *Schweitzer*, 149.

14. Schweitzer Miller, foreword to *Die Jahre vor Lambarene*, 6.

15. A. Schweitzer, *Out of My Life and Thought*, 188.

16. Marshall and Poling, *Schweitzer*, 157.

17. Ibid.

18. Nies-Berger, *Albert Schweitzer as I Knew Him*, 27–29.

19. Ibid., 33.

20. Audoynaud, *Le Docteur Schweitzer et son hôpital*, 73.

21. Ibid.

22. Seaver, *Albert Schweitzer*, 88.

23. A. Schweitzer, *Out of My Life and Thought*, 207.

24. H. Schweitzer, "Dr. Schweitzer's Hospital Work in Lambarene," unpublished lecture delivered in America, 1938, SU-Lemke Collection, 4.

25. Schweitzer left Strasbourg for Lambarene on February 14, 1924, and returned to Europe in mid-August 1927.

26. A. Schweitzer, *Predigten, 1898–1948* (Sermons, 1898–1948), Nov. 24, 1918, 1212.

27. *New English Bible*, John 11:25–26.

28. Heuss-Knapp, *Ausblick vom Münsterturm*, 104.

29. A. Schweitzer, *Out of My Life and Thought*, 185.

30. *New English Bible*, Ruth 1:16–17.

31. Kristeva, "An Interview with Julia Kristeva," 10.

32. Horst, "Le presbytère du quai Saint-Nicolas," 176, emphasis added.

33. Ernst Bresslau (1877–1935) would emigrate with his family from Germany to Brazil in 1934 and die of a heart attack a year later.

34. Minder, "Internement et retour en Alsace," 197.

35. A. Schweitzer, *Out of My Life and Thought*, 185.

36. Ibid., 190.

37. Ibid., 197.

38. Ibid., 198.

39. Minder, "Internement et retour en Alsace," 200.

40. AS to HS, "Easter Sunday Evening 23," Helene Schweitzer Bresslau Correspondence, 1919–1939.

41. AS to HS, Oct. 21, 1921, Helene Schweitzer Bresslau Correspondence, 1919–1939.

42. AS to HS, Dec. 23, 1921, Helene Schweitzer Bresslau Correspondence, 1919–1939.

43. Sorg, introduction to volume 1 of *Correspondance, 1901–1912*, 1:32.

44. A Schweitzer, *Out of My Life and Thought*, 198.

45. Comment by W. Hubert le Peet, quoted in Seaver, *Albert Schweitzer*, 86.

46. Mühlstein, *Helene Schweitzer Bresslau*, 193.

47. For further details on this challenging period, see ibid., 196–98.

48. Rhena Schweitzer Miller to James Brabazon, May 24, 1974, quoted in Brabazon, *Albert Schweitzer*, 341.

49. Brabazon, *Albert Schweitzer*, 341.

50. AS to HS, Feb. 14 (Letters I and II), 17, and 20, 1924, Helene Schweitzer Correspondence, 1919–1939.

51. HS to AS, Mar. 1924, quoted in Mühlstein, *Helene Schweitzer Bresslau*, 199.

52. AS to HS, Feb. 14, 1924, Helene Schweitzer Bresslau Correspondence, 1919–1939.

53. HS to AS, Oct. 11, 1924, quoted in Mühlstein, *Helene Schweitzer Bresslau*, 203.

54. AS to HS, Nov. 9, 1924, Helene Schweitzer Bresslau Correspondence, 1919–1939.

55. AS to HS, Aug. 7, 1924, Helene Schweitzer Bresslau Correspondence, 1919–1939.

56. A. Schweitzer, *Out of My Life and Thought*, 214.

57. HS to Breitkopf & Härtel, Sept. 22, 1930, Helene Schweitzer Correspondence with Breitkopf & Härtel, 1928–1932, ERJ-716, Nachlass A. Schweitzer, ZBZ.

58. This illness can only be surmised from a note Helene wrote in the upper-left corner of the letter quoted at the end of the paragraph. It is possible that Helene wrote this note to mask her tuberculosis.

59. AS to HS, Nov. 26, 1929, Helene Schweitzer Bresslau Correspondence, 1919–1939.

60. Secretan, "News from Lambarene," 15.

61. H. Schweitzer, "News from Lambarene," 13. See also A. Schweitzer, "News from Lambarene."

62. H. Schweitzer, "News from Lambarene," 14.

63. Ibid., 12.

64. Woytt-Secretan, "Souvenirs d'une infirmière," 232.

65. Ibid., 234.

66. H. Schweitzer, "Dr. Schweitzer's Hospital Work in Lambarene," 22. It should be noted, however, that Helene made an error in remembering the "Swiss lady doctor" on the 1931 expedition as Ilse Schnabel. In fact, it was Dr. Anna Schmitz

who accomplished this six-week journey with Emma Haussknecht. See Haussknecht, "On Trek."

67. Brabazon, *Albert Schweitzer*, 357.

68. Oermann, *Albert Schweitzer, 1875–1965*, 216.

69. HS to Marie Secretan, July 14, 1930, Helene Schweitzer Korrespondenz, DASZ.

70. HS to Breitkopf & Härtel, July 13, 1930, ERJ-716, Helene Schweitzer Correspondence with Breitkopf & Härtel, 1928–1932, ZBZ.

71. HS to Dr. Priestman, Hamburg, Tropenkrankenhaus (Hamburg, Tropical Disease Hospital), n.d. (c. 1930), Markus Brandes Private Collection.

72. *Würzburger General-Anzeiger*. "Bei Albert Schweitzer 'zwischen Wasser und Urwald.'"

73. H. Schweitzer, "Dr. Schweitzer's Hospital Work in Lambarene," 32.

5. Against the Current

1. HS to George Seaver, Mar. 24, 1945, quoted in Seaver, *Albert Schweitzer*, 159–60.

2. See H. Schweitzer, "Journal, 1941," SU-Lemke Collection; the details given here of Helene's journey from Lisbon to Lambarene rely on journal entries made between July 23 and August 2, 1941.

3. Klemmer, "Lisbon—Gateway to Warring Europe," 259.

4. Koestler, *Scum of the Earth*, 275.

5. H. Schweitzer, "Journal, 1941," June 10–July 8, 1941.

6. See H. Schweitzer, *Tagebuch*, 1913–15, Apr. 7, 1913, 13.

7. See, for example, HS to Cary and Harry Bresslau, July 18, 1913, quoted in Mühlstein, *Helene Schweitzer Bresslau*, 150.

8. H. Schweitzer, "News from Lambarene," 12.

9. See "Journal, 1940" and "Journal, 1941." Helene was in frequent contact with her daughter and numerous friends throughout 1940–41.

10. HS to Luise Bresslau-Hoff, Nov. 18, 1940, quoted in Mühlstein, *Helene Schweitzer Bresslau*, 242.

11. Ernst Bresslau was baptized as a child, along with his sister and brother, by a Lutheran pastor in 1886. Obviously, this baptism had no influence on his social or professional status in Germany under the rule of the Third Reich.

12. HS to George Seaver, Mar. 24, 1945, quoted in Seaver, *Albert Schweitzer*, 160.

13. HS to Luise Bresslau-Hoff, July 9, 1941, quoted in Mühlstein, *Helene Schweitzer Bresslau*, 245.

14. H. Schweitzer, "Journal, 1941," July 31, 1941.

15. Ibid., Aug. 2, 1941.

16. At age twenty, Rhena had traveled with her mother to Lambarene for a six-week visit in 1939. This was her first experience of the hospital she would one day help to manage.

17. A. Schweitzer, "Cahier 47, 1941," Aug. 2, 1941, SU-Schweitzer Papers. Note that Mr. Louvet-Jardin, who managed a lumber company near Lambarene, was in his later years treated by Dr. Walter Munz at the Schweitzer Hospital (Walter Munz in discussion with the author, Aug. 31, 2013).

18. H. Schweitzer, "Journal, 1941," Aug. 2, 1941. The women mentioned here are Emma Haussknecht and Dr. Ilse Schnabel.

19. Skillings, "Postscript," 259.

20. I am grateful to Jo and Walter Munz for sharing with me on August 31, 2013, their memories of this mission station where they stayed overnight in 1969 and enjoyed Father Bromberg's enormous enthusiasm for the Schweitzers and their work.

21. H. Schweitzer, "Dr. Schweitzer's Hospital Work in Lambarene," unpublished lecture delivered in America, 1937–38, SU-Lemke Collection.

22. I have relied on Helene Schweitzer's hand-written notes at the top of the first page of the typescript of her lecture in the SU-Lemke Collection, where dates and venues suggest a different or additional schedule than that found in Mühlstein, *Helene Schweitzer Bresslau*, 237–38. Mühlstein places the beginning of the lecture tour in Baltimore in November 1938 and brings it to a close before Christmas. Although it is certainly possible that the dates written on Helene's typescript—beginning on December 10, 1937, and running through March 13, 1938—may have changed, it is unlikely that all of them were cancelled. More likely, there were two lecture tours: one early in the winter of 1937–38 in the Northeast and another at the end of 1938 that took Helene Schweitzer to the Midwest. A combination of Helene's typescript and Albert's letter dated December 19, 1938 (quoted later), supports this interpretation.

23. Oermann, *Albert Schweitzer*, 224–25.

24. Mühlstein, *Helene Schweitzer Bresslau*, 238.

25. I am using the name that Helene Schweitzer would have known, "Kristallnacht," but it should be noted that the more appropriate name for this historical event in Germany today is "Pogromnacht."

26. Note that this headline erroneously implies restraint on the part of German propaganda minister Joseph Goebbels. In fact, he was the mastermind behind these coordinated riots.

27. AS to HS, Dec. 19, 1938, Helene Schweitzer Bresslau Correspondence, 1919–1939, SU-Schweitzer Papers. Note that this letter confirms that Helene was, indeed, engaged in a lecture tour at the end of 1938.

28. A. Schweitzer, *The Hospital in Lambarene during the War Years*, quoted in Skillings, "Postscript," 260.

29. See the foreword to this book by Sylvia Stevens-Edouard, which focuses on the Albert Schweitzer Fellowship.

30. See chapter 4 of this book.

31. See chapter 3 of this book.

32. Examples include their nephew Pierre-Paul Schweitzer, who survived deportation to Buchenwald, and Helene's girlhood friend Bertha Lenel, who was deported from Freiburg im Breisgau to the French camp Gurs. One of Schweitzer's first coworkers in Africa, Dr. Victor Nessmann, was arrested for his activities in the French Resistance, tortured, and murdered in 1944. Prior to this shocking and tragic loss, the Schweitzers' dear friend Margrit Jacobi died in Theriesienstadt, and Helene's beloved cousin Johanna Engel took her own life rather than be subjected to a similar fate.

33. Christiane Engel, in discussion with the author, Sept. 27, 2013.

34. HS to Luise Bresslau-Hoff, Nov. 28, 1943, quoted in Mühlstein, *Helene Schweitzer Bresslau*, 248.

35. H. Schweitzer, "Journal, 1941," Sept. 30, 1941.

36. HS to Luise Bresslau-Hoff, Dec. 16, 1941, quoted in Mühlstein, *Helene Schweitzer Bresslau*, 247.

37. Woytt-Secretan, "Vor fünfzig Jahren hielt Albert Schweitzer," Mar. 21, 1982.

38. A. Schweitzer, "One Hundredth Anniversary Memorial Address," 55–56. Note that the gender-specific usage of the term *man* in this 1948 translation should be interpreted to mean "person."

39. Ibid., 59.

40. Note that although Americans continue to use the name "Holocaust," the preferred name internationally for Hitler's systematic murder of six million Jews and other "undesirables" is the Hebrew "Shoah."

41. World War II is generally understood to have begun with Germany's invasion of Poland on September 1, 1939.

42. Suermann, *Albert Schweitzer als "homo politicus,"* 168.

43. Ibid., 173.

44. *The Deputy* by Rolf Hochhuth critiques the Catholic Church's position (or lack thereof) during World War II.

45. A. Schweitzer, preface to *The Deputy*, 7.

46. A. Schweitzer, *Out of My Life and Thought*, 225–27.

47. AS to HB, Aug. 28, 1911, *Correspondance, 1901–1912*, 3:559.A.S.

48. This international conference in the Spanish city of Algesiras took place from January to April 1906 with the goal of securing Moroccan ports.

49. HB to AS, Aug. 26, 1911, *Correspondance, 1901–1912*, 3:558.H.B.

50. Ibid.

51. A. Schweitzer, "Religion in Modern Civilization," 359. Note that the translator of this summary is unknown. Could it have been Helene?

52. It should be noted that thinking and the dangers of its absence became cornerstones of philosopher Hannah Arendt's postwar philosophical writings related to Hitler's Germany, such as *Eichmann in Jerusalem* (1960) and *Origins of Totalitarianism* (1973).

53. A. Schweitzer, "Religion in Modern Civilization," 364.

54. Ibid., 366.

55. The Freedom Prize of the German Booksellers Association has been one of the highest honors in Germany since its inception in 1950.

56. Heuss, "Laudatio," 4.

57. See Oermann, *Albert Schweitzer*, 217.

58. A. Schweitzer, *The Hospital in Lambarene during the War Years*, quoted in Skillings, "Postscript," 259.

59. Jennings, *La France libre fut Africaine*.

60. The Schweitzer Hospital's links and contributions to the larger goals of Charles de Gaulle's Free France directed from London deserve further study. Here my intention is simply to contextualize life in Lambarene as more engaged during the war than has been previously understood.

61. Note that the first radio station in the town of Lambarene became a reality in 1938. However, with the outbreak of war in 1939, communication "was completely severed" and not resumed until support was declared for Charles de Gaulle's French Provisional Government in London in 1942. See Seaver, *Albert Schweitzer*, 156–58.

62. Heuss, "Laudatio," 2.

63. Note that as of 1933 Schweitzer cancelled all concert dates in Germany and vowed not to return to that country as long as Hitler was alive. See Marshall and Poling, *Schweitzer*, 198, based on personal conversations with Schweitzer that took place in July 1962.

64. Heuss, "Laudatio," 4.

65. AS to HS, Jan. 22, 1936, and Feb. 20, 1936, Helene Schweitzer Bresslau Correspondence, 1919–1939. Note that Helene's letters related to this issue were not preserved.

66. Mühlstein, *Helene Schweitzer Bresslau*, 232.

67. AS to HS, Aug. 7, 1936, Helene Schweitzer Bresslau Correspondence, 1919–1939.

68. Seaver, *Albert Schweitzer*, 156.

69. In addition to the vegetable gardens and plantings, Emma Haussknecht supervised a number of building projects in Schweitzer's absences, including the last houses constructed in the leprosy village just months before her death in March 1956. See Silver, "Emma Haussknecht," AS-Gunsbach.

70. H. Schweitzer, "Journal, 1941," Aug. 3–4, 1941.

71. Office of the Gouverneur Général de l'Afrique Equatoriale Française to AS, Brazzaville, Jan. 29 and Apr. 20, 1946, Dossier 18.4, Nachlass A. Schweitzer, ZBZ.

72. AS to Governeur Général (Jean Louis Marie André) Soucadoux, Oct. 3, 1946, Dossier 18.4., Nachlass A. Schweitzer, ZBZ.

73. H. Schweitzer, "Journal, 1946–47," Sept. 8–11, 1946.

74. See H. Schweitzer, "Journal, 1946–47," Sept. 8–Oct. 9, 1946. Ironically, A. Biedermann's address, as written on the first page of this journal (22 place de la Gare), is next to the Salle Albert Schweitzer (Albert Schweitzer Room). This quiet, welcoming space was inaugurated in 2013 at the Strasbourg train station in conjunction with the Schweitzer Centennial as a place to comfort travelers in need.

75. HS to George Seaver, Mar. 24, 1945, quoted in Seaver, *Albert Schweitzer*, 159–60.

76. HS to Luise Bresslau-Hoff, Apr. 30, 1945, quoted in Mühlstein, *Helene Schweitzer Bresslau*, 250.

6. Madame Schweitzer in the Age of Obscurity

1. In 1947, apart from his brief visit to Gunsbach that lasted less than two weeks in January–February 1939, Albert Schweitzer had been in Lambarene since February 1937.

2. HS to Luise Bresslau-Hoff, June 9, 1944, suspension points in original, quoted in Mühlstein, *Helene Schweitzer Bresslau*, 250.

3. Brabazon quotes a letter from Helene dated June 25, 1948, to poet-biographer Hermann Hagedorn in which she reflects on her return to Königsfeld: "I was pretty miserable in Europe, more than I can tell you" (Collection of American Literature, Beinecke Rare Books and Manuscript Library, Yale Univ., New Haven, CT, quoted in Brabazon, *Albert Schweitzer*, 403).

4. Albert Schweitzer baptized Rhena's children—Monique, Philippe, Christiane, and Catherine Eckert—in the living room of their home on November 7, 1948.

5. HS to Luise Bresslau-Hoff, Jan. 1, 1946, quoted in Mühlstein, *Helene Schweitzer Bresslau*, 250.

6. See Mühlstein, *Helene Schweitzer Bresslau*, 251, regarding Mühlstein's communication with Carolina Bresslau-Hoff in 1994.

7. AS to HB, Dec. 21, 1904, in *Correspondance, 1901–1912*, 1:89.A.S.

8. AS to HB, Midnight 1904–5, in *Correspondance, 1901–1912*, 1:92.A.S.

9. It should be noted that more than ten thousand letters from Albert Schweitzer to numerous correspondents exist in the Archives Centrales Schweitzer Gunsbach, and hundreds more can be found in the Albert Schweitzer Papers in the Special Collections Research Center, Syracuse University Libraries. A count of Helene's letters available for study in public archives amounts to less than one percent of this figure.

10. As noted earlier, these texts became *The Quest for the Historical Jesus* and The *Philosophy of Civilization*, respectively.

11. In 1947, Helene could not know that Albert's manuscripts, typescripts, notes, and edits revealing the extent of her work would eventually be housed in the Manuscript Division of the Zentralbibliothek Zürich.

12. The Antje Bultmann Lemke Collection Relating to Albert Schweitzer at the Special Collections Research Center, Syracuse University Libraries, includes numerous journals written by Helene Schweitzer Bresslau between 1893 and 1951. Though most of the journals are small in size, these writings total more than one thousand pages. Note that this material did not enter these archives until 2010.

13. H. Schweitzer, "Journal, 1918," Mar. 27, 1918, SU-Lemke Collection. In German, the quoted stanza reads as follows:

Unfähig zur Arbeit sitze ich und weine
Bis hilfreiche Seelen sich meiner erbarmen
Drin hämmern und schaffen für uns die Armen
Im Parke liege ich träumend alleine.

14. H. Schweitzer, "Journal, 1941," July 12, 1941. I am grateful to the eldest child, the now-octogenarian Eliane Guillod-Kaltenrieder of Switzerland, who was able to name the ship on which her family traveled with Helene Schweitzer on board.

15. *LIFE*, "'The Greatest Man in the World,'" 95. It should be noted that although Helene was of Jewish descent, she had been baptized by a Lutheran pastor as a child. As far as we know, she did not practice Judaism in her adult life.

16. Arnold, "The Greatest Man in the World," 324.

17. Ibid.

18. Brabazon, *Albert Schweitzer*, 398. Reverend Joy's photos from that trip illustrate both articles mentioned here.

19. See the Melvin Arnold Papers, Albert Schweitzer Files 1945–1953, Ando-ver-Harvard Theological Library, Harvard Divinity School, Cambridge, MA.

20. H. Schweitzer, "Dr. Schweitzer's Hospital Work in Lambarene," unpublished lecture delivered in America, 1937–38, SU-Lemke Collection, 1.

21. H. Schweitzer, "With Schweitzer in Africa," 345–46.

22. Both magazines had been around for decades, but they became more popular than ever after the war.

23. Mellon, *My Road to Deschapelles*, 42.

24. Travers, "Angel of the Jungle," 101.

25. *Time*, "Religion: Reverence for Life," 72.

26. *Daily Boston Globe*, "A Visitor with No Message." Note that Schweitzer spoke little or no English. Fragments of dialogue such as this one came through American interpreters, whose tone may—or may not—have colored the meaning.

27. American missionary friends Myrta and Emory Ross hosted this event under the auspices of the Federal Council of Churches of Christ in America.

28. *Badische Zeitung* (Freiburg, Germany), "Frau Helene Schweitzer sprach in Freiburg," quoted in Fleischhack, *Helene Schweitzer*, 9.

29. See H. Schweitzer, *"Lebenslauf,* 1954," DASZ.

30. Ibid.

31. Filmed by Erica Anderson and directed by Jerome Hill, *Albert Schweitzer* won the Academy Award for best documentary feature in 1958.

32. See Brabazon, *Albert Schweitzer*, 445–47, for a detailed account of this event.

33. Oswald, *Mon oncle Albert Schweitzer*, 63.

34. Ibid., 139.

35. HS to Herr von Schleintz, Jan. 19, 1955, Markus Brandes Private Collection.

36. Mühlstein, *Helene Schweitzer Bresslau*, 266.

37. H. Schweitzer, "News from Lambarene," 14.

38. H. Schweitzer, "Journal, 1941," Aug. 15, 1941.

39. See SU-Lemke Collection for Helene's journals from 1950 and 1951.

40. AS to Erica Anderson, June 8, 1956, Erica Anderson Correspondence, 1950–1965, SU-Schweitzer Papers.

41. Zweig, *Greatness Revisited*, 67–68.

42. Quoted in Woytt-Secretan, "Introduction," n.p.

43. H. Schweitzer, "Journal, 1945," Aug. 5, 1945.

44. Sonja Müller Poteau, in discussion with the author, Feb. 13, 2013.

45. Ibid.

46. See Cousins, *Anatomy of an Illness.*

47. It should be noted that among Schweitzer's burdens in the 1950s were some Americans' efforts to portray him as a Communist.

48. At Norman Cousins's urging, Schweitzer had agreed to use his moral authority to make a public statement in opposition to atomic weapons. "Peace or Atomic War? A Declaration of Conscience" was broadcast on Radio Oslo and 140 other radio stations worldwide on April 23, 1957. Mühlstein notes that Helene assisted Schweitzer during the preparation of his speech, especially with regard to English translations of scientific articles and in concurring with the final form of his remarks (*Helene Schweitzer Bresslau*, 267–68).

49. Quoted in Cousins, *Dr. Schweitzer of Lambarene*, 109.

50. H. Schweitzer, "Journal, 1951," Nov. 23, 1951.

51. Kik, "Diary Entry," 12.

52. Schempp, "Helene Schweitzer," n.p.

53. See the Winnifred Wirckau Nachlass (Papers), DASZ.

54. Tau quoted in Mühlstein, *Helene Schweitzer Bresslau*, 264.

55. See H. Schweitzer, "Journal, 1950."

56. Woytt, "Helene Bresslau," 22.

57. W. Munz, *Albert Schweitzer dans la mémoire des Africains*, 154.

58. These letters are archived in the Erica Anderson Correspondence, 1950–1965.

59. AS to Erica Anderson, June 6, 1957, Erica Anderson Correspondence, 1950–1965.

Afterword

With thanks to my daughter, Lea Mühlstein, and her partner, Joshua Edelman, who polished my English. Translations from the German are my own unless otherwise noted.

1. Cesbron, *Albert Schweitzer Begegnungen*, 32.

2. Illies, *1913 Der Sommer des Jahrhunderts*, 99. The literal translation of Schweitzer's dissertation title is "The Psychiatric Evaluation of Jesus."

3. Quoted in Seaver, *Albert Schweitzer*, 160.

4. Sontag, *Krankheit als Metapher*, 5.

5. Meyer, *Jüdische Identität in der Moderne*, 133.

Bibliography

Naming women of the past as authors in bibliographies presents particular challenges. Please note that works by Helene Schweitzer Bresslau written prior to her marriage in June 1912 can be located here under "Bresslau, Helene." For works beyond that date, she is listed under the name she used most often in her published writings and in most of her letters written from midlife onward: "Schweitzer, Helene." Likewise, Marie Secretan's writings are listed under either her maiden name "Secretan" or her married name, "Woytt-Secretan," depending on date of publication.

Primary Sources: Archives and Collections

Albert Schweitzer Papers. Special Collections Research Center, Syracuse University Libraries.

    Erica Anderson Correspondence, 1950–1965.

    Helene Schweitzer Bresslau Correspondence, 1919–1939.

    Schweitzer, Albert. "Cahier 47 d'Albert Schweitzer." Unpublished document, 1941.

Antje Bultmann Lemke Collection Relating to Albert Schweitzer. Special Collections Research Center, Syracuse University Libraries.

    Schweitzer, Helene. "Dr. Schweitzer's Hospital Work in Lambarene." Unpublished lecture presented in diverse venues in the United States, 1937–38.

    ———. Journals and day books, 1918–51.

Archives Centrales Schweitzer Gunsbach.

    Lettres de Marie Roumanille-Blanc.

    Silver, Ali. "Emma Haussknecht." Unpublished document, n.d.

Archives départementales des Hautes-Pyrénées, 1917–18. Tarbes, France.

Colby College Special Collections. Waterville, ME.

Collection Marcel Bonnet, 1922–2007. Bibliothèque Municipale Joseph-Roumanille of Saint-Rémy-de-Provence.

Mayor of Saint-Rémy to his citizens. Mar. 13, 1915; Apr. 24, 1915; Nov. 29, 1915. Material related to Dr. Jacques Scheib, Dr. Albert Schweitzer, and the Dépôt d'Austro-Allemands de Saint-Rémy. Shelf M-261.

Schweitzer, Albert. "Declaration Alsace-Lorraine." May 30, 1918.

———. "Deux caisses avec adresses et un paquet, déposés au Sequestre au Dépôt de St. Rémy de Provence par moi souligné Albert Schweitzer" (Statement of goods sequestered). N.d. (c. spring 1918). Arch. Bouches du Rhône.

Collection of American Literature. Beinecke Rare Books and Manuscript Library. Yale University, New Haven, CT.

Deutsches Albert Schweitzer Zentrum, Frankfurt am Main, Germany.

Helene Schweitzer Korrespondenz.

Schweitzer, Helene. "*Lebenslauf.*" Unpublished document, 1954.

Winnifred Wirckau Nachlass (Papers).

Markus Brandes Private Collection.

Melvin Arnold Papers. Andover-Harvard Theological Library. Harvard Divinity School, Cambridge, MA.

Albert Schweitzer Files, 1945–1953.

Schweitzer, Helene. *Tagebuch* (diary), 1913–15. Unpublished document. Private collection.

Zentralbibliothek Zürich.

Helene Schweitzer Correspondence with Breitkopf & Härtel, 1928–1932. ERJ-716. Nachlass A. Schweitzer (A. Schweitzer Papers).

Nachlass A. Schweitzer (A. Schweitzer Papers).

Secondary Sources

Alsace-Lorraine Constitution of 1911. In *Quellen zur Deutschen Innenpolitik 1890–1914*, edited by Hans Fenske, 389–92. Darmstadt, Germany: Wissenschaftliche Buchgesellschaft, 1991. English version available at http://mjp.univ-perp.fr/constit/de1911alsacelor.htm.

Anderson, Erica. *Albert Schweitzer.* 1957. Independent documentary film directed by Jerome Hill. DVD, 83 min. Remastered and restored by Roan Archival Group, 2005, and by the International Association for Schweitzer of Lambarene, 2013.

————. *The Schweitzer Album: A Portrait in Words and Pictures.* New York: Harper & Row, 1965.

Arendt, Hannah. *Eichmann in Jerusalem: A Report on the Banality of Evil.* Introduction by Amos Elon. 1960. Reprint. New York: Penguin, 2006.

————. *The Origins of Totalitarianism.* New York: Harcourt, Brace, Jovanovich, 1973.

Arnold, Matthieu. *Albert Schweitzer: Les années alsaciennes, 1875–1913.* Strasbourg: La Nuée Bleue, 2013.

Arnold, Melvin. "The Greatest Man in the World." Special edition, *Christian Register* 126, no. 8 (1947): 324–27.

Audoynaud, André. *Le Docteur Schweitzer et son hôpital à Lambaréné: L'envers d'un mythe.* Paris: Editions L'Harmattan, 2005.

Badische Zeitung (Freiburg, Germany). "Frau Helene Schweitzer sprach in Freiburg." June 15, 1952.

Barry, John M. "The Site of Origin of the 1918 Influenza Pandemic and Its Public Health Implications." *Journal of Translational Medicine* 2, no. 3 (2004): 1–4. doi: 10.1186/1479-5876-2-3.

Bianquis, J. *In Memoriam: Madame Edouard Lantz (née Valentine Ehrhardt), 1873–1906.* 8th ed. Paris: Société des Missions Evangéliques, 1929.

Bixler, J. Seelye. "The Miracle of Lambarene: A Guest Editorial." *Saturday Review,* Jan. 15, 1955.

Brabazon, James. *Albert Schweitzer.* 2nd ed. Syracuse, NY: Syracuse Univ. Press, 2000.

Bresslau, Helene. "Gott." *Protestantenblatt,* 1904, n.p.

————. "Strassburger Mütterheim." *Blätter für das Straßburger Armenwesen,* no. 5 (Mar. 1908): 15.

Cameron, James. *Points of Departure: Experiment in Biography.* 1967. Reprint. London: Granta Books, 2006.

Cesbron, Gilbert. *Albert Schweitzer Begegnungen.* Berlin: Union, 1957.

Cousins, Norman. *Anatomy of an Illness as Perceived by the Patient.* 1979. Reprint. New York: Norton, 2005.

————. *Dr. Schweitzer of Lambarene.* New York: Harper and Row, 1960.

Couturier de Chefdebois, Isabelle. "Notre-Dame de Garaison." Preface to *Notre-Dame de Lourdes.* Montreal: Centre Marial Canadien, 1952. At http://biblisem.net/etudes/coutnotr.htm.

Daily Boston Globe. "A Visitor with No Message." July 30, 1949.

Denzel, Sieglinde, and Susanne Naumann. "Jenseits in Afrika, Helene Schweitzer." In *Ich bin was ich bin: Frauen neben grossen Theologen und Religionsphilosophen des 20. Jahrhunderts*, edited by Esther Röhr, 104–35. Gütersloh, Germany: Gütersloher, 1997.

Fleischhack, Marianne. *Helene Schweitzer: Einblick in das Leben einer Frau, der es gegeben war, sich selbstlos und aufopfernd einem grossen Werk der Nächstenliebe hinzugeben.* Konstanz, Germany: Christliche, 1968.

Grandhomme, Jean-Noël. "Les Alsaciens-Lorrains dans les camps d'internement du Finistère (1914–1919)." *Annales de Bretagne et des Pays de l'Ouest* 109, no. 4 (2002): 163–75.

Haussknecht, Emma. "On Trek." *British Bulletin of Dr. Schweitzer's Hospital Fund*, no. 7 (Spring 1932): 1–12.

Heuss, Theodor. "Laudatio." Speech in honor of Albert Schweitzer's Friedenspreis, delivered in Frankfurt, Germany, Sept. 16, 1951. At http://www.friedenspreis-des-deutschen-buchhandels.de/sixcms/media.php/1290/1951_schweitzer.pdf.

Heuss-Knapp, Elly. *Ausblick vom Münsterturm.* Tübingen, Germany: Rainer Wunderlich, 1952.

Horst, Madeleine. "Le presbytère du quai Saint-Nicolas." In Minder, *Rayonnement d'Albert Schweitzer*, 176–78.

Igersheim, François. "Le 'Reichsland,' un pays d'Empire." In Jung and Thiébaut, *1870–1910: Alsace*, 30–35.

———. "Un tournant pour l'Alsace." In Jung and Thiébaut, *1870–1910: Alsace*, 4–7.

Illies, Florian. *1913 Der Sommer des Jahrhunderts.* Frankfurt am Main: Fischer, 2012.

Jennings, Eric. *La France libre fut Africaine.* Paris: Perrin, 2014.

Jung, Dominique, and Jean-Marc Thiébaut, eds. *1870–1910: Alsace, le grand tournant.* Special issue of *Saisons d'Alsace*, no. 45 (Sept. 2010).

Kik, Richard. "Diary Entry Dated August 1956." *Rundbrief für den Freundeskreis von Albert Schweitzer*, no. 11 (Aug. 1957): 12.

Kingsley, Mary. *Travels in West Africa.* Washington, DC: National Geographic Society, 2002.

Klemmer, Harvey. "Lisbon—Gateway to Warring Europe." *National Geographic* 80, no. 2 (1941): 259–76.

Koestler, Arthur. *Scum of the Earth.* London: Jonathan Cape, 1941.

Kristeva, Julia. "An Interview with Julia Kristeva." Interview by Kathleen O'Grady. In "Julia Kristeva, 1966–96; Aesthetics, Politics, Ethics," special issue of *Parallax*, no. 8 (July–Sept. 1998): 5–16. At http://www.cddc.vt.edu/feminism/kristeva.html.

Laurent, François. *1914–1918: Alsaciens-Lorrains otages en France; Souvenirs d'un lorrain interné en France et en Suisse pendant la guerre.* Strasbourg: Presses Universitaires de Strasbourg, 1998.

Lee, Hermione. *Virginia Woolf's Nose: Essays in Biography.* Princeton, NJ: Princeton Univ. Press, 2007.

LIFE. "'The Greatest Man in the World': That Is What Some People Call Albert Schweitzer, Jungle Philosopher." Oct. 6, 1947.

Marshall, George, and David Poling. *Schweitzer: A Biography.* Baltimore: John Hopkins Univ. Press, 2000.

Mauran, Hervé, and Jean-Marie Ehret. "Les camps d'évacués alsaciens en Ardèche, 1914–1919." Parts 1 and 2. *La Revue du Vivarais* 102, no. 734 (1998): 95–125, and no. 735 (1998): 145–80.

Mauron, Marie. "Histoire de notre temps: La captivité du docteur Schweitzer." *Lettres françaises*, no. 556 (Feb. 17–24, 1955): 5.

Mellon, Gwen Grant. *My Road to Deschapelles.* New York: Continuum, 1998.

Meyer, Michael. *Jüdische Identität in der Moderne.* Translated by Anne Ruth Frank-Strauss. Frankfurt am Main: Jüdischer, 1992.

Minder, Robert. "Internement et retour en Alsace." In Minder, *Rayonnement d'Albert Schweitzer*, 189–202.

———, ed. *Rayonnement d'Albert Schweitzer: 34 Etudes et 100 Témoignages.* Colmar, France: Alsatia, 1975.

Morel, Léon. "Au Gabon avant l'arrivée du Docteur Schweitzer." In Minder, *Rayonnement d'Albert Schweitzer*, 185–89.

Mühlstein, Verena. *Helene Schweitzer Bresslau: Ein Leben für Lambarene.* Munich: Beck, 1998.

Munz, Jo, and Walter Munz. *Albert Schweitzer's Lambarene: A Legacy of Humanity for Our World Today.* Translated and edited by Patti M. Marxsen. Rockland, ME: Penobscot Press, 2010.

Munz, Walter. *Albert Schweitzer dans la mémoire des Africains.* Etudes Schweitzeriennes no. 5. Coproduction of l'Association Française des Amis d'Albert Schweitzer and the Fondation Internationale de l'Hôpital Albert Schweitzer de Lambaréné. Strasbourg: Editions Oberlin, 1994.

Originally published as *Albert Schweitzer im Gedächtnis der Afrikaner in meiner Erinnerung*. Bern: Haupt, 1991.

Nessmann, Victor. *Avec Albert Schweitzer de 1924–1926: Lettres de Lambaréné*. Etudes Schweitzeriennes no. 6. Coproduction of l'Association Française des Amis d'Albert Schweitzer and the Fondation Internationale de l'Hôpital Albert Schweitzer de Lambaréné. Strasbourg: Editions Oberlin, 1994.

The New English Bible: Oxford Study Edition. Edited by Samuel Sandmel. New York: Oxford University Press, 1976.

New York Times. "NAZIS SMASH, BURN AND LOOT JEWISH SHOPS AND TEMPLES UNTIL GOEBBELS CALLS HALT." Nov. 10, 1938.

———. "SCHWEITZER'S WIFE HONORED WITH HIM." July 19, 1949.

Nies-Berger, Edouard. 1995. *Albert Schweitzer as I Knew Him*. Translated by Rollin Smith. Hillsdale, NY: Pendragon Press, 2003.

Oermann, Nils Ole. *Albert Schweitzer, 1875–1965: Eine Biographie*. Munich: Beck, 2010.

Oswald, Suzanne. *Mon oncle Albert Schweitzer*. Preface by Robert Minder. Translated by Madeleine Horst. Colmar, France: Editions Alsatia, 1974.

Printz, Othon. *Avant Schweitzer: Les génies tutélaires de Lambaréné*. Colmar, France: Do Bentzinger, 2004.

Rehm, Max. *Rudolf Schwander und Kurt Blum: Wegbahner neuzeitlicher Kommunalpolitik aus dem Elsass*. Stuttgart: Kohlhammer, 1974.

Rinderknecht, Peter. "Helene Schweitzer: Eine Frau eines grossen Mannes." *Rundbrief für den Freundeskreis von Albert Schweitzer*, no. 11 (Aug. 1957): 14–18.

Rogers, Miriam. "Madame Schweitzer." In *A Tribute on the Ninetieth Birthday of Albert Schweitzer*, edited by Dr. Edward Prince Booth, Dr. Homer A. Jack, Mrs. Miriam Rogers, and Mrs. Robert Alfred Vogt, 35–36. Boston: Friends of Albert Schweitzer, January 14, 1965.

Scheib, Jacques. "Mémoires d'un médecin." Part 2. *L'Outre-Fôret* 3, no. 83 (1993): 1–33.

Schempp, Otto. "Helene Schweitzer: Am liebsten incognito." *Christ und Welt*, no. 42 (Oct. 19, 1956): n.p.

Schweitzer, Albert. *The African Sermons*. Edited and translated by Steven E. G. Melamed. Syracuse, NY: Syracuse Univ. Press, 2003.

———. *Albert Schweitzer—Essential Writings*. Selected with an introduction by James Brabazon. Maryknoll, NY: Orbis Books, 2005.

———. *Geschichte der Leben-Jesu-Forschung*. 2nd ed. Tübingen: Mohr Siebeck, 1984. Originally published in 1913.

———. *The Hospital in Lambarene during the War Years, 1939–45* (pamphlet). Boston: Albert Schweitzer Fellowship, 1947.

———. *J. S. Bach*. Translated by Ernest Newman. 2 vols. New York: Macmillan, 1950. Originally published in French in 1905 and in German in 1908.

———. *More from the Primeval Forest*. Translated by C. T. Campion. London: Adam & Charles Black, 1931. Originally published in German in 1931.

———. "News from Lambarene: Letter from Dr. Schweitzer, January 8, 1930." *British Bulletin of Dr. Schweitzer's Hospital Fund*, no. 4 (Spring 1930): 3–11.

———. "One Hundredth Anniversary Memorial Address." In *Goethe: Four Studies by Albert Schweitzer*, translated by Charles R. Joy, Goethe Bicentennial Edition, 29–60. Boston: Beacon Press, 1949.

———. *On the Edge of the Primeval Forest: Experiences and Observations of a Doctor in Equatorial Africa*. Translated by C. T. Campion. London: Adam & Charles Black, 1921. Originally published in Swedish in 1921.

———. *Out of My Life and Thought: An Autobiography*. Translated by Antje Bultmann Lemke. New York: Holt, 1990. Originally published in German in 1931.

———. "Peace or Atomic War? A Declaration of Conscience." Radio broadcast, Apr. 24, 1957. Printed as an appendix to Norman Cousins, *Dr. Schweitzer of Lambarene*, 227–35. New York: Harper and Row, 1960.

———. *The Philosophy of Civilization*. 2 vols. Translated by C. T. Campion. London: A. & C. Black, 1923. Originally published in German in 1923.

———. *Predigten, 1898–1948*. Edited by Richard Brüllman and Erich Grässer. Munich: Beck, 2001.

———. Preface to *The Deputy* by Rolf Hochhuth, translated by Richard and Clara Winston, 7. New York: Grove Press, 1964. Originally published in German in 1963.

———. *The Quest for the Historical Jesus*. Edited by John Bowden. Translated by John Bowden, J. C. Coates, Susan Cupitt, and W. Montgomery.

Minneapolis: Augsburg Fortress, 2001. Originally published in German in 1906.

———. "Religion in Modern Civilization." *The Christian Century*, Nov. 21 and 28, 1934. Reprinted as an appendix in George Seaver, *Albert Schweitzer: The Man and His Mind*, 359–66. 1947. reprint, New York: Harper Brothers, 1955.

Schweitzer, Albert, and Helene Bresslau. *Albert Schweitzer et Hélène Bresslau: Correspondance, 1901–1912.* Edited and translated by Jean-Paul Sorg. 3 vols. Colmar, France: Do Bentzinger, 2005–11.

———. *Die Jahre vor Lambarene: Briefe von 1902–1912.* Edited by Rhena Schweitzer-Miller and Gustav Woytt. Munich: Beck, 1992.

———. *The Albert Schweitzer–Helene Bresslau Letters 1902–1912.* Edited by Rhena Schweitzer Miller and Gustav Woytt. Translated from the German and edited by Antje Bultmann Lemke. Syracuse, NY: Syracuse Univ. Press, 2003.

Schweitzer, Helene. "News from Lambarene: Letter from Madame Schweitzer January 10, 1930." *British Bulletin of Dr. Schweitzer's Hospital Fund*, no. 4 (Spring 1930): 11–14.

———. "With Schweitzer in Africa." *Christian Century*, Apr. 21, 1948, 345–46.

Schweitzer Miller, Rhena. Foreword to *Die Jahre vor Lambarene: Briefe von 1902–1912*, edited by Rhena Schweitzer Miller and Gustav Woytt, 5–6. Munich: Beck, 1992.

Seaver, George. *Albert Schweitzer: The Man and His Mind.* 1947. Reprint. New York: Harper Brothers, 1955.

Secretan, Marie. "News from Lambarene: Letter from Fräulein Marie Secretan." *British Bulletin of Dr. Schweitzer's Hospital Fund*, no. 4 (Spring 1930): 14–18.

Sieber, Elfriede. "Helene Schweitzer: Frau eines grossen Mannes." *Frauen und Frieden*, no. 11 (1957): n.p.

Skillings, Everett. "Postscript: 1932–1949." In Albert Schweitzer, *Out of My Life and Thought: An Autobiography*, translated by C. T. Campion, 244–74. New York: Holt, Rinehart and Winston, 1961.

Sontag, Susan. *Krankheit als Metapher.* Frankfurt am Main: Fischer, 1992.

Sorg, Jean-Paul. Introductions to volumes 1 and 3 of Albert Schweitzer and Helene Bresslau, *Albert Schweitzer et Hélène Bresslau: Correspondance,*

1901–1912, 3 vols., edited and translated by Jean-Paul Sorg, 1:5–32, 3:5–73. Colmar, France: Do Bentzinger, 2005–11.

Spear, Otto. "Helene Bresslau: Fürsorgearbeit in Strassburg." *Rundbrief für den Freundeskreis von Albert Schweitzer und den Deutschen Hilfsverein*, no. 46 (Nov. 1978): 30–32.

Suermann, Thomas. *Albert Schweitzer als "homo politicus."* Berlin: BWV Berliner-Wissenschaft, 2012.

Time. "Religion: Reverence for Life." July 11, 1949.

Travers, Virginia. "Angel of the Jungle." *Woman Magazine*, July 1950.

Trensz, Frédéric. "Témoignage." In *Albert Schweitzer: Etudes et Témoignages*, edited by André Siegfried, 203–24. Brussels: Editions de la main jetée, 1951.

Urquhart, Clara. *With Doctor Schweitzer in Lambarene*. London: Harrap, 1957.

Vimont, Jean-Claude. "Garaison, un camp de familles internées dans les Hautes-Pyrénées, 1914–1919." *Criminocorpus revue*, June 8, 2012: 1–38. At http://criminocorpus.revues.org/1876. doi 10.4000/crimino corpus.

Wahl, Alfred. "Choisir la France: L'option de nationalité 1871–1872." In Jung and Thiébaut, *1870–1910: Alsace*, 44–49.

Wersinger-Liller, Anne. "Albert Schweitzer à St. Rémy." In Minder, *Rayonnement d'Albert Schweitzer*, 203–6.

Wolf, Roland. "Albert Schweitzer im Jahr 1912." *Rundbrief für die Freunde von Albert Schweitzer*, no. 104 (2012): 55–62.

Woytt, Gustav. "Helene Bresslau." *Rundbrief für den Freundeskreis von Albert Schweitzer*, no. 11 (August 1957): 22–26.

Woytt-Secretan, Marie. *Albert Schweitzer: Un médecin dans la forêt vierge*. Strasbourg: Editions Oberlin, 1947.

———. "Introduction: Servir dans la discrétion." Exhibition notes for *Mathilde Kottmann ou une vie de service dans la fidélité et la discrétion, (1897–1974)*, n.p. Molsheim-Mutzig, France: Paroisse Protestante, 2007.

———. "Souvenirs d'une infirmière." In Minder, *Rayonnement d'Albert Schweitzer*, 228–40.

———. "Vor fünfzig Jahren hielt Albert Schweitzer die Gedenkrede zu Goethes hundertstem Todestag: Erinnerungen einer Mitarbeiterin." *Dernières Nouvelles d'Alsace*, Mar. 21, 1982. Reprinted in "Albert

Schweitzer: Hundert Jahre Menschlichkeit," special edition of *Albert Schweitzer Rundbrief*, no. 105 (2013): 84–86.

Würzburger General-Anzeiger. "Bei Albert Schweitzer 'zwischen Wasser und Urwald': Frau Helene Schweitzer." Dec. 1, 1931.

Zweig, Friderike M. *Greatness Revisited*. Edited by Harry Zohn. Boston: Branden Press, 1971.

Selected Schweitzer Websites

Albert Schweitzer Fellowship. Boston. At http://www.schweitzerfellowship .org (in English).

Albert Schweitzer Hospital. Deschapelles, Haiti. At http://www.hashaiti .org (in English).

Albert Schweitzer Page. Privately maintained by Jack Fenner. At http:// home.pcisys.net/~jnf/ (in English).

Association Française des Amis d'Albert Schweitzer. Strasbourg, France. At http://www.afaas-schweitzer.org (in French).

Association Internationale Schweitzer de Lambaréné. At http://www .schweitzer.org (in French).

Deutscher Hilfsverein. German Schweitzer Association based in Frankfurt am Main. At http://www.albert-schweitzer-zentrum.de/ (in German).

Dr. Schweitzer's Hospital Fund of Great Britain. At http://www.reverence forlife.org.uk (in English).

Fondation Internationale de l'hôpital Albert Schweitzer de Lambaréné. At http://www.schweitzerlambarene.org (in French).

Schweitzer Haus. Königsfeld, Germany. At http://www.albertschweitzer haus.de/ (in German).

Schweitzer Hilfsverein für das Albert-Schweitzer Spital in Lambarene. Swiss Schweitzer Association. At http://www.albert-schweitzer.ch (in German).

Index

• • •

Italic page numbers denotes illustrations.

absence (invisibility): Helene's, at
  Schweitzer Hospital, 2–3, 5, 110–
  11; Helene's, in Albert's writings,
  xvii, 7–9; Helene's, in media, 129;
  Helene's, in standard narratives, xi,
  xv, xvii, xxi, 133, 141
Adolinanongo, 7, 89, 91, 94, 155, 161
African Sermons, The (Melamed), xxi
African Stories (A. Schweitzer), 158
Albert. *See* Schweitzer Bresslau, Albert
  "Bery" (ASB)
Albert Schweitzer (Brabazon), xxi
Albert Schweitzer (film), 19–20, 129,
  183n31
Albert Schweitzer Fellowship, Boston
  (ASF), xii–xiii, xix, 102
Albert Schweitzer Festival, Boston,
  xii
Albert Schweitzer Hospital, Haiti,
  125
*Albert Schweitzer's Lambarene: A
  Legacy of Humanity for Our World
  Today* (Munz and Munz), xxi
Alembé, 1, 44, 153
Alsace-Lorraine, Germany, xviii,
  50–51, 54, 165n9; Albert's decla-
  ration regarding, 61; annexation

of, 25–26, 165n9, 172n40; constitution of, 26–27
Andende, 7, 44, 45, 87, 89, 121, 153,
  155
Anderson, Erica, 126, 131; Albert's
  correspondence with, 133, 138–39;
  documentary film by, 19–20, 129,
  183n31; on Helene's wifely role,
  10–11; at Nobel Prize ceremony,
  130; photographs of, 138
"Angel of the African Jungle" (Travers), 126
Anna O., 31–32
anti-Semitism: Harry Bresslau's
  experiences with, xviii, 26; Jewish
  question and, 99. *See also* Nazism
Antje Bultmann Lemke Collection
  Relating to Albert Schweitzer, xx,
  168n5, 182n12
Arnold, Matthieu, xxi, 33, 37–38
Arnold, Melvin, 123–24, 125–26
ASB. *See* Schweitzer Bresslau, Albert
  "Bery" (ASB)
A. Schweitzer Papers, 37
ASF. *See* Albert Schweitzer Fellow-
  ship, Boston
atomic weapons, 135, 161, 183n48

Audoynaud, Andre, 77, 79
"Auntie Etiquette" nickname, 24, 130
Azowani, Joseph, 8, 9, 45, 46, 49

back pain, 38–39, 152
Badische Zeitung, xv
Bagnaud, Jean, 54, 61
baptism: Ernst Bresslau's, 149,
    177n11; of grandchildren, 118,
    159, 181n4; Helene's, xviii, 3,
    21, 81, 143, 149, 182n15; Rhena
    Schweitzer-Miller's, 79
Barrès, Hélène, 15, 20
Bern Accords, 61
biblical metaphors, xxii, 31; for
    Albert, 80–81; for Helene, 81–82
bicycle: Albert's gift of, 75; club, 14,
    150; excursions, 28, 150
biographies: of Albert, xv, xxi, xxii; of
    Helene, xvi–xvii, xix, xx
birth: of Albert, 19, 26; of Helene,
    xvii, 26, 149; of Rhena, 20, 58–59,
    61, 76, 154
Bixler, Julius, xviii–xix, 164n13
Black Forest: Helene's tuberculosis
    treatment in, 16, 39, 152; Helene's
    vacations in, 32, 151; Königsfeld
    house in, 24, 85, 117, 119, 155, 156
*Blätter für das Strassburger Armenwe-
    sen*, 34
Born, Max, 109
Brabazon, James, xxi, xxii, 10, 14, 17,
    86, 93
Brazzaville, 96, 100, 114, 159,
    168n24
Breitkopf & Härtel, 89, 93–94
Bresslau, Ernst (brother), 25, 33, 82;
    baptism of, 149, 177n11; death of,
    98, 112, 157, 175n33

Bresslau, Harry (father), xvii, 62,
    74–75, 153, 154; anti-Semitism
    affecting, xviii, 26; death of, 87,
    155; at University of Strasbourg,
    xviii, 32, 128, 142, 149, 151
Bresslau, Helene. *See* Schweitzer
    Bresslau, Helene
Bresslau, Hermann (brother), 33, 149,
    153
Bresslau-Hoff, Carolina (niece), 119
Bresslau-Hoff, Luise (sister-in-law),
    82, 122, 160; as Helene's confi-
    dante, 142; Helene's correspon-
    dence to, xvi, 49–50, 98, 103–4; at
    Strasbourg Mother's Home, 34
Bresslau-Isay, Caroline "Cary"
    (mother), 26, 62, 98, 149, 153,
    158; death of, 103–4, 123, 159
Brooke, Edward, xii
burial site, 3, *69*, 161

Cahn, Arnold, 85–86
Cameron, James, 11
Campion, C. T., 30
careers, of Helene, xv–xvii; develop-
    ment of, xxi–xxii; linguistic skills
    and, xviii–xix, xxii, 1, 11, 37, 144;
    teaching, xviii, 33, 142, 149, 150.
    See also nursing career; social work
Catholic Missions, 96, 100
celebrity and media representations,
    xi, 123–27, 138
Cesbron, Gilbert, 140
childhood, xvii–xviii, 4
Christian: identity, 124; stereotypes,
    xvi
City Orphan Administration: Helene,
    as first female inspector for, 4, 23,
    32, 143; Helene's resignation from,

38, 152; Helene's work for, 14,
32–36, 78, 128–29, 144, 151
civil prisoner of war, xx, xxii, 20;
at Garaison, 15, 50–53, 56,
61, *65–66*, 142, 153–54; house
arrest and, 28, 47, 153. *See also*
Saint-Rémy-de-Provence
Clasen, Richard, 47, 73, 74, 174n3
collaborations, 4–5, 94, 107, 141; on
J. S. Bach (Schweitzer, Albert), 15,
28, 89, 120, 127; on "Peace or
Atomic War" (Schweitzer, Albert),
161, 183n48; on *The Philosophy of
Civilization* (Schweitzer, Albert),
28, 49, *71*, 86, 120; on *The Quest
for the Historical Jesus* (Schweitzer,
Albert), 16, 27–28, 37, *70*, 120,
127, 151, 167n54; on *Wir Epigonen* (Schweitzer, Albert), 15, 28,
71, 120, 168n23
collaboratrices. *See* female staff members (*collaboratrices*)
collections, of correspondence and
diaries, xx, 13, 24, 168n5, 181n9,
182n12
comrade, 29–30, 35, 81. *See also*
friendship
concentration camps: French, during
World War I, 50–51; of World War
II, 101–2, 103, 159, 179n32. *See
also* civil prisoner of war
Congo evening, 35, 40, 151, 170n69
Conrad, Willibald, 25, 27, 150
Constitution of Alsace-Lorraine,
26–27
correspondence: Albert and Helene's
early, xxi, 8, 14, 22–24, 29–30,
40; Albert's, with Anderson,
133, 138–39; collections of, xx,
13, 24, 181n9; during Garaison

internment, 52–53; Helene's, with
Luise Bresslau-Hoff, xvi, 49–50,
98, 103–4; Helene's compiling and
editing of, 117–20; publication
of, xiv, 30, 140; Schweitzer-Miller
on Albert and Helene's, 30, 140,
163–64n7; Sorg on Albert and
Helene's, xx, 13, 84, 166n36
Council of Women, Berlin, 32
courtship, 17. *See also* pact of
friendship
Cousins, Norman, xv, 6, 11, 21, 126,
135, 183n48
Couve, Daniel, 43
Curtius, Gerda, 16

day books. *See* diaries
death: of Albert, 161; of Ernst
Bresslau, 98, 112, 157, 175n33;
of Harry Bresslau, 87, 155; of
Bresslau-Isay, 103–4, 123, 159; of
Haussknecht, 133; of Helene, xv,
69, 136, 138, 139, 161; of Louis
Théophile Schweitzer, 87, 155
de Brazza, Savorgnan, 29, 42, 168n24
"Declaration of Alsace-Lorraine" (A.
Schweitzer and J. Bagnaud), 61
"Declaration of Conscience" (A.
Schweitzer), 161, 183n48
dedications, 15, 21, 29–30, 81, 155
de Gaulle, Charles, xxi, 110,
180nn60–61
Deputy, The (Hochhuth), 106
diaries, xvi, 165n14; collections of,
xx, 182n12; during fifth sojourn
to Lambarene, 122–23; intentional
nature of, 123, 140; of 1913–15, 6,
7–8, 44, 45–46, 121; during 1940–
41, 122–23; during Saint-Rémy

diaries (*cont.*)
    internment, 60–61, 121; during
    second sojourn to Lambarene,
    121–22
Dittrich, Nicole, xx
documentary film, 19–20, 129, 183n31
Dr. Schweitzer of Lambarene (Cous-
    ins), xv, 11
"Dr. Schweitzer's Hospital Work in
    Lambarene" (H. Schweitzer), *72*,
    93

Eckert, Jean (son-in-law), 98, 103, 158
education: at Lindner School for Girls,
    4, 149; nursing, 24, 31, 32, 37–38,
    129, 151, 152; at Strasbourg Music
    Conservatory, xviii, 33, 150;
    teacher training, xviii, 33, 142,
    149; at University of Strasbourg,
    33, 128, 142, 150
Ehret, Jean-Marie, 50, 51
Ehretsmann, Paul (nephew), 115
emancipation, xx, xxi–xxii, 4, 30, 40,
    81, 128. *See also* independence;
    modernity
Emane, Augustin, xxi
engagement, 20, 38, 39, 152
Engel, Johanna (cousin), 86, 112,
    152, 159, 179n32
equal partnership: Helene's longing
    for, xxiii, 119; Helene's role in,
    11–12, 37, 75–76, 141, 143; with-
    out marriage, 14, 81; at Schweitzer
    Hospital, 3–4, 9, 91, 116
escape: Helene's, from Nazism, xx, 5,
    96–98, 100, 122, 142, 158–59;
    Schweitzer-Miller's, during World
    War II, 103, 159
Europa, 1, 6, 44, 153

family planning, 35
feelings: Helene's, about Albert's
    female friends, xxiii, 20, 92–93;
    Helene's, about female staff mem-
    bers, 112, 131–35
Fehling, Helene, 34
Fellowship of the Mark of Pain, 7, 94
female friends, of Albert, xxi, 8, 14,
    15, 83; Helene as prototype for,
    xxiii, 13, 17; Helene's feelings
    about, xxiii, 20, 92–93
female staff members (*collaboratrices*),
    131–35
feminist discourse regarding Helene,
    xvi, xix, 8
Fischer, Annie, 15, 20, 155, 166n46
Fleischhack, Marianne, xvi
Forrow, Lachlan, xiii
frailty stereotypes, xv, xxii, 3, 76, 78,
    87, 126–27
France: concentration and internment
    camps of, 27, 50–51; Free France
    regions of, xxi, 110, 180n60; Ger-
    man invasion of, 158
Franco-Prussian War, 4, 50, 164n10
Free France regions, xxi, 110, 180n60
French Equatorial Africa, 4, 52,
    170n69; as Free France region, xxi,
    110, 180n60; Helene's wartime
    travels in, 96, 114, 159; mission-
    aries in, 19, 42–44; Schweitzer
    Hospital in, xxi, 1, 5
Friedenspreis, 109, 111, 160
friendship: Albert and Helene's
    early years of, 28–29; Albert and
    Helene's marriage as, xvii, 3;
    Albert and Helene's secrecy about,
    29, 30, 37; Helene as Albert's
    "most loyal," 3, 13, 29–30, 81,
    155. *See also* equal partnership;

female friends, of Albert; pact of friendship

Friendship House museum, 138

Friends of Albert Schweitzer (Boston), 10

fund-raising, xi, xix, xxii, 102, 111, 141, 144

Gabon, xi, 42, 44, 134

Garaison. *See* Notre Dame de Garaison (Garaison)

German Schweitzer Association, 11, 136

Germany: Alsace-Lorraine annexed by, 25–26, 165n9, 172n40; France invaded by, 158; Strasbourg influenced by, 14, 16, 25; Treaty of Frankfurt, 25–26

Gerson, Max, 93, 102–3, 107, 113, 156

Gifford Lectures, 108

Gillespie, Noel, 87, 155

"God" (H. Bresslau), 32, 151

"God's Eager Fool" (*Reader's Digest*), 127

Goebbels, Joseph, 102, 111, 178n26

Goethe, Johann Wolfgang: Albert's prize regarding, 88, 156; Albert's speech regarding, 104–8, 156; bicentennial celebration of, 5, 126, 160

"Gott." *See* "God" (H. Bresslau)

grandchildren, 118, 137, 158, 159, 160, 181n4

gravestone, 3, *69*, 161

"Greatest Man in the World, The" (Arnold), 123

"'Greatest Man in the World, The': That Is What Some People Call

Albert Schweitzer, Jungle Philosopher" (*LIFE*), 123

Gunsbach, France, 23, 24, 31; as Albert's family home, 26, 31, 82–83, 88, 154, 156; marriage in, 39, 153; Martin in, 77, 133; Schweitzer House in, 77, 88–89, 131, 133, 134, 157

Gussman, Larry, xii

Gütschow, Elsa, 34

Haas, Lina, 25, 27, 150

Harth, Constance, 20

Haussknecht, Emma "Miss Emma": death of, 133; expedition of, 93, 176–77n66; Helene's relationship to, 92, 114, 132–33, 159; at Schweitzer Hospital, 13, 21, 87, 91, 113, 131, 180n69

heart problems, 132, 160

Helene. *See* Schweitzer Bresslau, Helene

"Helene Schweitzer: Am liebsten incognito" (Schempp), xv

Helene Schweitzer Bresslau: A life for Lambarene (Mühlstein), xvi

Helene Schweitzer Bresslau: Ein Leben für Lambarene. See Helene Schweitzer Bresslau: A life for Lambarene (Mühlstein)

Helene Schweitzer Papers, at Syracuse, xx

"Helene Schweitzer: The Wife of a Great Man" (Rinderknecht), 11

heroic image: Albert's, xix, xxii, 2, 80; Helene's, 17, 78, 134–35

Herrenschmidt, Adèle "Tata," 14, 20

Heuss, Theodor, 73, 109, 110, 111, 136, 160

Heuss-Knapp, Elly, 15, 27, 34, 73, 80, 136, 160; in bicycle club, 14, 150
Hibbert Lectures, 108
historians, of Schweitzers, xxi
Historic Zone, 2, 7, 69, 161
Hitler, Adolf: Albert regarding, 105–9; Holocaust (Shoah) of, 105, 179n40; rise of, 98, 103, 157, 158; thinking regarding, 108–9, 180n52
Hochhuth, Rolf, 106
Holocaust (Shoah), 105, 179n40
home for unwed mothers. See Strasbourg Mother's Home
Horst, Madeleine, 82
Hospital Aid Association, 78
house arrest, 28, 47, 153
humanitarian work: of Albert, xi, 21, 108; Albert and Helene's shared ideals about, 5, 24, 25, 28, 127–28; Schweitzer Hospital as, xxi; World War I's shaping of Albert's, 21, 28, 47–48, 61, 108
Hume, Edward, 101

"identity crisis," 30–32
Illies, Florian, 141
illnesses, 78, 144–45; back pain, 38–39, 152; heart, 132, 160; during internments, 52, 56, 57; phlebitis, 49, 171n29; pleurisy, 39, 149; pneumonia, 90, 92; separation rationalized by, 75–78. See also tuberculosis
Iltis, Jean, 55
independence: Helene's, xix, xx, 22–25, 112, 137, 141; Helene's evolution of, xviii, xxi–xxii, 40–41; Helene's loss of, 131–33; Helene's

role models for, xviii, 32, 142; Helene's struggles with, 36; Mühlstein on, 16, 131; Sorg on, xviii, 16–17, 40
influence: Germany's, on Strasbourg, 14, 16, 25; Helene's, on Albert, xi–xii, xviii, 11–12, 14, 17, 19, 140–41; Jewish, on Helene, xvii, 3, 31–32, 141–42, 143, 182n15
International Red Cross, 5, 57, 115, 122, 158
internment. See civil prisoner of war
internment camps, 27. See also concentration camps

Jennings, Eric, xxi
Jewish influence, xvii, 3, 31–32, 141–42, 143, 182n15
"Jewish question," 99
journals. See diaries
Joy, Charles R., 123–24
J. S. Bach (A. Schweitzer), 15, 28, 89, 120, 127

Kaiser Wilhelm I, 25–26, 168n13
Kaiser Wilhelm II, xxi, 26–27, 168n13
Kaiser Wilhelm Universität. See University of Strasbourg
Kaltenrieder, Emile, 122
Kik, Richard, 136
Kingsley, Mary, 42–44
Knapp, Elly. See Heuss-Knapp, Elly
Knapp, Marianne, 34
Koestler, Arthur, 97
Königsfeld, Germany, 77, 85–86; Helene's house requisitioned in, 98, 117, 158; house in, 24, 85, 117, 119, 155, 156

Kottmann, Mathilde, 13, 21, 87, 90, 92, 131; as Albert's secretary, 157; Helene's feelings about, 112, 132, 134

Kristallnacht, 101–2, 178n25

Kristeva, Julia, 81–82

Kulturphilosophie. See Philosophy of Civilization, The (A. Schweitzer)

Kurrentschrift, 7–8, 171n15

Lambarene, xvi; descriptions of, xxi, 1–2, 12–13; eighth sojourn to, 130–31, 160; fifth sojourn to, 114, 115, 159; first sojourn to, 44–50, 76, 78, 144, 153; fourth sojourn to, 158; as Helene's "home," 5, 6, 102, 113, 135–36, 138; house in, 2, 12; ninth sojourn to, 136, 161; second sojourn to, 90–93, 156; seventh sojourn to, 160; sixth sojourn to, 159; third sojourn to, 96–101, 102–4, 113–14, 158. *See also* Schweitzer Hospital

Lambarene Fellows Program, xii–xiii

Lantz, Edouard, 43

Lantz, Valentine, 43

Lausanne, Switzerland, 112, 157, 158

Lauterburg, Markus, 21

League of Jewish Women, 32

Lebenslauf (H. Schweitzer), 128–29, 130

lecture tour, United States: notes from, xx, *72*, 94–95; as publicity campaign, xii, xix, 5, 11, 111, 125–26, 144; schedule of, 101–2, 157–58, 178n22; venues of, 124

Lee, Hermione, 3

legacy, 140–45

Lenel, Bertha, 98, 122, 179n32

letters. *See* correspondence

Leyrer, Karl, 37

Libreville, 1, 44, 114

LIFE, 123

Lindblad Publishing, 73

Lindner School for Girls, 4, 149, 150

linguistic skills, xviii–xix, xxii, 1, 11, 37, 144

lives, of Helene, 3, 5

Loeb, Georgina, 101

Loeb, Leo, 101

"*Madame Docteur*" nickname, 2, 46, 131

Maison Schweitzer. *See* Schweitzer House, Gunsbach

marriage, 16; Albert's resistance to, 14, 22–23, 30; ceremony for, 39, 153; of convenience, 38, 77, 84; engagement for, 20, 38, 39, 152; equal partnership without, 14, 81; as friendship, xvii, 3; unconventional nature of, 18–19, 30. *See also* separations

Marshall, George, 76–77

Martin, Emmy, 13, 77, 83, 86, 89, 130, 133, 157

Mauran, Hervé, 50, 51

media representations and celebrity, xi, 123–27, 138

medical missionary service, xvii, 29, 40, 43, 123, 153, 170n1

Melamed, Steve E. G., xxi

Mellon, Gwen, 125

Mellon, Larry, 125

Meyer, Michael, 145

Minder, Robert, 47, 59, 83

"Miracle of Lambarene, The" (Bixler), xix

missionaries: in French Equatorial
Africa, 19, 42–44; Helene on,
124–25; medical, xvii, 29, 40, 43,
123, 153, 170n1. *See also* Paris
Mission Society
modernity, 14, 16, 18, 20, 21, 30, 46,
85; Helene as prototype for, xiii,
13, 17; Helene's self-image of, 19,
141–42
Mon Oncle Albert Schweitzer
(Oswald), xv
Morel, Georgette, 47, 49, 73, 93
Morel, Léon, 49, 73
Mother's Home. *See* Strasbourg
Mother's Home
Mühlstein, Verena, xvi–xvii, xix, 85;
on Helene's friendship with Albert,
30; on Helene's "identity crisis,"
31–32; on Helene's independence,
16, 131; on Helene's influence on
Albert, 14
Munz, Jo, xxi
Munz, Walter, xxi, 8, 137, 178n17,
178n20

Nachlass A. Schweitzer. *See* A.
Schweitzer Papers
Nassau, Robert H., 42
National Socialist Worker's Party
(Nazi Party), 103, 157
Nazism: Albert's politics regarding,
xxii, 104–12; Helene's escape
from, xx, 5, 96–98, 100, 122, 142,
158–59. *See also* anti-Semitism
Nessmann, Victor, 9, 21, 46,
179n32
New York City, xix, 101–2, 113, 126,
157–58
Nies-Berger, Edouard, 13, 77, 79

1913 Der Sommer de Jahrhunderts
(Illies), 141
Nobel Peace Prize, xi, *68*; Anderson
and Martin at, 130; Helene's atten-
dance at, 5, 130, 137, 160
Notre Dame de Garaison (Garaison),
15, 50–53, 56, 61, *65–66*, 142,
153–54
nursing career, 1, 4, 5, *64*; Helene's
education for, 24, 31, 32, 37–38,
129, 151, 152; at Schweitzer Hospital, xvi, 9, 45, 102, 158

obscurity. *See* absence (invisibility)
Oermann, Nils, xxi
Ogowe River, *65*; beauty of, 42, 46,
91, 97; descriptions of, 1–2, 6–7,
19–20
Olaus-Petri Foundation, 83
On the Edge of the Primeval Forest (A.
Schweitzer), 83, 130, 155, 174n3;
Helene unnamed in, xvii, 8
orphans. *See* City Orphan
Administration
Oswald, Suzanne (niece), xv, 130–31
Out of My Life and Thought (A.
Schweitzer), xvii, 9, 37, 94, 156,
164n8

pact of friendship, 14, 19, 84, 104,
153; Helene's struggles with,
22–23, 30–31; initiation of, 150;
secrecy of, 29, 30, 37
Pappenheim, Bertha, 31–32
Paris Mission Society: Albert's joining
of, 10, 14, 29, 30, 35; "Schweitzer
question" of, 39–40, 43, 152–53;
support from, 2, 40, 153

partnership. *See* equal partnership

patriarchal culture: Albert and, xix–xx, 8; Helene viewed through, xxii, 77–78, 126–27. *See also* stereotypes

"Peace or Atomic War? A Declaration of Conscience" (A. Schweitzer), 161, 183n48

Philosophy of Civilization, The (A. Schweitzer), 48, 53, 106, 164n4; dedications in, 15, 21, 29–30, 81, 155; Helene's collaboration in, 28, 49, *71*, 86, 120

phlebitis, 49, 171n29

pleurisy, 39, 149

pneumonia, 90, 92

Pogromnacht (Kristallnacht), 101–2, 178n25

Polczek-Gütschow, Elsa, 15, 23, 34

Poling, David, 76–77

posthumous reputations, 3, 8, 79, 137

Poteau, Sonja Müller, 134–35

prisoner of war. *See* civil prisoner of war

Protestant Seminary, 18, 29, 55

prototype, xxiii, 13, 17

publications, about Helene, xv–xvii, xx, xxi. *See also* biographies

publicity campaign. *See* lecture tour, United States

public speaking, 94, 124, 128. *See also* lecture tour, United States

Quest for the Historical Jesus, The (A. Schweitzer), 16, 27–28, 37, *70*, 120, 127, 151, 167n54

Reader's Digest, 127

Reichsland, 26

Reimarus zu Wrede, Von: Eine Geschichte der Leben-Jesu-Forschung. See Quest for the Historical Jesus, The (A. Schweitzer)

Reinach, Fanny, 14–15, 20

"Religion in Modern Civilization" (A. Schweitzer), 108

religious views, of Albert, 40, 43, 48, 153

repatriation: after World War I, 61–62, 154; after World War II, 114–16

Republic of Gabon, xi, 42, 44, 134

Reverence for Life, xi, xiii, 13, 48, 61, 99, 106

Rinderknecht, Peter, 11

Rogers, Miriam, 10, 11

roles, Helene's: as cofounder, xvii, 5, 8–9, 129–30, 141; misperceptions about, xvii, 119, 125–27; at Schweitzer Hospital, 3–4, 12, 91, 94, 116, 131; wifely stereotype, xi, xv, 10–11, 46, 76, 123, 127, 141. *See also* collaborations; equal partnership

Rolland, Romain, 48

Ross, Emory, xii, 101

Roumanille, Barthélemy, 59

Roumanille, Simon, 58

Roumanille-Blanc, Marie, 58, 59

Russell, C. E. B. Lillian, 89

sacrificial stereotypes, xv, xix, xxii, 76, 78–80

Saint-Rémy-de-Provence: Albert as physician at, 57–58, 59; Helene's diary at, 60–61, 121; internment at, 53–56, 142, 154; repatriation from, 61–62, 154

Salomon, Alice, 32
schedules: of Albert, 17–18, 29,
83, 84–85, 89, 112, 153–54; of
lecture tour, United States, 101–2,
157–58, 178n22
Scheib, Jacques, 56, 57, 58
Schempp, Otto, xv, 136
Schlienger, Xavier, 55, 57
Schmalz, Ella, 34, 151
Schmitz, Anna, 90, 92, 156,
176–77n66
Schnabel, Ilse, 93, 176–77n66
scholars, of Schweitzers, xxi
Schwander, Rudolf, 33, 34, 73, 151,
154, 165n8
Schweitzer, Albert. See Schweitzer
Bresslau, Albert "Bery" (ASB)
Schweitzer, Louis Théophile (Albert's
father), 26, 82–83, 87, 155,
166n43
Schweitzer, Pierre-Paul (nephew),
179n32
Schweitzer Album, The (Anderson),
10–11
Schweitzer Bresslau, Albert "Bery"
(ASB), 64–72; biblical metaphors
for, 80–81; bicycling of, 28, 75,
150; biographies of, xv, xxi, xxii;
birth of, 19, 26; "blind organ" of,
53, 57; celebrity and media coverage of, xi, 123–26; death of, 161;
Goethe prize of, 88, 156; Goethe
speech of, 104–8, 156; Gunsbach
family home of, 26, 31, 82–83,
88, 154, 156; Helene's absence
in writings of, xvii, 7–9; Helene's
influence on, xi–xii, xviii, 11–12,
14, 17, 19, 140–41; Helene's introduction to, 22, 25, 27, 150; heroic
image of, xix, xxii, 2, 80; initials

used by, 2, 45, 83, 102, 164n2;
lectures of, 108, 155, 156; Nobel
Peace Prize of, xi, 5, 68, 130, 137,
160; as organist, xix, 11, 27, 29,
81, 83, 112, 150; patriarchal views
of, xix–xx, 8; as physician during
internment, 57–58, 59; politics of,
xxii, 104–12; schedule of, 17–18,
29, 83, 84–85, 89, 112, 153–54;
Schweitzer-Miller's relationship
with, 86, 120, 158; as "the Great
Doctor," xi, 2, 8, 164n1; United
States visit of, xv, 5, 10, 123–27,
160; at University of Strasbourg,
29, 153. See also correspondence;
female friends, of Albert; friendship; humanitarian work; marriage;
Paris Mission Society
Schweitzer Bresslau, Albert "Bery"
(works): African Stories, 158;
"Declaration of Alsace-Lorraine,"
61; "Declaration of Conscience,"
161, 183n48; On the Edge of the
Primeval Forest, 83, 130, 155,
174n3; J. S. Bach, 15, 28, 89, 120,
127; Kulturphilosophie (see The
Philosophy of Civilization); Out of
My Life and Thought, xvii, 9, 37,
94, 156, 164n8; "Peace or Atomic
War? A Declaration of Conscience," 161, 183n48; The Quest
for the Historical Jesus, 16, 27–28,
37, 70, 120, 127, 151, 167n54;
"Religion in Modern Civilization," 108; Wir Epigonen, 15,
28, 47, 71, 120, 168n23. See also
Philosophy of Civilization, The (A.
Schweitzer)
Schweitzer Bresslau, Helene, 63–72,
164n2. See also specific topics

Schweitzer Committee of the USA.
  See Albert Schweitzer Fellowship,
  Boston
Schweitzer-Eckert, Rhena. *See*
  Schweitzer-Miller, Rhena
Schweitzer Fellows for Life, xiii
Schweitzer Fellows Program, US, xiii
Schweitzer Hospital, *69*; at Adolinanongo (first expansion), 7, 89,
  91, 94, 155, 161; at Andende (first
  location), 7, 44–45, 87, 89, 121,
  153, 155; female staff members
  at, 131–35; in French Equatorial
  Africa, xxi, 1, 5; Haussknecht at,
  13, 21, 87, 91, 113, 131, 180n69;
  Helene as cofounder of, xvii,
  5, 8–9, 129–30, 141; Helene's
  absence (invisibility) at, 2–3, 5,
  110–11; Helene's equal partnership
  in, 3–4, 9, 91, 116; Helene's fund-
  raising for, xi, xix, xxii, 102, 111,
  141, 144; Helene's nursing work
  at, xvi, 9, 45, 102, 158; Helene's
  roles in, 3–4, 12, 91, 94, 116, 131;
  Historic Zone of, 2, 7, *69*, 161; as
  humanitarian work, xxi; modern,
  of 1981, xii, 161; as oldest hospital
  in Africa, 7; during World War II,
  xii, 110, 144, 159
Schweitzer House, Gunsbach, 77,
  88–89, 131, 133, 134, 157
Schweitzer-Miller, Rhena (daughter),
  xi, xvi, *66*, 73, 85–86, 90, 98, 112,
  161; on Albert and Helene's correspondence, 30, 140, 163–64n7;
  Albert's relationship with, 86,
  120, 158; baptism of, 79; birth of,
  20, 58–59, 61, 76, 154; escape of,
  during World War II, 103, 159;
  on Helene's influence on Albert,

11–12; Helene's single motherhood
  of, 4–5, 21, 75, 78, 88, 144, 155,
  157; in New York City, xix, 101–2,
  113, 157–58
Schweitzer-Schillinger, Adèle (Albert's
  mother), 26, 49, 82, 153
Seaver, George, xxii, 77–78, 115
Secretan, Marie. *See* Woytt-Secretan,
  Marie
separations, 84, 145; during courtship, 17, 31, 32; of 1924–27, 21,
  75–78, 79, 86–88; post–World
  War I, 81–82
Shoah (Holocaust), 105, 179n40
sickness. *See* illnesses
Silver, Ali, 13, 131, 132, 134
single motherhood, 4–5, 21, 75, 78,
  88, 144, 155, 157
Skillings, Everett, xii, 101, 122
Social Congress in Frankfurt, 34
social conscience, 13–14
social work, xx, 1, 4, 31–32, 128–29,
  143, 150–51. *See also* City Orphan
  Administration; Strasbourg
  Mother's Home
Söderblom, Nathan (Archbishop), 75,
  83, 154
sojourns. *See* diaries; Lambarene
Sontag, Susan, 144
Sorg, Jean-Paul: on Albert's female
  friends, 15; on Helene's correspondence with Albert, xx, 13, 84,
  166n36; on Helene's independence,
  xviii, 16–17, 40; on Helene's influence on Albert, 17, 19
stereotypes: Christian, xvi; frailty,
  xv, xxii, 3, 76, 78, 87, 126–27;
  sacrificial, xv, xix, xxii, 76, 78–80;
  wifely role, xi, xv, 10–11, 46, 76,
  123, 127, 141

Stettin, Germany, 24, 31, 32, 40, 151, 169n32
St. Paul-de-Mausole. *See* Saint-Rémy-de-Provence
Strasbourg, France: German influence on, 14, 16, 25; progressive nature of, xxi, 4, 27, 32–33, 142–43
Strasbourg Mother's Home, 129, 168n5; family planning for, 35; Helene's founding of, 4, 23, 34–35, 78, 143–44, 152; success of, 36–37
Strasbourg Municipal Hospital, 73, 82, 83, 152, 154
Strasbourg Music Conservatory, xviii, 33, 150
Stucki, Walter Otto, 123
Suermann, Thomas, xxi, 106

Tagebuch. *See* diaries
Talagouga, 42–43, 44
Tau, Tove, 137
teaching career, xviii, 33, 142, 149, 150
theology, as action, xii, 48
Time, 126–27
tombstone, 3, *69*, 161
travels, of Helene, 5, 16–17, 111, 150, 152, 154, 157. *See also* lecture tour, United States
Travers, Virginia, 126
Treaty of Frankfurt, 25–26
Trensz, Frédéric, 9, 46
tropes. *See* stereotypes
tuberculosis, xix, 5, 144–45, 170n66, 176n58; Helene cured of, 93–94, 100–101; Helene diagnosed with, 85–86; Helene's attacks of, 152, 155, 156, 173n51; Helene's attitude toward, 85, 176n58; Helene's Black Forest convalescence for, 16, 39, 152; Helene's early signs of, 4

unconventionality, of Helene, 14, 18–19, 30
Unitarian Church, 123–24
United States: Albert and Helene's media coverage in, 123–26; Albert and Helene's visit to, xv, 5, 10, 126–27, 160; Schweitzer Fellows Program in, xiii. *See also* lecture tour, United States
University of Strasbourg, 23, 164n6; Albert at, 29; Albert's forced resignation from, 153; Harry Bresslau at, xvii, 32, 128, 142, 149, 151; Helene at, 33, 128, 142, 150
unwed mothers, 35, 40. *See also* Strasbourg Mother's Home
Urquhart, Clara, 11
USAID, xii

Van Leer, Tony, 136, 139, 161
von Treitschke, Heinrich, xviii

Waiseninspektorin (orphan inspector). *See* City Orphan Administration
Weimer Republic, 103
Wersinger-Liller, Anne, 57, 59–60
Wetterle, Abbott Emile, 61
Widor, Charles-Marie, 48, 57
wifely role stereotype, xi, xv, 10–11, 46, 76, 123, 127, 141
Wirckau, Winnifred, 136–37, 160

Wir Epigonen (A. Schweitzer), 15, 28, 47, *71*, 120, 168n23. *See also The Philosophy of Civilization* (A. Schweitzer)

Wolf, Mark L., xii–xiii

women. *See* female friends, of Albert; female staff members (*collaboratrices*)

World War I: Albert's humanitarianism shaped by, 21, 28, 47–48, 61, 108; Albert's postwar experiences, 82–83; beginning of, 27, 46–47, 48–49; France's concentration camps during, 50–51; Helene's postwar experiences, 82; Helene's repatriation after, 61–62, 154. *See also* civil prisoner of war

World War II, 1, 125; build up to, 105–6, 107, 158; concentration camps of, 101–2, 103, 159, 179n32; end of, 114–16; Helene's escape during, xx, 5, 96–98, 100, 122, 142, 158–59; Helene's house requisitioned during, 98, 117, 158; Helene's repatriation after, 114–16; Kristallnacht, 101–2; Schweitzer Hospital during, xii, 110, 144, 159; Schweitzer-Miller's escape during, 103, 159

Woytt, Gustav (nephew), xv–xvi, 92, 137

Woytt-Secretan, Marie, 9, 46, 90, 91–93, 104, 156

Zimmermann, Karl, 11

Zweig, Friderike, 133

Zweig, Stefan, 133